C0-CBU-035

The Economist Intelligence Unit Guide to Eurobonds

Also Published by McGraw-Hill

Andrea Mackiewicz
THE ECONOMIST INTELLIGENCE UNIT GUIDE TO BUILDING A GLOBAL IMAGE

Shirley B. Dreifus, Editor
BUSINESS INTERNATIONAL'S GLOBAL MANAGEMENT DESK REFERENCE

Thomas J. Ehrbar, Editor
BUSINESS INTERNATIONAL'S GUIDE TO INTERNATIONAL LICENSING

Gray Newman and Anna Szterenfeld
BUSINESS INTERNATIONAL'S GUIDE TO DOING BUSINESS IN MEXICO

The Economist Intelligence Unit Guide to Eurobonds

Noël Clarke
of Capital Markets Partners Ltd.
with contributions from

**Robert Chillcott,
Clifford Chance,**
Solicitors
Ken G. Cox

McGraw-Hill, Inc.

New York   San Francisco   Washington, D.C.   Auckland   Bogotá
Caracas   Lisbon   London   Madrid   Mexico City   Milan
Montreal   New Delhi   San Juan   Singapore
Sydney   Tokyo   Toronto

I dedicate this to my wife, Alicia

336.31
C59e

Library of Congress Catalogue Number 92-40379

Copyright © 1993 by Noël Clarke. All rights reserved. Printed in the United States of America. Except as permitted under the United States Copyright Act of 1976, no part of this publication may be reproduced or distributed in any form or by any means, or stored in a data base or retrieval system, without the prior written permission of the publisher.

1 2 3 4 5 6 7 8 9 0   DOC/DOC   9 8 7 6 5 4 3

ISBN 0-07-009338-5

The sponsoring editor for this book was David Conti and the production supervisor was Suzanne W. Babeuf. This book was set in Baskerville by North Market Street Graphics.

Printed and bound by R. R. Donnelley & Sons Company.

 This book is printed on recycled, acid-free paper containing a minimum of 50% recycled de-inked fiber.

For more information about Eurobonds, contact:
Noël Clarke
Capital Markets Partners Ltd.
20 Parliament Hill
London, England NW3 2TU
Tel: 071-794-0288
Fax: 071-435-2386

For more information about other McGraw-Hill materials, call 1-800-822-8158 in the United States. In other countries, call your nearest McGraw-Hill office.   MH93

Contents

University Libraries
Carnegie Mellon University
Pittsburgh, Pennsylvania 15213

Contributors

Noël Clarke is managing director of Capital Markets Partners Limited. His international banking career began in 1977 when he joined London Multinational Bank, later to become Chemical Bank International. After working for two securities houses, including Deutsche Bank Capital Markets, he launched Capital Markets Partners Limited (CMP) in 1988 to advise on the origination and execution and debt financings by way of international syndicated bank loans and bond issues for borrowers and banks. In a consulting role CMP advises financial institutions on their investment banking and capital markets operations. In 1988 CMP set up a division to evaluate and provide the financing for investments in Central Europe. CMP is currently advising on several privatizations in Central Europe and on the establishment of an investment banking division of a major Central European bank. Chapters are by him unless otherwise indicated.

Robert Chillcott has held senior positions in the fields of investment management, international finance, and Eurobonds. His range has encompassed a wide variety of securities of many different countries and currencies, including equities, fixed interest, and floating-rate notes (FRNs). In 1980, as investment manager of the Co-operative Bank, he was at the forefront of developing the now accepted method of assessing FRNs by margin calculations. He also created the concept of actively managing an FRN portfolio. In 1985, while a director of Enskilda Securities, he invested FRN funds for clients, where both assets and liabilities were managed. He is presently working with Chartered WestLB in London.

Kenneth Cox has been in banking for over 20 years in a variety of capacities spanning the lending, capital markets, and corporate finance areas both domestically and internationally. For the last four years, he has been a Director of Baring Brothers & Co. Ltd. where he has developed the bank's securitization and property business.

Stephen Hood and Andrew Taylor are partners in the Capital Markets department of Clifford Chance, an international law firm, with offices in London, Tokyo, New York, Paris, Hong Kong, and Frankfurt. The Capital Markets department concentrates exclusively on Euro-issues, both debt and equity, complex structured finance, and debt securitization.

Lawrence de V. Wragg is managing director of LWA Associates Limited. He began his career as a consultant with Price Waterhouse Associates, before moving into merchant banking in 1974. As a director of Charterhouse Bank, he was head of the worldwide capital markets division. He now runs LWA Ltd., which is an advisory firm specializing in managerial and control issues in financial organizations.

Foreword

The modern Eurobond market has been shaped by the same kind of powerful forces that have shaped modern industry. Aggressive competition among players of truly international activities has been accelerated by the provision of information on a scale undreamed of at the market's inception. The result is an industry that is not only extremely responsive to the needs of the participants, but highly efficient and transparent. This outcome has been achieved largely by virtue of its hitherto unregulated status, allowing innovation unparalleled in any solely domestic environment.

Market participants are making increasing use of high technology for the quotation, trading and settlement of ever more sophisticated instruments. But I have always maintained that no matter how fast the technology becomes, nor how widespread the transparency, someone always has to think and feel and act, to determine price levels. Thus the most prized skills of the successful practitioner remain within the area of a 'gut feel' instinct, for an issue cannot be priced correctly by simply performing calculations.

It is necessary to establish a 'feel' for the instrument and the issuer, and use this subjective assessment as a way of gaining the best possible terms for both borrower and investor. This work surpasses other books on the Eurobond market by giving the first detailed breakdown of this process, illustrated by easily comprehensible case studies. Though issuance is placed within the context of the market and the participants whose activities shape that market, this is a hands-on guide intended for practical use.

During 40 years in the securities business, I was fortunate enough to witness the debut of the Eurobond market with its first issue, a mere $15 mn in 1963, but which went on to become a $200 bn a year industry. Mr Clarke, on the other hand, is a relative newcomer with a track record of 15 years. Nevertheless I think his book provides a truly comprehensive guide to this everchanging, exciting and challenging market place.

Stanley D. L. Ross
Member of the Board
Deutsche Bank Capital Markets Limited
March 10, 1990

Preface

The purpose of this book is to introduce the Eurobond market and provide practical guidance on the origination and structuring of new issues. The second edition follows the basic outline of the first, which was prepared in 1989, but is updated to reflect various changes of practice and market patterns. Fixed-price reofferings are now a standard procedure for launching new issues. Trends in Eurobond currency sectors have changed considerably and U.K. securities regulation has been virtually redrafted. On the other hand, the chapters on documentation and calculations of value, the worked examples of different financings, and case studies have not required any change. The book is not exhaustive and does not address, for example, Eurobond trading, Eurobond portfolio management, or advanced financial engineering techniques such as options pricing, all of which are dealt with in other current publications. Nor does a book of this kind deal with historical material or with a discussion of broader macroeconomic and financial issues which would limit its practical use. Some recent developments, however, are likely to have a lasting impact on the function of the market, and it is appropriate to review some of these in these pages.

One significant development in the Eurobond market is the continuing effect of the dismantling of exchange controls and deregulation of national securities markets, particularly in Europe. Generally speaking, deregulation has opened up domestic securities markets to competition from foreign intermediaries, including brokers, market makers, and issuing houses. In most instances, the arrival of more players has increased the pressure for the reform and modernization of domestic bond markets, and the first issuer to benefit has often been the government itself. In promoting more openness of their securities markets, governments vastly broadened their investor audience to encompass domestic, offshore, and foreign investors. This trend has also benefited Eurobond issues. First, where the sovereign has issued in a sufficiently wide range of maturities, a homogeneous yield curve has been created which serves as a vital reference for more precise pricing of new Eurobond issues denominated in their currency. Second, Eurobond investors have a means of hedging the currency and interest exposure of their investments. Third, issues denominated in the currency of the borrower's country of origin are less dependent on foreign investors for their placement and therefore less vulnerable to sudden disinvestment by foreign investors for currency rather than credit reasons. Thus, the opening up of domestic bond markets, in providing more placement, clear pricing benchmarks, and good hedging instruments has provided more liquidity and depth to the Eurobond currency sectors concerned.

The gains and losses realized from currency exposure are one of the principal short-term motivations of international investors in Eurobonds. In the medium term, investors' preference currency tends to reflect longer-term influences on the strength or weaknesses of individual currencies. Thus, the Australian dollar Eurobond sector is presently shrinking while the Euro-French franc sector, historically at the mercy of political events in France, took seventh place in 1991. An important development was the Treaty of Maastricht of December 1991 which, while providing in the short term opportunities for gains (and losses) driven by the perception of convergence of yields, has underlined the emergence of a single currency in Europe, which is likely to be a derivative of the ECU, if not the ECU in its present form. It is possible to visualize now a polarization of the world financial markets by the end of the century into three zones: (1) the U.S. dollar, (2) the yen, and (3) the ECU which, clearly, will reduce, among other effects, the opportunities of international investors for short-term "currency play"—though without necessarily affecting the growth of the market as a whole.

Another development of lasting impact is the realization that has finally dawned in many bankers' minds that capital adequacy ratios are not only here to stay but are already affecting the lending business of commercial banks. True, commercial banks were confronted already in 1986 by the pressure on their traditional lending brought by new instruments such as Euro-commercial paper and, later, Euro-medium-term notes (see p. 45). But heavy provisions against LDC and East and Central European debt and the practice of marking-to-market quoted investments have conspired to shrink shareholders' funds of many banks to the point where their capital adequacy ratios are in question. The implication of this for borrowers raising medium-term finance is clear: many investment banks presently anticipate a significant growth of debt funding by private sector corporations through bond issues and are increasing their resources in skills such as credit analysis to meet this development.

Although new issues and Eurobond trading businesses recovered sharply in 1991, there is still excess capacity among the intermediaries, and withdrawals from the market and closures are still occurring. This is not surprising if analyzed from the point of the ever-growing capital commitment required of issuing houses not only to different Eurobond currency sectors (which can be managed out of London) but, equally important, to the government bond markets in those same currencies (which require an additional physical presence in the financial center concerned). Global bond issues, now an established instrument, depend in particular on (1) an accurate perception of the issuer in the domestic market and (2) the depth and degree of access to investors in that market. The same principles apply to conventional Eurobonds where the trend is for large liquid issues which depend for their successful placement on a clear perception of the issuer and wide distribution. This points to the need for more investor education and professional investor relations maintenance—a subject until recently sorely neglected by issuers and intermediaries.

Acknowledgments

This preface should not conclude without some words of thanks for help in completing this book to friends and former colleagues, including Ken Cox, Jonathan Price, Alan Taylor, Hans-Ulrich Wiemann—and to several institutions, including Euromoney, IFR Publishing Ltd., the London Stock Exchange, and the International Securities Market Association for providing market statistics.

Noël Clarke
16 July 1992

Introduction

The subject of Eurobonds has long enjoyed a mystique that has relegated it in most people's minds to the realms of the esoteric, that is, intelligible only to the initiated. This is perhaps not surprising. To begin with, the Eurobond market is a market of some considerable technical complexity. It is also an international wholesale market, where the average size of issue is large, the numbers of eligible issuers comparatively small, and where the names of issuers are often unfamiliar to households in their own country, never mind overseas. As for investors, their identity is not known at all, since Eurobonds for the most part are bearer instruments. All in all, the Eurobond market was remote from the parochial environment of a domestic capital market.

Nor were the intentions of the players designed to throw light on the market. Historically, Eurobonds were subscribed in large part from funds held offshore, that is, outside the country of residence of the owner. The capital gains and interest revenue on portfolios of Eurobonds held "offshore" were in many cases only liable for tax if repatriated to the investor's country of origin. Many investors still buy Eurobonds—among other securities—legitimately to shelter their wealth from tax. Issuers, for their part, had recourse to the Eurobond market to escape the fiscal, exchange control, or registration requirement imposed by national governments and which made raising money in their home capital market expensive, time-consuming, or even impossible. The recent constraint on lending forced on banks by strict capital adequacy ratios is also likely to encourage borrowers further to resort to the bond markets to raise their large-scale medium-term finance requirements.

Yet for all the mystique, Eurobonds are straightforward debt instruments. Thanks to gradual deregulation of domestic financial markets, they are today accessible to an ever-growing population of issuers and investors—hitherto confined to their home capital markets. The recent emergence of the global Eurobond, for example, is helping to break the barrier between the offshore bond market and the United States domestic bond market, the largest of its kind. There is a need, therefore, which this book attempts to meet, to dispel the myths and make intelligible the nature of Eurobonds and the large variety of derivative products, currency sectors, and investor markets which the market encompasses.

At a practical level, this book aims also to explain basic calculations of value performed both manually and using the Hewlett-Packard calculator HP-12C which by now is standard issue to every practitioner. The structure of an issue is also illustrated by its documentation, whose components are reviewed by Clifford Chance, leading legal advisor in London to the market.

Practitioners also acquire subjective skills to assess bond market conditions and to price a new issue. There is no substitute for experience in this area, yet most Eurobond investment bankers are unable or unwilling to impart these skills to their new recruits, let alone new issuers. Therefore an attempt is made here to introduce some of the thought processes which are applied in the delicate task of pricing. The exercise of judgment is then combined with resourcefulness in some case studies in financial engineering. These studies are drawn from actual financings and provide examples of finance structures used daily in Eurobond issues.

This book would not be complete without a review of the trend in securities' regulation as it affects the Eurobond market. Although the Eurobond market is technically offshore, it has its principal physical location in London. Most new issues are managed out of London and more than three-quarters of the secondary market trading in Eurobonds is conducted by securities houses located there. Since 1986, securities markets in the United Kingdom have been the subject of detailed and at times onerous regulation. The Securities and Futures Authority (resulting from the merger of the Securities Association with the Association of Futures Dealers and Brokers), and today the principal regulatory body for the U.K. securities industry, has demonstrated a pragmatic approach to the accommodation of the Eurobond market, which has brought about a much needed rationalization in trading houses' reporting procedures. Mindful of the risk of overregulation and the burden in time and expense of compliance, the SFA has produced a framework which is capable of evolution and whose principles are serving as inspiration for the regulation of dealings in international securities in continental European markets.

Short History of the International Bond Markets

At the turn of the twentieth century, the world international bond markets consisted solely of "foreign" issues, that is, bonds issued, placed, and traded in a bond market which was foreign to the issuer's country of incorporation.* These markets had most of the features recognizable in bond markets today:

- Issuers were typically foreign governments or private sector utilities such as railway companies.

- Issues were subscribed by retail and institutional investors.

- Issuers and investors were intermediated by continental private banks and old London merchant houses versed in the art of rechanneling surplus capital to finance development projects.

- Underwriting and the syndication of underwriting risk were established practices, and the structure of a bond—under English law—was similar to that prevailing today.

The Emergence of the United States as a World Economy. The period of the First World War saw little activity in the international bond markets, and the upheaval of the war itself had little impact on financial markets. In the early 1920s attention was focused on the rapid growth of the United States economy. The U.S. dollar, underpinned by large foreign trade surpluses, became a strong currency and boosted the appeal of U.S. industry for portfolio investment by foreigners. In this period, the world capital markets served primarily to channel European savings into the United States economy. Issuance activity elsewhere in the international markets remained small.

With European nations demoralized and impoverished by the war, the United States took the lead among industrialized nations and the ground was laid for the dollar to become the leading currency in the world economy. This emerging dominance was upset, however, by defaults by borrowers in Latin America, a key market for the United States, and later the New York stock market crash of 1929 which triggered further defaults and bankruptcies and led to the Great Depression in the United States and overseas. The collapse of confidence brought the international bond markets to a standstill in the early 1930s, and issuing activity did not resume until after the Second World War. The U.S. economy itself was resilient and by the mid-1930s had recovered its stance and, thanks to its substantial overseas markets, was able to continue prospering during the Second World War.

The Dollar as an International Currency. By the end of the Second World War, the dollar, already a familiar currency to international investors, was achieving worldwide acceptance for the settlement of international trade transactions. From being a local currency, it was consecrated as an

---

* The concept of an international bond issue goes back to the 14th century. Edward I financed his wars through bond issues launched in Italy by the then big banking families.

international reserve asset at a conference at Bretton Woods (U.S.A.) in 1944. The conference, which brought together representatives of the major developed countries, laid the groundwork for a new international monetary order,* in particular to supplement and eventually supplant the ailing pound sterling as a reserve asset. Worldwide confidence and the inherent strength of the U.S. dollar made it a clear choice. Central banks henceforth agreed to use dollar reserves held in New York for the routine settlement of trade balances and, where necessary, the defense of their currencies.

Thus, the U.S. dollar was established as an international reserve asset and the primacy of the currency was reinforced when Britain imposed exchange controls in 1947 and devalued sterling by 30 percent in 1949. As the leading international currency, demand for U.S. dollars continued to rise from international investors, from entities active in international trade, and from monetary authorities keen to boost their reserves. Yet the supply of dollars remained limited and the scarcity value of the currency underpinned its appreciation. At the same time, the preeminence of the dollar was matched by the ascendance of the U.S. capital markets while issuance activity in Europe by foreign and domestic borrowers after the war was scant. Following the introduction of exchange controls, London ceded its role in international bond finance to New York, which attracted both borrowers and issuing houses from overseas.

The Eurodollar. As the Cold War broke out in the early 1950s, several communist countries, including China and the Soviet Union, fearful of the possibility of their dollar assets in New York being frozen, transferred their dollar accounts to European banks. The first such transfer was by the Soviet Union to a bank established in France, Banque Commerciale pour l'Europe du Nord, whose telegraphic address was *Eurobank*. This was the first instance in which the expression *Euro-* was used in a financial market and soon a dollar held in a deposit in a bank outside the United States became known as a *Eurodollar.*

Continued demand for U.S. dollars in the early 1950s kept the currency strong. However, the high value of the dollar made U.S. goods become uncompetitive abroad and the trade surpluses turned gradually into deficits. The currency did not weaken at first because dollar balances accumulated by non-U.S. residents were not sold. Instead, continued confidence in the currency led foreign central banks and foreign suppliers to the United States to accumulate U.S. dollar holdings, much of which were in offshore accounts. However, the U.S. trade deficits were compounded by massive investment by U.S. corporations abroad, by foreign loans by U.S. banks, and by military procurement to NATO bases in overseas countries. By the end of the decade, the continuous outflows had turned the dollar into a weak currency.

---

* The Bretton Woods Conference led directly to the creation of the International Monetary Fund (1945) and the International Bank for Reconstruction and Development (1945).

In an attempt at defensive measures, the U.S. authorities enacted a series of regulations starting with the Interest Equalization Tax (IET)* in 1963. The IET did little to help the U.S. balance of payments,[†] but succeeded in discouraging U.S. investors from buying foreign securities. This was to prove the catalyst for the emergence of the Eurobond market.[‡]

Thus denied their principal source of foreign capital, foreign borrowers (mainly European) looked for alternative sources of capital which would not be constrained by exchange controls (United Kingdom), fiscal disincentives (United States) or capital controls (West Germany and Switzerland). Shortly after the introduction of IET, S.G. Warburg & Co. launched the first offshore bond issue denominated in U.S. dollars for the Italian state motorway agency, Autostrade.[§] In the same year a total of US$145 million in new Eurobond issues was raised, and by 1968 the volume of new issues had risen to US$3 billion.

On the strength of its early success, the Eurobond market quickly established itself:

- It had a *marketplace* in London and could draw on a sophisticated capital markets infrastructure.

- The British authorities looked favorably on the market, which was allowed to develop without regulation or restriction. London became, and remains today (despite capital adequacy and investor protection rules), the principal center for new issues and the trading of U.S. dollar-denominated Eurobonds.

- The relative *speed* and *simplicity* of issuing in the Eurobond market compared with the principal foreign bond market, the U.S. "Yankee" market,[1] attract numerous issuers.

- The establishment in 1969 of a *voluntary trade organization,* the Association of International Bond Dealers (AIBD)—now known as the International Securities Market Association (ISMA)—provided a forum for

---

* The IET was levied on purchases by U.S. residents of debt and equity instruments issued by foreign entities. The effect of the tax was to increase by around 1 percent the annualized cost of funds to borrowers, thus raising issuance costs in the United States to the level of cost of issuance overseas—hence the name.

[†] The IET was followed by the Foreign Direct Investment Regulations in 1964–1965 with a similar objective of stemming the outflow of dollars and obliging U.S. corporations to finance their foreign operations offshore. This gave a substantial boost to Eurobond issuance.

[‡] The first Eurobond issue actually predates IET and was launched in 1961 for a Portuguese oil company in European Units of Account (the composite currency originally used for accounting purposes by the European Community).

[§] The issue, for US$15 million, was guaranteed by state development agency IRI and had a maturity of 15 years. The U.K. lead manager underwrote the issue jointly with other European banks and thus made up an international syndicate; the issue was sold internationally throughout Europe.

[1] The Yankee bond market is the new issue and secondary market for dollar issues issued by non-U.S. borrowers in the U.S. domestic market.

the formulation of Eurobond trading and settlement practices, the study of technical issues, and rules for the orderly functioning of the market.

- The early establishment of *clearing systems,* Euroclear and Cedel in 1969 and 1970, respectively, resolved the problems of delivery and custody.

The Dominance of the U.S. Dollar. The huge supply of offshore U.S. dollar liquidity alone has assured the dollar its continued role as dominant currency of issue in the Eurobond market. It is also the largest pool of *unregulated* and *freely convertible* investment funds worldwide, replenished each year by large reflows of interest and principal repayments on outstanding issues. Thus, where a borrowing requirement is very large, there is no other resort. Sovereign borrowers such as Italy and Canada have raised as much as US$1 billion and more in a single issue. The larger the issue, the better its liquidity and popularity with investors. In contrast, the principal European currencies did not achieve full convertibility until 1958, and issuance restrictions and exchange controls applied in some cases until the late 1980s.

Other factors reinforce the prominence of the U.S. dollar in the Eurobond market. The U.S. domestic capital market was and still is the largest in the world and arbitrage between the domestic and offshore U.S. dollar bond markets provides the largest and most liquid interest rate exchange (or swaps)* market. Currency swaps are all quoted against floating-rate Eurodollars. Eurodollar interest rate futures contracts are the second most traded contracts, after U.S. Treasury stock.

Despite the central role of the U.S. dollar in the international money markets, there came about a gradual decline in the use of the currency in international bond issuance. The devaluations of 1971 and 1973, the subsequent floating of the currency, and its steady decline throughout the 1980s led to a marked fall in international confidence in the dollar as a store of wealth. The change of emphasis in U.S. domestic monetary policy toward the control of monetary aggregates, instituted in 1979 by the New York Federal Reserve head Paul Volcker, brought about higher volatility of interest rates which had a further destabilizing effect on investor confidence.

By contrast, European currencies over the same period became more stable, first by loosely coalescing in the "snake" in 1973 and later by adhering to a formal exchange rate mechanism embodied in the European Monetary System (EMS) in 1979 whose benefits in terms of currency stability and the control of inflation are now widely accepted. The EMS encouraged institutional investors, notably central banks which were unhappy about the U.S. dollar to diversify the currency exposure of their international securi-

---

* An *interest rate swap* is an exchange of an obligation to pay interest at a fixed rate for an obligation to pay interest at a floating rate. The debt financings which these obligations relate to are usually raised in separate markets. Borrowers enter into such exchanges on the basis that each wants to pay interest on the (fixed/floating) basis of the debt of the counterparty, which can raise money at a lower cost than would be the case in their own market.

ties portfolios. Other institutions, such as insurance companies and pension funds with prudential currency exposure strategies, followed suit and reinforced the trend in growing shares of different currencies in the new issues market.

Definition of the Eurobond Market. While the Eurobond market's existence is predicated on the postwar international monetary order, the actual impetus which led to its creation was an opportunistic response to the closure of the U.S. domestic capital markets to foreign borrowers. In the early years of its growth, the market depended on continuing restrictions and regulations in domestic capital markets to offer itself as an alternative. In time, however, the market has grown to establish itself as the leading international market in its own right.

During the three decades of its activity, various domestic events, such as the abolition of IET in 1974 and the abolition of U.S. withholding tax in 1984, were thought to herald the absorption of the Eurodollar bond market into the U.S. Yankee bond market. When IET was abolished, the share of Yankee bonds in the international bond market did indeed rise. However, international issuers, tired of the delays and costs of registering new issues with the SEC and international investors, for their part were wise to the inherent weakness of the dollar and were eager for bond investments denominated in other currencies. By the time U.S. withholding tax was abolished, U.S. issuers, who were the most likely to return to the U.S. domestic market, were by then well-versed in the technique of interest rate and currency swaps introduced in early 1980. The art was to launch Eurobond issues in third currencies and attach currency and interest-rate swaps to obtain floating-rate funding in U.S. dollars at below normal market cost. The gain in cost was achieved by arbitraging the domestic and Eurodollar capital markets. The U.S. domestic capital markets on their own could offer no such mechanism. The widespread use of swaps in the international capital markets enabled newly enfranchised borrowers, without any commercial reason to launch an international issue, to issue Eurobonds and thereby avail themselves of the value added of financial arbitrage techniques not available in domestic markets.*

The abolition of withholding tax in the United States triggered similar fiscal liberalization in European countries and was followed by the dismantling of exchange controls regulating access of domestic investors to foreign securities markets. The value of this in terms of size of issue and liquidity was soon realized. Eurobond issuing houses quickly identified the potential and harnessed new markets of onshore investors to the benefit of international issuers. As regards countries such as the United States, Japan

---

* Many such issues were bought by the investors of their own country and led to the paradox that domestic savings (e.g., in the United Kingdom and Japan) were channeled into their respective domestic industries via the international debt securities markets. This was a signal commentary on the efficiency of international capital markets.

and Australia, where access to the domestic securities markets is heavily regulated, the Eurobond has been adapted into a new Euro-investment, the global bond, which is capable of being placed with both offshore and domestic investors.

The definition or delimitation of the Eurobond market is thus no longer an issue. From having been a market for an anonymous and invisible breed of offshore investors, the target investor audience is now bounded only by the resourcefulness of the issuing houses.

Vulnerable Areas.   A more genuine challenge to the Eurobond market is its poor profitability. Historically, this was due to high proportion of U.S. dollar-denominated debt traded by the market. Investors and issuing houses alike, which hold positions in dollar securities, are vulnerable to measures by the U.S. monetary authorities to control domestic demand and to defend the currency. The danger to issuing houses has taken the form of sudden increases in short-term interest rates which caused losses (or *negative carry*) on their holdings of bonds as a result of the excess of the cost of funding over the coupon income. This occurred markedly in 1974, again in 1978, 1979, in 1980 and later, following the steady decline in rates over 1982–1985, to a lesser extent in 1987. Increases in short-term interest rates have usually heralded an increase in rates throughout the entire maturity spectrum. Anticipating this development, active investors have often compounded the banks' running losses on new (fixed-income) issues by selling holdings of medium-term bonds and reinvesting the proceeds in higher-yielding (short-term) money market instruments until the rate structure had risen, at which point they reinvested in bonds. Market makers then accumulated investor paper in addition to their existing positions. These inventories were partly hedged but, if the negative carry costs were too high, positions were realized and losses taken. Prime intermediaries suffered large losses in this way and many second-tier or poorly capitalized houses withdrew from the market altogether.

The other problem of the Eurobond market is excess capacity and the attendant problem of cutthroat competition for business. Following the stock markets crash of October 1987, issuing houses and investment banks were under increased pressure to produce fee revenue. The unrelenting competition for new issue business, the cost of compliance with statutory regulation, and capital adequacy ratios, in addition to poor trading conditions, caused by the gradual rise in U.S. dollar interest rates also led to large losses and, hence, withdrawals and closures. Among these were some prime issuing houses such as Orion Royal Bank, Lloyds, Bank of America, the Euromarket operations of U.S. investment banks (such as Paine Webber, Dean Witter), and brokering houses (such as Purcell Graham). Many closures were decided on a refusal to commit further capital for a minimal or negative return. The larger and better capitalized houses, however, were able to postpone or ignore the decision. But these were few in number and by the mid-1980s there was already a trend towards an oligopolistic market, dominated by a dozen highly capitalized investment banks and securities subsidiaries of universal banks. This trend has now become the established pattern of intermediaries of the Eurobond market.

These houses alone have been able to withstand adverse trading conditions and to indulge continuously in ferocious price-cutting for the sake of buying market share. These institutions, too, sustained losses on their securities underwriting operations; however, loss-making Eurobond operations were tolerated so long as they could be cross-subsidized by more profitable activities. At industry level, these collective loss-making activities had the effect not only of accelerating the withdrawal of competitors but, equally, of discouraging potential entrants.

Over the last two years, the industry has become leaner and has fewer participants. At the same time, there has been a marked improvement in bond trading conditions and the leading Eurobond issuing and trading houses are trading profitably again. And, while there is still excess capacity, a focus on the "bottom line" has taken over from aspirations of prestige. Attention is now turning to bringing the Eurobond trading houses into line with regulatory and market standards presently enforced in domestic markets. For investors, the introduction of systems to promote greater transparency in secondary market trading—hitherto rejected by Eurobond houses to protect their securities trading revenue—is one of the priorities on the agenda. Institutional investors who have sophisticated facilities and account for three-quarters of all trading, expect that their Eurobond dealings are conducted by trading houses on the same footing—in terms of ethical practices and price transparency—as their securities dealings in the principal regulated domestic markets.

The market's scope is thus in continual change, reflecting not merely the opening or closing of new frontiers but also the changing requirements of issuers and investors. In so doing, early notions are being continually challenged. Many sovereign and public sector issuers now eschew public offerings in favor of private placements. New issues are not necessarily sold through an international syndicate. Bearer form is considered dispensable in the interests of enhanced liquidity. The definition of the market is thus never static and international legislation such as the European Community Directives on a single financial market will undoubtedly cause it to change yet again. Yet the market's versatility and ability to adapt to a changing environment appears to be a constant and is the best guarantee of its continued service and survival.

Table 1-1. New Issue Volume of International Debt Securities (1984–1991) (in US$ millions)

	1984	1985	1986	1987	1988	1989	1990	1991
Foreign bonds*	25,529	29,574	36,850	38,865	48,464	44,259	50,974	49,514
Eurobonds†	79,290	132,875	180,182	135,023	175,913	211,819	175,857	247,773
Total international issuance of public debt securities	104,819	162,449	217,032	173,888	227,377	256,078	226,831	297,287

* Twenty-one currency sectors including the U.S. dollar, the Deutsche mark, the European Currency Unit, the Canadian dollar, sterling, the Australian dollar, the Austrian schilling, the Belgian franc, the Danish kroner, the Dutch guilder, the French franc, the Hong Kong dollar, the Italian lira, the Luxembourg franc, the New Zealand dollar, the Singapore dollar, the Swiss franc, the Finnish marrka, the Irish punt, the Spanish peseta, and the Portuguese escudo.

The principal sectors in the world foreign bond markets, ranked in decreasing order, over the period 1984–1991 are the Swiss franc (50.4 percent), the U.S. dollar (Yankee bonds) (21.1 percent), the Japanese yen (Samurai bonds) (14.6 percent), the Luxembourg franc (3.9 percent), the Spanish peseta (2.2 percent), the pound sterling (Bulldog bonds) (1.4 percent). Together these account for 93.6 percent of all issuance of foreign bonds in that period.

† Twenty-two currency sectors excluding the Swiss franc (there is no Euro-Swiss franc bond market). For shares of the different Eurobond currency sectors, see Table 4.3 on p. 93.

SOURCE: Euromoney Bondware.

Table I-2. Comparison of New Issues of Domestic and International Medium-Term Debt Securities in 1991 (in US$ millions)*

International		Domestic		
Eurobonds	Foreign bonds	United Kingdom	United States[†]	Japan
247,773	49,514	37,061	621,032	754,718

* Exchange rate assumptions: US$1.00 = Yen 130 and US$1.85 = £1.00.
† Medium-term notes included.
SOURCES: Euromoney Bondware; Daiwa Europe Limited; Salomon Brothers International.

Table I-3. The Eurobond Market: Volume of Outstanding Issues at Year End, 1967–1991 (in US$ billions)

1967	7	1972	25	1977	62	1982	182	1987	659
1968	11	1973	27	1978	76	1983	227	1988	755
1969	14	1974	29	1979	90	1984	300	1989	887
1970	18	1975	40	1980	108	1985	423	1990	998
1971	20	1976	43	1981	130	1986	565	1991	1148

SOURCE: International Securities Market Association.

Table I-4. Estimated Volumes of Outstanding Medium-Term Debt Securities at Year End, 1991 (in US$ millions)*

International	Domestic[†]		
Eurobond	United Kingdom	United States[‡]	Japan
1,148,000	289,945	5,623,900	2,754,995

* Exchange rate assumptions: US$1.00 = Yen 130 and US$1.85 = £1.00.
† Issues by domestic borrowers, including government and municipal authorities in their own currency.
‡ Medium-term notes included.
SOURCES: ISMA; Daiwa Europe Ltd.; Salomon Brothers International; International Stock Exchange.

Table I-5. Eurobond New Issue Volume, 1963–1991

Year	$M (equiv.)	No. of issues
1963	150	14
1964	1,155	76
1965	852	72
1966	991	61
1967	1,679	80
1968	2,925	116
1969	2,620	103
1970	2,605	120
1971	3,783	141
1972	4,800	191
1973	2,603	80
1974	1,307	60
1975	6,167	198
1976	11,365	283
1977	14,838	312
1978	11,381	233
1979	14,193	252
1980	18,958	307
1981	25,189	387
1982	45,516	565
1983	40,065	466
1984	81,080	761
1985	118,490	1,186
1986	168,798	1,533
1987	141,939	1,377
1988	178,167	1,561
1989	221,710	1,703
1990	158,566	1,115
1991	227,730	1,307

SOURCE: IFR Bondbase.

1
The Nature of a Eurobond

The Eurobond is an international debt security and draws its conception and structure from standard debt securities used in domestic bond markets. In these respects it shares with them the basic characteristics which define the role of bonds in financial markets:

- A Eurobond is a debt contract between a borrower and an investor, which records the borrower's obligation to pay interest and the principal amount of the bond on specified dates.*
- A Eurobond is transferable; that is, its ownership is capable of being transferred from one investor to another.*
- A Eurobond is a medium- to long-term debt security.
- A Eurobond is intended to be tradeable, that is, bought and sold during the period up to its maturity.
- A Eurobond issue is generally launched through a public offering and listed on a stock exchange.

Thus Eurobonds are no different in their purpose, function, or contractual form than domestic or "foreign" bonds. How then are they differentiated? These domestic, "foreign," and Eurobond markets are defined and differentiated most clearly by their respective underwriting, syndicate, and pri-

---

* For a full account of the legal nature of a Eurobond and a Eurobond issue, see Chapter 10, "Anatomy of a Eurobond Issue."

1

mary placement practices, and the following examples will best illustrate the distinctions between them:

- *Domestic bonds:*

  General Motors Inc., a U.S. corporation, issues bonds in the United States for placement in the U.S. domestic market, i.e., with U.S. investors resident in the United States.

  The issue is underwritten by a syndicate of domestic underwriters, i.e., a group of U.S. securities houses.

  The issue is denominated in the currency of the investors, i.e., U.S. dollars.

- *Foreign bonds:*

  Volvo (Sweden), a foreign corporation, issues bonds in the United States, for placement in the U.S. market alone.

  The issue is underwritten by a syndicate of U.S. securities houses.

  The issue is denominated in the currency of the intended investors, i.e., U.S. dollars.

- *Eurobonds:*

  Volvo, a foreign corporation, issues, in a major international financial center, bonds to be placed internationally (subject only to selling restrictions of individual national jurisdictions).

  The issue is underwritten by an *international* syndicate of securities houses.

  The issue is denominated in any currency, including even the currency of the borrower's country of incorporation.

Further distinctions between domestic, foreign, and Eurobonds arise in secondary market trading. While domestic and foreign bonds are traded in the domestic market, Eurobonds may be traded in any financial center (subject to local securities regulations). There are separate procedures, too, for settlement and custody.

Together the "foreign" bond and Eurobond markets make up the international bond market. These definitions, however, while of some help in clarifying the role of each market, are no longer of lasting importance and as domestic markets deregulate, the distinction between the international and domestic markets is becoming blurred too. Thus, foreign bond issues have been sold into both the domestic and international markets through the inclusion of international banks in the syndicate. Conversely, Eurobond issues by U.K. private sector borrowers, denominated in sterling, with British syndicates and intentionally placed mainly with U.K. institutional investors are domestic issues in all but name. Until recently, Eurobond issues in Deutsche mark were required to be issued out of Germany under all-German syndicates, which assimilated them to foreign issues with international placement. These and other distinctions are examined in detail in the review of the currency sectors in Chapter 4.

Structure of a Eurobond

Each issue of Eurobond securities is subject to the *terms and conditions* which make up its structure. A typical structure comprises some twenty such terms and conditions which recur in most issues. Some of these, such as the prepayment provisions and covenants, are adapted in each issue to reflect the conditions in the bond markets, the circumstances of the borrower, and the particular financing which is the subject of the issue. Other provisions such as bearer form, payments of interest free of withholding tax, remain unchanged and are considered as "market practice." However, few such terms have the force of standards, far less that of a statutory requirement.

The full terms and conditions of an issue are printed on the actual bond, which for practical (rather than legal) purposes, has three components:

- *The face.* Sets out the name of the borrower, short details on maturity, the interest-rate coupon (or, in the case of floating rate securities, the interest base and margin), and the formal promise to pay interest and principal.

- *The reverse.* Sets out (1) the terms and conditions of the issue and (2) the details of the banks responsible for payments of interest and principal (*the paying agents*).

- *The coupons.* The third component of the bond is a series of detachable coupons which are presented on interest payment dates as evidence of entitlement to payment. These are identical in all respects except the date of payment (see following).

The principal features and the terms and conditions of an issue and their relationship to the structure are examined in the following pages, while legal relationships are reviewed in Chapter 10 under "Documentation."

Face of the Bond

The Issuer. Traditional issuers in the Eurobond market are major international entities with (1) substantial business operations, (2) sufficient credit standing to permit of unsecured borrowing, and (3) visibility among international investors. Thus typical issuers include:

- Supranational bodies (World Bank, EEC, European Coal and Steel Community, Euratom, etc.)

- Sovereign governments (Italy, Sweden, Austria, etc.)

- Public sector agencies (Hydro-Quebec, State Electricity Corporation of Victoria, etc.)

- State-owned corporations (Japanese Air Lines, Gaz de France, etc.)

- Regional development banks (Inter American Development Bank, Asian Development Bank, etc.)

- International commercial banks (Deutsche Bank, Credit Lyonnais, J. P. Morgan, etc.)
- Private sector multinational corporations (IBM, Volkswagen, British Airways, etc.)

Issuers of lesser international standing but prominent in their domestic market have also tapped the Eurobond market including:

- Private sector corporations financing overseas operations (e.g., U.S. corporations, in the wake of IET)
- During the late 1980s, middle-ranking Japanese corporations with low international profile and little borrowing requirement issued very extensively in the Swiss franc and Eurodollar bond markets. Issues typically included warrants giving the investor a right to purchase the equity of the borrower. The resulting cost of funds was very low and the proceeds were often applied to reinvestment in securities.
- Another class of issuer to emerge in the late 1980s is the "one purpose" company with no prominence internationally or at home. These are set up by one or a syndicate of financial institutions to acquire and hold financial assets, including mortgages, commercial receivables, or existing securities. The portfolio of assets, hitherto financed by bank loans, is refinanced through a Eurobond issue. The share capital of the issuer is small and the borrowing entity may even be a trust, i.e., without shareholders. The income from the asset portfolio is pledged in priority to the service of the debt. Such issues are said to be *collateralized* or *asset-backed* and the loan portfolio is said to be *securitized*. (See Chapter 2, p. 48.)
- The last category of issuer—and a common one—is the small one-purpose company incorporated offshore as a subsidiary of a private sector corporate borrower. These companies, known as *finance vehicles,* are purposely incorporated in jurisdictions which do not levy withholding tax and are used as alternative issuers in the instance where the borrower, by issuing in its domestic or in a "foreign" bond market would have to withhold tax on the interest payments of such an issue and thereby deny itself access to the Eurobond investor market.

The Guarantee.   Guarantees feature in Eurobond issues principally for reasons of:

- *Withholding tax.*   Where the issuer is an offshore finance vehicle, the credit of the issuer is supported by a guarantee of the parent company (see previous); payments under the issue are guaranteed by the parent and are free of withholding tax. If the guarantee were called, payments under the guarantee by the parent in some cases could be subject to withholding tax and would have to be "grossed-up" (see tax section following).

- *Credit.* Guarantees are also found where the issuer is a company or overseas subsidiary whose size or strength of credit is insufficient to support an unsecured Eurobond obligation and where the parent is reluctant to borrow in its own name because of balance sheet or accounting considerations and buys the guarantee of a third party. This notion has been adapted by little known Japanese corporate borrowers which have launched issues under the guarantee of a major international Japanese bank which lends its own credit to the issue.

Similarly, one-purpose companies created to hold a parcel of financial assets (see previous) are funded by an issue of Eurobonds under guarantee of a bank or even a financial insurance policy issued by an insurance group which lends its credit rating to the issue.

To comply with guidelines issued by the Eurobond International Primary Markets Association, a guarantee on a Eurobond issue should:

1. cover all amounts due including principal, premium (on early redemption), interest and additional amounts on gross-up
2. stand alone and be valid independently of the bonds
3. be enforceable whether or not prior action is taken to enforce the terms and conditions of the bonds
4. not be affected by any waiver or modification in terms given in respect of the bonds

Guarantees offering protections (1–4) are termed *indemnities;* other guarantees offering protection on amounts due only (item 1) are termed *sureties.* Guarantees may take one of several forms and are:

1. contractual (i.e., purposely created to support the credit of the issuer, as private sector corporations and banks, etc.)
2. contained in the statutes of the borrower (e.g., government agencies and government-owned corporations)
3. established by decree or parliamentary act (e.g., government agencies)

Issue Size. The size of an issue varies as a function of:

- the borrower's financing requirement
- the size and appetite from time to time of the investor market (US$ and Deutsche mark markets offer the largest amounts in a single issue)
- the choice of instrument (fixed or floating rate)
- the professional bond market and investors' perception of the borrower's industry, ranking, and financial condition

- general economic data including interest rate, inflation, and currency expectations
- bond market conditions (i.e., heavy or light issuance activity; expectation of movement in yield on benchmark issues)
- restrictions on amount, if any, placed by the monetary authorities of the currency of denomination

The first fixed rate Eurobond issue launched in 1963 was for US$15 million but as the market acquired depth, issue sizes of US$100 million were soon commonplace. The current range of issue size is US$100–400 million and rising, mainly because of the continuing demand for liquidity. Larger-size issues are more widely distributed and thus more readily tradeable. The single largest fixed rate offering is an issue of ECU2.75 billion (approx. US$3.5 billion) raised in 1991 by the United Kingdom. The Republic of Italy has raised ECU2.5 billion and issues of US$1.5 and US$1 billion. In the floating rate sector, the largest issue size is US$4 billion for the United Kingdom.

Final Maturity. The maturity date stated on the face of the bond denotes the last date of redemption or repayment of the bonds (see p. 9 for early redemption dates). The maturity of a Eurobond issue is determined by three considerations:

- *Currency perception.* In an international market, investors have a concern not only for quality of risk and yield, but also currency exposure. The relevance of currency perception to maturity preference is best illustrated by the case of the U.S. dollar. Among the first Eurobond issues in the mid 1960s were some fixed rate Eurodollar offerings with maturities of 15 years. As U.S. inflation rose and the trade deficit grew, the weakness of the currency became more apparent and interest rates, which were used to defend the currency, became volatile. The lack of confidence and increased volatility in the bond markets led to a gradual disappearance of international demand for long-term fixed rate Eurodollar bonds.* Since the early 1980s, the range of maturities in U.S. dollars has been 3–7 years reflecting shorter-term investment strategies, imperfect hedging instruments, and illiquidity of longer-term issues.
- *Market considerations.* In the fixed rate sector, a key determinant for the borrower's choice of maturity is the differential in coupon cost for different maturities, which is shown by the yield curve (see Chapter 3).

The maturity is also dictated by the choice of instrument: the longest fixed rate maturity is 30 years while floating rate issues have been issued

---

* This is not the case in all markets: Eurobonds denominated in sterling, whose perception in the international currency markets is often weaker than the U.S. dollar, has consistently offered long maturities because of national—rather than international—demand for long-dated sterling debt.

without final maturity. Occasionally regulatory constraints have been imposed on longer maturities so as to reserve these for the government's own debt financing.

Where market conditions did not permit, a number of devices have been used to offer issuers longer maturities including (1) issues in two tranches with different maturities; (2) with investor options to extend the maturity (extendable) or reduce it (retractable). In general, issues with these features have suffered from poor liquidity.

- *Borrower requirements.* The selection of a maturity will clearly take account of the borrower's funding requirement and cost target. In order to optimize the cost of the financing, it may be cheaper to issue in another currency and swap the proceeds into the desired currency of exposure, in which case the maturity of the bond issue is subject to the choice of maturity offered in the swaps markets. An opportunistic borrower may then select a maturity offering the most cost attractive swap in priority to the maturity of his funding requirement.

The TEFRA Legend. The United States Tax Equity and Fiscal Responsibility Act of 1982 requires debt securities held by U.S. residents to be in registered form so as to prevent evasion of U.S. income tax. The breach of this regulation carries sanctions not only against investors but against issuers as well, whether or not incorporated in the United States. However, in order not to jeopardize the access of U.S. incorporated borrowers to the Eurobond market, Eurobond issues were exempted from the scope of the Act, regardless of the issuer, provided:

- the issue is intended to be issued to non-U.S. residents only (and thus qualify for the "foreign offering" exemption from registration under the Securities Act of 1933).

- the issue paid interest only outside the United States.

- the bonds carried a statement, known as the *TEFRA* legend, to the effect that "the holder was subject to limitations under the U.S. Income Tax laws," in effect the loss of a right to offset capital gains or losses on the bonds against gains or losses on other assets.

The TEFRA Act is the prime example of how domestic legislation has served to circumscribe the scope of the Eurobond market. Taken in conjunction with the U.S. Securities Act, the primary distribution of Eurobonds is in effect denied access to the U.S. market, except in the form of private placements in registered form.

Authentication. From being mere pieces of paper, the bonds become valid instruments by being *authenticated* or certified as authentic on the face of the Note at the time of *closing* or payment of the proceeds of the issue.

Certification is performed either by an officer of the borrower or the paying agent.

Terms and Conditions
(Reverse of Bond)

Redemption. The redemption provisions deal with the program of scheduled mandatory repayment of principal and takes the form of:

- a *BULLET* repayment (i.e., a single payment of the full face amount of the bond on the maturity date)
- an *amortization* schedule, which is a series of partial repayments on specified interest payment dates prior to and including the final maturity date

Amortization is effected in one of three ways:

- *A sinking fund* (or *sinker*) is a program of mandatory redemption of a stated principal amount of bonds each year at 100 percent of face value. Sinking funds typically take effect some years after the issue date and consist of equal or increasing annual repayments, leaving a balance or *balloon* repayment due on the final maturity date. The obligation is met by drawing bonds by lot and publishing their serial numbers in the financial press. The amount of drawings may be reduced by prior purchases by the issuer of its own bonds in the secondary market, usually at prices below the redemption price of 100 percent. The drawing of lots, the publicity, and the payments are normally managed by the paying agent acting on behalf of the issuer.
- *A purchase fund* is a program of repurchases of bonds in the secondary market either (1) up to a stated principal amount or (2) by reference to a period of time. The program is triggered by a fall in price of the bonds in the secondary market, below a certain level, usually par. Because of the potential difficulty of purchasing bonds which are illiquid, purchase fund programs are undertaken on a "best-efforts" rather than a mandatory basis.
- *Serial Notes* are bonds where a fixed portion of each security is repaid and canceled on scheduled redemption dates; the face value of the securities and the interest payable thereon are reduced pro rata. Serial amortization is rare and, in the past, associated with FRN issues by weaker sovereign credits; it provides an easier repayment scheme and lends support to the issue.

Sinking funds typically allow a longer grace period than purchase funds before repayment begins but can be unfavorable to the investor: if the bonds are trading *above* par, the investor suffers a capital loss. Both amortization schemes are now comparatively rare, while serial notes are usually associated with Eurobonds issued in registered form.

The effect of amortization programs is to reduce the period during which the borrower has the use of 100 percent of the proceeds of the issue (see Chapter 3 for worked examples and calculations). The issuer is aware at the outset of the average life of the issue but from the investors' point of view, the concept is potentially misleading: with the exception of serial notes, there is no guarantee that an individual holding will be redeemed according to the schedule of redemption of the issue taken as a whole.

Optional Redemption. Some issues give the borrower the option (or *call*) to redeem or *prepay* all or part of the issue prior to final maturity. The option becomes available normally after the issue has run a half to two-thirds of its life and is exercisable generally on the anniversary of the issue and thereafter on interest payment dates, by repayment at par or at a small premium which declines in successive years. The feature is valuable to a borrower whose issue was launched in a period of high interest rates. The exercise of the call will be determined by the cost of refinancing prevailing at the time of the call in relation to the coupon on the existing bond.

Issues also have the option to prepay when the fiscal authority with jurisdiction over the issuer modifies the provision of exemption from withholding tax. In such an instance, the issuer is required to make investors whole or *gross-up* through additional payments. Such additional payments are themselves subject to withholding tax and the increased costs of servicing the issue would normally lead the issuer to prepay, provided the cost of refinancing was not prohibitive.

Finally, major issuers may also require a right to purchase their own bonds in the secondary market and either hold the bonds as if they were investors, resell, or cancel.

Status. This term denotes the ranking of the issue in relation to the borrower's other debt. Eurobonds are normally (but not always) direct, unconditional, and unsecured, and rank on an equal footing or *pari passu* with all other unsecured obligations of the issuer. In effect, holders of a Eurobond with this status have the highest ranking as creditor (except for unsecured obligations which may be preferred by statute).

Gradations have been introduced and Eurobonds have been issued by commercial banks on a *subordinated* basis (i.e., with a ranking below that of depositors) and even on a *junior subordinated* basis to qualify as capital funds under capital adequacy rules. Bonds convertible into common stock or equity are by similar reasoning issued with a subordinated status.

Negative Pledge. This is an undertaking by the borrower not to enhance the status of other debt unless the benefit of such enhancement is also given to the issue. The undertaking affords little actual protection and, in the event of a breach by the issuer, the bondholders have no remedy but to accelerate repayment of the issue (under "Events of Default" following) and, in the event of a liquidation, to contest their claim, still unsecured against newly secured creditors.

Interest. Interest on Eurobonds is set either at a *fixed* rate, a *floating* rate, a combination of both, or a *nil* rate.

- *Fixed rate.* A Eurobond with a fixed rate of interest or fixed *coupon* pays interest annually in arrears and interest is calculated by convention on the basis of twelve months of 30 days each and a year of 360 days.

- *Floating rate.* A floating rate of interest on a Eurobond is expressed as the sum of an Interbank rate (e.g., the London Interbank Offered rate—LIBOR*—for 3 or 6 months' deposits) plus a margin.† Floating rate interest is calculated on a "money market" basis (i.e., the number of actual days elapsed in a year of 360 days and on a standard issue is paid in arrears semiannually or quarterly in keeping with the interest period of 6 or 3 months).

- *Zero rate.* Eurobonds which pay no interest are fixed-rate bonds with a zero coupon and are designated *zero-coupon bonds.* These are issued at a deep discount such that the redemption yield to the investor is similar to standard or "full coupon" fixed-rate bond of equivalent maturity (see Chapter 2).

Events of Default. Events of default are events which trigger the right of immediate repayment (i.e., prior to the final maturity date). Such events denote primarily active breaches of covenants by the borrower including:

- nonpayment of interest or principal when due, usually with a short grace period
- breach of undertakings (e.g., negative pledge)

Events of default are also designed to anticipate impending default or insolvency by including circumstances which, if realized, give the holders the opportunity to accelerate repayment prior to the collapse of the issuer, including:

- cross-default (i.e., default on payment or other obligations, as the case may be, under other borrowings)
- petition or order to wind up the issuer
- cessation or threatened cessation of business
- insolvency
- substantial disposals of assets affecting the ability of the issuer to service the issue

Where a trustee is appointed to represent the bondholders, the trustee *declares* an event of default and convenes the bondholders to decide on

---

* The London Interbank Bid Rate or LIBID is also used as reference base rate, and so is the mean of LIBOR and LIBID, referred to as LIMEAN.

† The margin is on a scale of a fraction of 1 percent, in the range of ⅟₁₆–⅜ percent. Some FRNs have a NIL or even a negative margin.

whether to require repayment. On issues where no trustee is appointed, the bondholders only have a direct recourse to the borrower.

Event-Related Put Options. Event-related investor put options are found in issues by private sector corporations and allow investors either to redeem their bonds at par or occasionally to be compensated for a higher risk by receiving higher coupon payments. Event risks which may trigger the put are normally tailored to the issuer and might typically include:

- a hostile or friendly takeover of the issuer
- a takeover by the issuer of another party
- a recapitalization
- a repurchase program by the issuer of its own shares
- a distribution of assets above a certain percentage of the issue's net worth

The guiding principle in the formulation of event risk is the possibility of circumstances or events which could lead to a much higher ratio of borrowings to shareholders' funds and/or deterioration of the ability of the issuer to service the debt. The borrower would normally require an objective assessment of the impact of such events, and a trigger such as a downgrading of the original rating of the issue is usually specified.

Taxation. Eurobond issues by design pay interest gross (i.e., without deduction of withholding or income taxes). Historically, the intention was to maximize yield by enabling investors to defer paying tax until the end of the fiscal year. The alternative would have been for issuers where applicable to make deductions of income tax at source, but this would have led to prohibitive tax management for investors.

- Different fiscal jurisdictions levied witholding tax on interest or coupon income paid to nonresidents at different rates.
- There were and still are few double taxation agreements to enable investors to offset the withholding tax against their other tax liabilities.

Investors holding securities offshore were not required in many cases to account for (or pay income tax on) the income on their holdings and, for such investors, a high-quality bond paying interest gross was an ideal instrument. Many offshore investors—both retail and institutional—managed Eurobond portfolios quite legitimately in this way and, for many years, the market developed in large measure thanks to its ability to supply offshore investors with tax free bonds. Recently, as Eurobond investors have become predominantly institutional, audit requirements and sophisticated tax management have reduced the importance of tax free coupon payments. Nonetheless, these are likely to remain a key attraction of Eurobonds for some time.

Compliance by the issuer with a requirement of its fiscal jurisdiction to withhold tax on interest or other payments triggers an obligation on the issuer to gross-up (i.e., to make additional payments to make investors whole). Where an issuer makes such additional payments, the issuer may pre-pay under the *tax call* option (see earlier section, "Optional Redemption").

Form.   A security is either in registered or bearer form. Eurobonds are mostly in bearer form, that is, without record of the owner, in keeping with traditional investor preference for anonymity. There are exceptions, including some issues by the Kingdom of Belgium and U.S. government agencies; Eurobonds issued as private placements to U.S. investors (to conform with U.S. securities legislation) are also in registered form to comply with U.S. fiscal legislation (TEFRA 1982, see previous section).

Recent research on investors has shown that a majority of international institutional investors have significant holdings of bonds in registered form (e.g., U.S. Treasury securities). This has opened up the possibility of Eurobond issues in registered form which could be launched not only in the Eurobond market but also the U.S. domestic market. The first such issue or so-called *global bond* was launched in the autumn of 1989.

Title.   This is a legal concept relating to quality of ownership. As regards bearer Eurobonds, the legal owner at any time is considered to be the holder of the bond. Thus, for the purpose of claiming interest and principal payments, it is sufficient that the holder presents, either directly or through agents, the coupons or the bond to the Paying Agent and on selling or transferring the securities, ownership is transferred by the act of physical delivery to the subsequent holder (see Chapter 10, section on "Documentation").

Denomination.   The denomination of a bond is the currency and amount of its face value. An issue whose distribution is targeted to institutional investors is commonly offered in denominations of US$10,000 rising to US$100,000 or even US$1 million. Conversely, issues targeted at retail investors include small denominations of US$1000 or even Aus$1000. Higher administration costs make these less popular with issuers.

Governing Law and Jurisdiction.   The legal documentation of the issue normally provides (1) for a system of law to govern the interpretation and enforcement of the terms and conditions of the issue and distribution agreements and (2) a jurisdiction agreed by the issuer in whose courts claims by investors may be heard. The system of law most commonly used is English law. For practical purposes, issuers will often agree to the jurisdiction of the courts of the country of the chosen system of law but may also stipulate the courts of their own country. Issues by sovereign governments normally include a waiver of sovereign immunity.

Prescription.   This term denotes a time limitation on the right of investors to present coupons or bonds to claim payment of interest or principal after the final maturity date. This is a common occurrence and the anonymity of investors precludes any measure to trace them. Typically, prescription provides for up to 10 years delay on payments of principal and 5 years on interest payments.

Other Terms and Conditions.   The terms and conditions of the bonds also provide for a number of practical matters including:

- *Further issues.* The borrower may reserve for itself the right to launch further issues on the same terms and conditions. These issues have in particular the same coupon, maturity, and any amortization provisions, so that the second issue may be "added," as it were, onto the first. Bonds under such further issues are termed *fungible* with the original issue and generally benefit the issuer and investors, who gain from a broader distribution of the same instrument.

- *The substitution of the borrower by a successor corporation or other body within a group, including the guarantor of an issue.* This provision is usually seen where the issue is guaranteed and a change of issuer is unlikely to affect the strength of the credit which relies more on the guarantor than the issuer.

- *The Fiscal Agent and the Paying Agents.* These are appointed by the borrower to effect, on its behalf, payments of interest and principal to the investors. Fiscal and Paying Agents generally do not assume obligations to the holders (aside from holding in trust for the investors funds received from the borrower to meet the payments).

- *The Trustee.* Issues under English law may provide for the appointment of a trustee whose function is to represent bondholders (see Chapter 5). Where a Trustee is appointed, the Fiscal Agent takes the title of Principal Paying Agent.

- *A currency rate indemnity.* Where an investor sues and obtains judgment in a currency other than the denomination of the bond, a delay in payment of the judgment could result in an exchange rate loss against which the investor is further protected by an indemnity.

The bond also carries other provisions concerning the administration of the issue including:

- provisions for convening meetings of bondholders
- the replacement of lost or stolen bonds and/or coupons
- the publication of Notices in the financial press

Nonstandard issues also include terms and conditions which are tailored to the structure of the issue and also printed on the bonds, including:

- on an issue of bonds convertible into shares, provisions for conversion
- on an issue of Eurobonds with debt or equity warrants attached, an additional page setting out (1) on the face, the entitlement under the warrant and (2) on the reverse, the terms and conditions of subscription, method of exercise and, in the case of equity warrants, calculations for the adjustment to subscription price following issues of shares
- on an issue whose repayment is linked to a currency or stock index, provision for the calculation of the repayment amount

- on an issue of guaranteed Notes, the full text of the guarantee printed on the face of the bond

- on an issue of collateralized Notes, the terms and conditions including further events of default relating to the nonperformance of the underlying assets

Market Characteristics

The terms and conditions of a bond issue provide a definition of its structure which to all intents and purposes remains static or unchanged throughout the life of the issue. By contrast, the behavior of a bond issue in the marketplace, after it is launched, is a matter of constant change. Reviewed here are the concepts of tradeability, liquidity, ratings, and listings which relate to the secondary market performance of an issue.

Tradeability. The majority of Eurobonds are tradeable.* They are assets which may be freely bought and sold during their life. For the investor, this is essential for speedy and effective management of a bond portfolio in response to changes in interest rates, currency, performance, and bond markets. For registered bonds the method of transfer of ownership is by book entry in a register kept for that purpose. For bearer bonds (which predominate), transfer of ownership or *title* is said to *pass by delivery* alone. Tradeability makes Eurobonds a convenient store of wealth which may be readily realized.

Liquidity. The liquidity of an issue is a measure of the ease of trading in that issue during its life in the aftermarket or secondary market (i.e., from the time when the issue is launched until its final maturity date).

To trade their bonds, end investors deal with investment banks or trading houses (or intermediaries) which intermediate between investors. Trading houses perform a key function in the aftermarket and thereby promote the liquidity of an issue depending on the degree of their commitment:

- Securities houses which merely match buyers and sellers are called *brokers* and provide liquidity which is conditional on their ability to trade.

- Intermediaries which buy or sell without matching the bargain with an equal and opposite transaction with third parties take a position; they provide liquidity to the issue, but this is an ad hoc commitment and dependent on their own trading strategy.

- Intermediaries who consistently quote a buy price and a sell price and deal on those prices are called *market makers*. Market makers' willingness to trade continuously regardless (in theory) of yield movements or bond market conditions provides the only unconditional guarantee of liquidity.

---

* The tradeable character of Eurobonds is sometimes referred to as *negotiability*. This is misleading: negotiability is a concept of English law dealing with the rights of the eventual holder of the bond and an attribute which is available to Eurobonds in bearer form only. Registered Eurobonds are *not* negotiable but are still tradeable.

Liquidity can be assured by a single market maker fulfilling its two-way quote function. More often a "liquid" issue denotes an *active two-way* market with a large number of buyers and sellers served by 6 to 12 market makers at any time. Large Eurobond issues tend to be more actively traded and more liquid than smaller ones—having been distributed in theory to a broader international investor base. Liquidity ultimately depends on the willingness of market making intermediaries to deal and hold positions in an issue. It has to be admitted that only relatively few houses in the Eurobond market have consistently fulfilled these functions:

- Many issues are of small size and institutional investors often hold their bonds to maturity. Thus the majority of issues including large size offerings are "tightly" held and the absence of trading volume discourages aggressive position taking.

- Senior market makers will generally claim to make markets in 500–2000 issues. However, the resource requirements for a consistent commitment, in terms of information technology, professional staff, and capital commitment are prohibitive even for the leading international intermediaries. All of these make a market in the larger-size issues where liquidity then becomes self-generating. On smaller issues, many houses display less consistency and decline to offer two-way prices in conditions of volatile interest rates.* The range of Eurobond issues in which there is genuine liquidity is thus relatively small.

Ratings.　A rating is an evaluation of an issuer's ability to service an individual debt in relation to other borrowings and the overall creditworthiness of the borrower. These evaluations are conducted by independent *rating agencies.*† By convention the best rating is AAA, followed by AA, A, and BBB which is the lowest rating for "investment grade" bonds. Clearly, ratings assist investors, few of whom have the means to undertake the credit analysis of a large number of issues. But issuers also benefit in that a sustained high rating will generally lead to a lower cost of funds.

Ratings are assigned to issues, not the issuers. Over half of all Eurobond issues are rated and the practice is increasing. Collateralized issues, which depend on the quality of the underlying assets are "ratings-driven," i.e., without a rating, there is no issue (see section on "Rating Agencies," Chapter 5).

---

* Intermediaries intent on trading an issue in a poor market engage in the practice of selling short, i.e., selling bonds which they do not own and thus creating a "short" position which they close by buying back bonds when their price has fallen. This practice is beneficial by providing liquidity in the short term; however, it can trigger rapid price falls when the market perceives a lack of investor interest in the bonds. A notorious instance of this arose in the perpetual FRN market which, by the autumn of 1986, was saturated by new issues. Short selling led to sharp falls in prices, market makers withdrew from the market, and liquidity in this US\$17 billion market disappeared altogether.

† The best known Eurobond rating agencies are Moody's Investor Services and Standard and Poor's Corporation.

Listings. Most Eurobond issues are listed on at least one stock exchange, usually London or Luxembourg (but never New York*). A stock exchange is the traditional forum for secondary market trading in a security. In practice, the volume of Eurobond trading on the floor of the exchanges is minimal and most trading is conducted instead between market makers direct. This is referred to as *over-the-counter* trading.

A listing remains nonetheless an important feature of an issue because many institutional investors such as insurance companies and pension funds are required to invest the greater part of their cash liquidity in listed securities. However, the efficiency of a listing in promoting liquidity or transparency of price on the exchange is only as good as its members' willingness to deal on it. In practice, a listing offers little comfort in these respects to Eurobond investors who, rather than rely on a listing, will evaluate an issue's liquidity from the size and rating of the issue. A large-size issue with an AAA rating is likely to be—though not always—more liquid than a single-A-rated issue for $75 million.

The purpose of a listing is therefore to provide an alternative trading forum, but is no guarantee as such of liquidity. Should all market makers withdraw from making a market in an issue, the listing on its own will not provide counterparties for dealings.

The practical benefits of a listing are the requirements for admission to the exchange's official list. European stock exchanges stipulate on Eurobond issues disclosure of information on the issuer at the time of the issue and the supply of financial accounts on an annual basis until the final maturity date. Evidence is also required of a system for disbursement of payments of interest and principal undertaken by the paying agent. (See sections on stock exchanges, Chapter 5, p. 143, and documentation, Chapter 10.)

Elements of Price[†]

This section introduces the basic concepts relating to the price of a Eurobond, and the expression *bond* or *Eurobond* in this section refers to a fixed-income debt obligation (i.e., with level interest payments). Bonds with floating-rate payments are reviewed in Chapter 2, and worked examples and exercises in the relevant calculations of value of both types of bonds are provided in Chapter 3.

The price of a bond is defined in terms of a percentage of its nominal or face value. The nominal value is always 100 percent or *par* regardless of whether the face value of the bond is £100, US$500, or DM10,000. A price of 98 means 98 percent of face value, i.e., a *discount* of 2 percent to *par*

---

* The U.S. Securities Act of 1933 requires detailed information on the issuer to be set out in a prospectus which is filed or registered with the U.S. Securities and Exchange Commission before the offering. The extent of disclosure and registration procedures is one the principal reasons for the recourse of many international borrowers to the Eurobond market.

[†] Lawrence de V. Wragg and Noël Clarke coauthored this section.

(100 percent) and a price of 101.5 percent means 101.5 percent of face value or a *premium* of 1.5 percent over par (100 percent).

When the price of a bond is quoted as par, then the yield will be automatically identical to the interest coupon or coupon rate. In other words, a five-year bond with a coupon rate of 8.5 percent standing at par will yield 8.5 percent per annum. Where the price of the bond is other than par, then the yield to the investor (or cost, from the viewpoint of the issuer of the bond) must be calculated to take account of the premium or discount from par in terms of price, as well as the coupon rate.

There are two types of yield which may be calculated. The first is the *current* or *running yield*, which evaluates the coupon rate in terms of the price paid for the bond. The formula is simple:

$$\text{Running yield} = \frac{\text{Coupon rate}}{\text{Price (excluding accrued interest)}}$$

Thus the running yield of a bond with a coupon of 8.5 percent and a price of 98 is expressed as follows:

$$\frac{8.5\%}{98} = 8.67\% \text{ per annum}$$

This yield takes no account of the value of the 2 percent discount (i.e., 100 − 98) to the investor at maturity of the bonds, but simply expressed the day-to-day return on the price actually paid for the bonds. The second type of yield, *maturity yield* or *yield to redemption,* overcomes this deficiency. It does so by applying discounted cash flow techniques to discount all the cash flows in a bond back to their present value. The calculation makes the necessary but simplifying assumption that the intermediate coupons received can be reinvested for the remaining life of the bond at the same yield as the maturity yield of the bond itself.

Like any other bond, a Eurobond is a series of interest and principal payments, and the value of the series at any one moment is equal to the *sum* of the *present values* of the future payments discounted at the rate of interest rates or *yield* sought by the market on debt of similar maturity and credit quality. The sum of the present values is the *price* of the bond which may be calculated manually (see Chapter 3) or by preprogrammed calculator.

The same concepts apply in the pricing of a new issue of fixed-rate bonds. Usually the known price elements are the maturity and issue amount sought by the issuer, the current market yield level for a given maturity, and credit quality and the principal repayment which is normally 100 percent. The unknowns are the price at which the bonds are issued and the coupon rate. If the bonds are issued at 100 percent, the yield to maturity will equate to current market yield levels, provided the coupon is set at the same level.

The principal elements of price of a bond may thus be summarized as follows:

Maturity/Remaining Life. The maturity date is the date of repayment or redemption of the bond. The period of time to the maturity date or the "remaining life" of the bond, is the basis for most calculations of yield to maturity. Where the bond has a sinking fund, the average remaining life is calculated and is sometimes used as an alternative basis of yield calculation, known as the yield to average life (see earlier section, "Redemption").

The concepts of remaining life and average life are accepted practice in new issues (origination). However, bond investors and fund managers, in performing calculations of yield on issues trading in the secondary market, use a further concept which relates the average life of a bond to current yield levels. This concept is known as *duration* and takes into account the phenomenon that for a given average life, the percentage change in the price of a bond caused by a given percentage change in market yields will vary at different absolute yield levels. Duration is therefore responsive to yield levels and is widely considered as a more accurate assessment of the life of a bond.

Coupon Rate. This is the interest coupon on a bond. On a new issue the coupon rate is set at a level which ensures that the yield to redemption of the bonds is equal to current market yield levels at the time of launch. The coupon is calculated on the basis of the desired maturity, the issue price, the redemption price, and current market level of yield. This calculation (see Chapter 3) produces the coupon figure which is rounded to the nearest ⅛ percent.

Issue Price. Given a market-related coupon, the issue price of a new issue of bonds is normally par or 100 percent. Rounding the coupon to the nearest ⅛ percent may lead to an adjustment to the issue price to obtain the desired level of current market yield. An issue price may also be deliberately set:

- above par, to meet investor demand for a particular level of coupon, in which case investors ignore the corresponding increase in outlay to purchase their bonds.

- below par, on issues with a below market coupon. Low coupons are often designed to minimize income tax for the investor who buys at a discount to a standard issue price but obtains a similar yield as on a conventional bond. Zero-coupon bonds are the extreme case of "discount bonds" and are issued at a steeper discount still.

Redemption Price. The price at which the bond is redeemed, expressed as a percentage of the face or nominal amount. This price is normally par or 100 percent of the face value. In the case of a prepayment, redemption is usually at a premium, say 101½ percent, and thereafter declining on later prepayment dates (see previous section, "Optional Redemption").

18

Current Market Price.   The current market price of a bond is the price at which it trades in the secondary market and is expressed as the sum of the present values of the stream of coupon and principal payments over the remaining life of the bond, discounted at a rate equal to the current market yield.

Current Market Yield.   The current market yield is the level of yield quoted in or sought by the market for debt risk of a particular credit and maturity. Where the bond is denominated in a currency of country with a major government bond market, the market yield is commonly expressed in terms of a *spread* or margin over the redemption yield of the appropriate *benchmark* or reference issue of similar maturity (e.g., U.S. Treasury stock for Eurodollar bond issues; U.K. government stock for Eurosterling issues). At any one moment the spreads quoted on a selection of issues with the same maturity will vary according to (1) the quality of credit and market perception of the issuer and (2) bond market conditions. Where no benchmark issue is available, for example, as was the case with ECU denominated issues, the market yield is derived from a *yield curve* which indicates the level of yield sought by the market in a range of maturities for a given quality of credit.

Redemption Yield.   This is the yield to maturity of the bond calculated on the basis of the period to final maturity or average life (see previous). The price of a bond in the secondary market should stabilize where its redemption yield is the same as the current market yield of bonds of similar credit quality and maturity.

Other elements of price relate to the fees, costs and expenses of launching a new issue, as follows:

Fees.   Issuing houses charge fees for managing, underwriting, and selling new issues. On fixed- and zero-coupon issues, these are standard and deducted from the proceeds of the issue—in accordance with a scale applied throughout the industry. Fees are expressed as a percentage of the issue size and include:

- a *management fee* of ³⁄₁₆–½ percent out of which the lead manager levies a *praecipuum* of up to 40 percent of the management fee before distribution of the remainder to the management group of the issue pro rata to their underwriting commitments

- an *underwriting commission* of ³⁄₁₆–½ percent paid to managers and underwriters pro rata to their underwriting commitments

- a *selling concession* of ¾–1½ percent paid pro rata to allotments of bonds by the lead manager to other managers, underwriters, and selling group members

Fees on floating-rate note issues are negotiated and have ranged from ¹⁄₁₀–1 percent or more of the principal amount, to include all three categories of fees. Fees on floating-rate notes are lower since the risk to the underwriters of adverse movements of interest rates is technically nil.

In recent years, a new (but not altogether permanent) trend in practices of launching new issues has been used whereby the underwriters agree to sell at a minimum price for a minimum period. This practice, which is known as a *fixed-price reoffering*, ensures a more orderly primary market and eliminates short selling in that period. In such cases, there is less risk of price movement from short selling and fees have been negotiated downwards.

Expenses. The expenses incurred in arranging a new issue can run into substantial sums. Competition among securities houses for mandates have enabled issuers to negotiate a maximum figure of reimbursement on nonrecurring expenses. Depending on the frequency of issue, the sum may be as little as US$25,000, rising to US$100,000 for first-time or infrequent issuers. A larger figure is agreed upon in the case of a first-time issuer. This is to take account of the process of *due diligence* required of the lead manager to acquaint itself with the issuer's business, where appropriate, to make a physical inspection of premises, plant and other tangible assets and to have audited by independent accountants the financial accounts which are set out in the prospectus. Due diligence is required on each subsequent occasion but the process is quicker for a frequent borrower.

The principal items of expense comprise:

- *Nonrecurring items:*

    printing (securities, offering circular, and legal agreements)

    fees to legal advisers to (1) the issuer and, where applicable, the guarantor, (2) the management group; on first-time issues, legal advisers are appointed both in the country of origin of the borrower (and, where applicable, the guarantor) and the country of origin of the law governing the agreements

    fees to accountants for the audit report to be submitted to the stock exchange and comfort letters to the managers

    publicity expenses: press releases, box advertisements (London listing only)

    travel expenses (for lead managers, lawyers, and accountants)

    out-of-pocket expenses (telex, telephone, fax)

- *Recurring items:*

    Trustee fees (where applicable)

    paying agency fees

    listing fees

2

The Principal Medium-Term Euro-Debt Instruments

Unsecured Instruments

This chapter reviews the main categories of Eurobond instruments which have an enduring role in the market. Every Eurobond financing is individual and the permutations of structure—comprising an issue of bonds and combined, say, with derivatives and/or swaps—are numerous. But the structure of a bond itself is also continuously reexamined and new debt securities are conceived in a marketing response to perceived investor expectations, different types of borrower cash flow, yield optimization in times of rising interest rates, or better liquidity. Most new bond structures are short-lived, but a few have stood the test of time and have opened up major new investor markets. The successful adjustments in structure have focused on:

- the interest base (e.g., fixed-income bonds, floating-rate notes, zero-coupon bonds)
- form (bearer versus registered form)
- status (unsecured versus asset-backed issues)
- maturity (finite redemption versus undated issues)
- public issues versus private placements

The great majority of debt securities financings are issues of unsecured instruments. This chapter reviews first, the different categories of unsecured instruments which for the sake of convenience are distinguished by their interest base, namely:

fixed-rate issues

zero rate

floating rate

This review also considers these instruments as issued by way of public offering. A subsequent section is devoted to the same set of instruments but issued by way of private placements. A third section examines a more recently established Euro-instrument, which is not a bond instrument but a hybrid of commercial paper and bonds, namely medium-term notes. The last section is devoted to asset-backed or collateralized issues.

Fixed-Income Eurobonds

A fixed-income Eurobond or "straight" bond can be viewed, like bonds in domestic markets, as cash flow of level interest payments on a specified date over a period of years together with a repayment of principal on the last such date. The interest rate or coupon is expressed as a percentage of the issue amount and is fixed at launch.

In the Eurobond market, interest is payable annually in arrears, normally on the anniversary of the issue up to and including the final maturity date. Interest accrues on the outstanding principal and, by convention, for the number of days in twelve months of 30 days and a year of 360 days. Interest is calculated according to the following formula:

$$I = P \times \frac{D}{360} \times C$$

where I = Interest accrued
P = principal outstanding
C = interest rate or coupon
expressed as a percentage
D = number of days*

For the issuer, the attraction of a fixed-rate issue is the knowledge of level payments on interest and, provided there is no tax-driven prepayment, a set

---

* *Example:* If an investor held a fixed-income Eurobond from 1 January–31 May, the period of investment would be expressed as 5 whole months of 30 days or 5 × 30 = 150 days. A broken period extending 1 January–15 June would be expressed as 5 months of 30 days plus 15, i.e., (5 × 30) + 15 = 165 days).

repayment schedule. The debt service is known both as to amount and its timing and can thus be set against budgeted revenues to calculate in advance the return on a proposed project. Historically, bonds have almost always paid interest at a fixed rate and this is by far the most common interest payment scheme on Eurobonds. For investors, the attractions of fixed-income bonds lie in a known income and relative safety of capital. As a series of known future cash flows, a bond presents less risk of large or sudden movement in price than an equity stock. Aside from insolvency or liquidation, the principal factor capable of affecting the value of a bond is a change in interest rates which might make alternative (known) cash flows more or less attractive.

A further concern for international investors is currency fluctuation. A risk-averse investor will prefer a Eurobond denominated in a currency which is strong and of a country where interest rates are stable. In such an environment, the price of the bond fluctuates within a narrow range and the investor has confidence his or her investment may be realized without significant capital loss. These conditions have prevailed in the Deutsche mark, Swiss franc and yen bond markets which attract permanent investors and serve as a refuge in times of currency weakness or volatility of interest rates in other sectors. Conversely, the weakness of the U.S. dollar and at times volatile interest rate environment are the direct causes of the decline in the share of the U.S. dollar in international bond issuance.

The scope for adapting standard or "plain vanilla" fixed-income Eurobonds is limited. Changes have been made to the structure of payment dates (e.g., partly paid bonds) and maturity dates (e.g., extendable and retractable bonds), but neither of the resulting instruments have had a lasting impact. Second to plain vanilla issuance, the most common Eurobond structure is a standard fixed-rate issue by a private sector corporate borrower with medium-term options attached entitling the holder to purchase equity stock of the issuer. (These instruments are discussed in Chapter 8.) Other significant variants include the high-yielding bond issued by borrowers of lesser credit standing and the global bond, which is in registered form so as to be capable of primary distribution in both international and domestic bond markets.

Partly Paid Bonds. Partly paid bonds were adapted from the United Kingdom bond market and introduced to the Eurobond market in 1980. These are standard fixed-income bonds in all respects but for the payment of principal by investors on the closing date of the issue—which is limited to 0–33 percent of the principal amount, with the balance falling due up to six months later. These issues were launched in an expectation of a fall in market yields by the time of the later or second payment date. The coupon rate reflects the expectation of falling rates and was set at a lower than market rate. The device was popular with issuers who could tailor the second payment to their cash flow requirements. Interest is payable pro rata to the

Table 2-1. Issue Volume and Issue Type for All Eurobonds, 1984–1991

Issue type	1984 ($M)	Iss.	1985 ($M)	Iss.	1986 ($M)	Iss.
Fixed rate	36,131.61	457	66,817.79	869	105,508.75	1,037
Fixed rate extendable	—	—	150	1	107.99	—
Fixed rate zero coupon	1,724.65	20	1,721.43	25	2,931.58	45
Fixed rate conv. to floating	150.00	2	—	—	500.00	3
Fixed rate + wrts. for equity	2,395.51	48	2,743.40	57	14,811.90	196
Fixed rate + wrts. for debt	1,707.06	17	138.43	2	—	—
Fixed rate deep discount	171.83	4	—	—	—	—
Fixed rate adjustable	1,167.96	15	1,630.52	16	1,897.91	15
Fixed rate + wrts. for currency	—	—	—	—	197.34	1
Fixed rate + other wrts.	—	—	—	—	—	—
Total fixed rate	43,448.62	563	73,201.57	970	125,955.47	1,298
Convertible	4,160.70	49	4,637.78	68	5,983.18	73
Convertible preference shares	—	—	—	—	430.00	3
Total convertible	4,160.70	49	4,637.78	68	6,413.18	76
Floating rate	31,015.82	181	54,735.98	272	46,697.07	219
Floating rate extendable	50.00	1	—	—	143.16	1
Floating rate conv. to fixed	235.69	2	—	—	215.37	3
Floating rate + wrts. for debt	129.03	2	300.00	1	477.28	4
Floating rate + wrts. for equity	250.00	1	—	—	280.00	2
Total floating rate	31,680.54	187	55,035.98	273	47,812.88	229
Total (US$)	79,289.86	799	132,875.33	1,311	180,181.53	1,603

SOURCE: Euromoney Bondware.

part payment until the second payment date, when the issue becomes a standard fixed-income bond. Many issuers attached interest rate swaps for the full amount of the issue on the basis of quotes ruling as of the date of launch. If their expectation of falling rates were fulfilled, they then achieved significant cost savings over a standard structure.

The attraction to the investor lies in the behavior of the bond until the second payment date. A movement in bond market yields would be almost fully reflected in the price, as if the bond were fully paid. In the case of a fall in yields, the capital gain on the price was thus disproportionately larger in relation to the smaller initial capital outlay. However, this leverage effect holds good both for price gains and falls and, at the time of a heavy volume of issues in the early 1980s, interest rate expectations (far from being fulfilled) were disappointed. Some investors even had difficulty in meeting their second installment and many investors suffered paper losses which made for little secondary market trading. In the light of this experience, the instrument has fallen into disuse.

High-Yielding Bonds. High-yielding bonds are bonds which offer a significant yield premium in relation to investment-grade bonds of equivalent maturity. The concept was used as early as the 1960s in the U.S. domestic market for low-grade corporate issuers, and a handful of issues for Latin American borrowers were launched in the Eurobond market.

1987		1988		1989		1990		1991	
($M)	Iss.	($M)	Iss.	($M)	Iss.	($M)	Iss.	($M)	Iss.
82,382.62	813	120,264.98	1,100	115,710.52	1,088	110,860.41	821	192,638.79	971
—	—	—	—	—	—	—	—	—	—
1,334.96	27	973.56	22	1,862.24	34	1,665.76	29	4,450.92	77
268.62	3	432.68	3	71.67	1	—	—	—	—
23,535.10	210	28,490.59	217	67,112.18	259	19,575.64	110	27,345.28	200
382.85	3	47.13	1	—	—	—	—	—	—
—	—	—	—	—	—	—	—	—	—
407.32	6	—	—	116.22	2	118.00	1	—	—
763.64	10	477.14	7	4.59	1	26.21	1	—	—
836.43	10	—	—	—	—	—	—	—	—
109,911.54	1,082	150,686.08	1,350	184,877.42	1,385	132,244.02	962	224,524.99	1,248
13,093.16	125	4,885.07	41	4,130.35	31	3,251.3	26	7,138.51	61
975.00	4	908.79	6	1,118.75	8	927.67	4	—	—
14,068.16	129	5,793.86	47	5,249.10	39	4,178.97	30	7,138.51	61
10,579.22	80	19,012.50	107	21,077.72	132	39,327.27	195	16,109	108
234.19	1	—	—	—	—	—	—	—	—
230.30	2	420.91	2	278.01	2	106.40	1	—	—
—	—	—	—	337.21	1	—	—	—	—
—	—	—	—	—	—	—	—	—	—
11,043.71	83	19,433.41	109	22,290.65	135	39,433.67	196	16,109.91	108
135,023.41	1,294	175,913.35	1,506	211,819.46	1,506	175,856.66	1,118	247,773.41	1,417

In 1977, the concept of high-yielding bonds was applied in the United States domestic capital markets to finance corporate acquisitions. The typical issuer was an acquiror smaller than the target company and with too weak a credit to issue a large amount of new equity. In such an instance, the funding of the acquisition often comprised:

1. equity put up by the acquiror(s) from its/their own resources
2. senior debt which was secured against the assets of the target company

Where equity and senior debt together did not suffice, the balance was made up from a new class of finance, mezzanine funding, i.e., halfway between equity and senior debt. Mezzanine finance is subordinated debt, not secured against assets but often convertible into equity or with equity warrants attached. Since most commercial banks were averse to providing mezzanine finance, a number of investment banks resorted to the bond markets to raise the finance requirement. These bonds are standard fixed-rate bonds but for a premium in yield of 2–5 percent to compensate the subordinated and unsecured status of the risk.

In the 1980s many corporate acquisitions were contested and the acquisition price exceeded by far the net asset value of the target company and, on individual transactions, the share of mezzanine finance rose to as much as 40 percent of the total consideration. The financial charges on the acqui-

Table 2-2. Share (%) of Instruments in Eurobond New Issues, 1984–1991

	1984	1985	1986	1987	1988	1989	1990	1991
Fixed rate[a]	49.60	51.73	60.05	62.98	68.91	54.72	63.10	77.75
Zero coupon	2.17	1.30	1.63	0.99	0.55	0.88	0.95	1.83
Floating rate[b]	39.64	41.42	26.38	8.18	11.05	10.24	22.43	6.50
Equity-related	8.59	5.55	11.94	27.85	19.49	34.16	13.52	13.92
Convertibles[c]	5.25	3.49	3.56	10.42	3.29	2.48	2.39	2.88
Fixed and floating rate with equity warrants attached	3.34	2.06	8.38	17.43	16.20	31.68	11.13	11.04
Total	100.00	100.00	100.00	100.00	100.00	100.00	100.00	100.00

[a] Includes plain vanilla straights, extendables, fixed rate issues convertible into floating, fixed rate with warrants for debt, deep discount bonds, adjustable rate bonds, fixed rate issues with warrants for currency options, and other features.
[b] Includes plain vanilla FRNs, extendable FRNs, FRNs convertible into fixed rate bonds, FRNs with warrants for debt.
[c] Includes issues for convertible preference stock.

SOURCE: Euromoney Bondware.

Table 2-3. New Issues of Fixed, Floating, and Zero Coupon Issues in the Eurobond Market, 1984–1991 (in US$ millions)

	1984	1985	1986	1987	1988	1989	1990	1991
Total issuance	79,290	132,875	180,182	135,023	175,913	211,819	175,857	247,773
Fixed income[a]	45,885	76,118	129,437	122,644	155,506	188,264	134,757	227,122
Floating rate[b]	31,681	55,036	47,813	11,044	19,433	21,693	39,434	16,110
Zero coupon	1,724	1,721	2,932	1,335	974	1,862	1,666	4,541

[a] Includes: plain vanilla fixed rate bonds, extendables, fixed rate convertible to floating rate, fixed rate issues with warrants for debt, equity and currency options, deep discount bonds, adjustable rate bonds, equity convertibles, and other fixed rate bonds.

[b] Includes: plain vanilla floating rate bonds, extendables, floating rate convertible to fixed, floating rate bonds with warrants for debt and equity.

SOURCE: Euromoney Bondware.

sition finance were usually met entirely out of the cash flow of the target company and mezzanine bonds, being unsecured and subordinated, were particularly vulnerable to an economic downturn when the cash flow of the business became less capable of supporting high interest payments. Principal repayments which depended on the sale of assets reaching a certain price were also at risk. In times of stock market crisis, such as October 1987, high-yielding bonds registered disproportionately large falls, and in the course of subsequent recession, experience of the U.S. high-yielding corporate bond market shows a higher default record than on standard corporate debt securities, hence the name *junk bonds*.

The attraction of the yield premium enabled U.S. investment banks (notably Drexel Burnham Lambert) to place large volumes of securitized mezzanine financings with U.S. pension funds, savings institutions, and insurance companies. In 1989 total junk bonds outstanding in the U.S. domestic market stood at approximately US$200 billion, or 38 percent, of total corporate issuance. By diversifying their exposure among several issues, investors were able to compensate losses on individual holdings by the higher yield on the portfolio as a whole. Some institutions failed to diversify, suffered large capital losses on some holdings and, in liquidating their remaining investments, accelerated the collapse of the market in December 1990. The market recovered the following year and in different form. Many issues were retired and reissued in the form of equity. Investor interest, although firm, was mainly professional or speculative. Institutional investors with prudential investment policies have in the main stayed away from this sector, which has been tainted by the experience of risks which in many instances were not properly evaluated. Up to that time, a growing volume of paper was placed outside the United States. The 1989 acquisition of RJR Nabisco by Kohlberg Kravis Roberts was financed in part with US$5 billion of junk bonds of which $900 million were placed with Japanese insurance and leasing companies and with banks in Switzerland, the United Kingdom, France, Germany, Italy, Austria, and Scandinavia—the main providers of mezzanine finance in Europe. Demand for U.S. paper is explained by the dearth of supply from issuers in Europe where the proportions of equity and senior debt are higher and the mezzanine finance content correspondingly smaller. In the United Kingdom, which has the most active of the European markets in leveraged corporate acquisitions, mezzanine finance deals reached their peak in 1989, but amounted to less than £600 million, or 16 percent, of the finance requirement of some 40 buy-out acquisitions worth £3.75 billion. Other European markets are smaller still and more regulated. France imposes interest rate ceilings and controls the issue of equity warrants, while Italy imposes gearing ratios. Often the acquisition price is not high enough to warrant mezzanine finance at all.

High-yielding securitized issues have made a debut in the Eurobond market but with some important distinctions in relation to U.S. junk bonds. Eurobond investors look for liquid instruments and are traditionally risk-averse, preferring to forego yield for the sake of quality. Junk bonds may qualify on the first but not on the second count. Funding packages launched in the Euromarket to date have therefore been targeted principally to banks and priced in floating-rate form. Offerings are usually tiered with a choice of (1) bonds secured against portfolios of senior loans whose credit quality has been enhanced by financial insurance and (2) a smaller proportion of unsecured mezzanine risk offering a large premium in margin. These structures combine diversification of risk with a high yield. Although they are unlikely to appeal to retail investors, a small number of institutional investors in mezzanine funds are emerging outside the United States, and the foundations of a new Eurobond market sector are gradually being laid.

Zero-Coupon Bonds. A zero-coupon bond is a fixed-rate bond with no schedule of periodic interest payments. The cash flow comprises two payments, the receipt of the proceeds on issue date and the repayment of principal on maturity. For the investor to receive a yield equivalent to that of a standard straight issue, the issue price of the zero-coupon bond is set at a percentage discount to face value such that the yield to redemption is equivalent to that of a standard "full coupon" issue of equivalent maturity. In the secondary market, the price of the zero-coupon bond fluctuates in function of subsequent changes in market yields and, as the bond's life becomes shorter, the price rises gradually to par.

The first "0"-coupon Eurobond was denominated in U.S. dollars and launched in 1981 at a time of high and volatile interest rates. This structure, which was borrowed from the United States domestic market, resolves the problem of the nominal rate at which coupon payments on fixed-rate issues are reinvested. The purchase price of a standard fixed-rate bond reflects a stream of payments which, it is assumed, are reinvested at an identical rate. In practice, this never occurs. Bond market yields change constantly and the investor certainly has no guarantee of investing his coupon payments at the same rate throughout the life of the bond. Thus, if interest rates on subsequent interest payment dates are lower, coupon payments are reinvested at a lower rate and the total return on the bond falls. By eliminating coupon payments altogether, investors holding the zero-coupon bonds to maturity have no risk on the reinvestment "rate" and lock in the redemption yield which applied at the time of purchase. In return for the guaranteed redemption yield, some earlier issues offered a somewhat lower yield than equivalent full-coupon straight bonds.

For the issuer, a zero-coupon bond issue is ideal financing for a project which generates no income for some years. Tax authorities often treat the discount or notional accrued interest as a charge against profits whose payment may be deferred until maturity. On the other hand, the loading of the debt service of the bond into a single payment some years hence creates a higher credit risk, and the market has been confined to highly rated borrowers. United States corporates, familiar with the concept from the U.S. domestic market are the principal category of issuer (Atlantic Richfield, Campbell Soup, Exxon, General Electric, General Motors Acceptance Corporation, Gulf Oil, Pepsico, Philip Morris, Prudential, and Sears). Only a handful of European corporates (such as Siemens and Fiat) have joined their ranks. International banks (Banque Nationale de Paris, Bank of Tokyo, Deutsche Bank, and Swiss Bank Corporation) have launched issues which are generally linked to interest rate swaps. Chemical Bank has issued serial zero-coupon bonds, i.e., a series of issues with maturities in 15 successive years, which reproduces the cash flow of a financing with equal repayments but no interest payments. Some European government agencies (Electricité de France, Gaz de France, Exportfinans) have issued zero-coupon bonds and Caisse Centrale de Coopération Economique has issued 20-year serial zero-coupon bonds. Few sovereign governments have zero-coupon bonds outstanding (Austria and Denmark) because of the impact of the cash flow on their budget, the increased currency exposure, and the inability to avail themselves of the tax advantages.

Investors are attracted to zero-coupon bonds to meet future liabilities and the more distant the liability, the smaller the initial outlay. Revenue authorities in many jurisdictions allowed, at least initially, the treatment of the gradual increase in price not as income but capital gain which attracted lower rates of taxation. A notable category of investor has been the retail investor looking to meet education fees or make additional provision for retirement. To meet this need, many issues have launched in small denominations of US$1000.

Secondary market experience demonstrated that zero-coupon bonds have a volatility all of their own. As interest rates fell, investors sought the protection of high reinvestment rates and would buy zero-coupon bonds which then would rise in price more than conventional bonds. Conversely, when interest rates rose, investors would be tempted out of zero-coupon bonds for a higher redemption yield and the price of the zeros would fall relatively faster.

Many issues were firmly placed at the time of launch but when favorable tax treatment was curtailed, investor demand for the instrument, which had always been finite, wavered. Market makers found themselves holding and financing positions in bonds which paid no income, and thus became reluctant to provide liquidity.

Global Bonds. Global bonds attempt to address one of the frequent shortcomings of Eurobond issues, namely their relatively poor liquidity. This is not a matter of unreliable market makers so much as primary distribution capability into established and liquid bond markets. The Eurobond market addressed itself for many years primarily to offshore investors which, though substantial, tended not to trade actively. For a Eurobond issuer to become more liquid meant having access to major domestic bond markets such as those of the United States and Japan and overcoming the regulatory embargo on the primary placement of Eurobonds imposed by their respective securities authorities. Clearly, access to a wider range of markets facilitates launching issues in larger size and, provided there are committed market makers in each market, a larger-size and well-placed issue makes for better liquidity, smaller trading spreads in the secondary market and, hence, a lower cost of funds to the issuer.*

The segmentation of the Eurobond and U.S. domestic bond markets has had measurable consequences in terms of yield differentials. Issues by frequent international borrowers in the U.S. dollar bond markets have tended to trade at significantly higher yield than their corresponding issues in the Eurobond market. Thus The World Bank has issued extensively in the U.S. "foreign" or Yankee bond market and in the Euromarkets where issues of similar maturity have yielded 10 to 20 basis points less.

The orthodox explanation for the differential is the absence of any requirement of registered form in the Eurobond market where issuers are able to take advantage of the preference of investors for anonymity by issuing at a lesser cost. This theory, however, was challenged by research conducted by the World Bank in 1988, which suggested that over a third of non-U.S. resident holdings of U.S. dollar-denominated debt were U.S. Treasury or other U.S. domestic securities issued in registered form. While this did not disprove the so-called preference of Eurobond investors for bearer form, it did demonstrate willingness on the part of international investors to hold registered debt securities.

This evidence paved the way for a Eurobond issue launched simultaneously in the U.S. domestic and Eurodollar bonds markets. Clearly, the ability to trade an issue freely in both European and U.S. domestic markets would enhance its liquidity and in due course lead to a possible reduction

---

* A glance at domestic government bond markets puts the problem into context. Offerings of US$5 billion (equivalent) are commonplace and these markets are very liquid. Until the advent of global bonds, the only device available to issuers seeking to improve the liquidity of their Eurobonds has been to issue bonds which are fungible with outstanding issues.

in issuance costs in relation to current yield levels in either market. The World Bank realized this ambition in the autumn of 1989 with a "global" bond issue of U.S. dollar-denominated debt for distribution in both markets. The principal distinguishing feature of the bonds was their *registered form* which satisfied the U.S. TEFRA Act. The further requirement of registration under the U.S. Securities Act of 1933 was dispensed with under an exemption. The other terms of the issue are as follows:

Issue size:	US$1.5 billion, the largest fixed rate international offering to date
Maturity:	10 years
Call option:	None
Interest and interest payments:	8⅜ percent per annum payable semiannually in arrears (U.S. style) and computed on a 360 day year of 12 × 30 day months (Euro)
Tax status:	Standard Eurobond provisions of freedom from withholding tax
Form and denomination:	The bonds are issued in book entry form through the Federal Reserve Bank of New York and may be held: 1. by holding institutions in the Federal Reserve's book-entry systems 2. in accounts with Euroclear or Cedel

Book-entry bonds are exchangeable for physical certificates in denominations of US$1000 or multiples thereof and vice versa.

Listing:	Luxembourg (Euro-style)
Governing Law:	Law of the State of New York (U.S. style)
Sales restrictions:	Sales subject to applicable laws of relevant jurisdictions; however bonds under the issue are classed as exempted securities under U.S. Securities Act of 1933 and 1934 and may be sold into the U.S. market
Settlement:	7 days (Euro) and delivery against payment (U.S. and Euro)
Clearing:	Special purpose links are established between the U.S. clearing system, Fedwire and the Eurobond market systems, Euroclear, and Cedel; Eurobond dealers are able to access the U.S. market for repurchases without the penalty of a day's interest normally lost in transfers of bonds between the Eurobond and the U.S. domestic markets
Syndicate:	Deutsche Bank Capital Markets Ltd. Salomon Brothers Inc. The First Boston Corporation Goldman, Sachs & Co. IBJ International Ltd.

Merrill, Lynch, Pierce, Fenner & Smith Incorporated
J. P. Morgan Securities Ltd.
Morgan Stanley & Co. Incorporated
Nomura International plc
Paribas Limited
Shearson Lehman Hutton Inc.
Swiss Bank Corporation
UBS Phillips & Drew Securities Limited
Yamaichi (Europe) Limited

The experience of these issues has been conclusive. The World Bank's global bond issues trade at yields which are lower than both their U.S. domestic bonds (10–20 basis points) and their U.S. Eurobonds (5–10 basis points). As a result, the World Bank now raises bond finance primarily in this form.

Other lessons have been drawn from these coordinated offerings as follows:

- *Which markets?* The word *global* is misleading: there is no legal or other requirement for a global bond issue to be capable of placement in domestic bond markets worldwide. Apart from the Eurobond market, a global issue may cover a selection of domestic markets chosen on the basis of:

  markets where the borrower is already well established

  markets where there is strong investor demand

  the domestic market of the currency in which the issue is denominated; thus distribution of a U.S. dollar global issue among U.S. domestic investors will help to support the price of the issue against selling by international investors concerned about the occasional weakness of the U.S. dollar in foreign exchange markets

- *Credit perception.* A homogeneous perception of the borrower's credit is necessary in both the domestic and the international investor markets for the global concept to be effective. In the case of the World Bank, global issues are now traded in the United States by dealers specializing in U.S. government-sponsored agencies, instead of the "corporate" desks which traditionally handled World Bank issues. This is intended to promote a change of market perception of the borrower within U.S. domestic trading houses which, notwithstanding its AAA rating, have a less favorable perception of the World Bank than their Eurobond counterparts, because of its lending activity in the Third World.

- *Issue size.* The issue size has to be significant in order to reach several markets in depth and provide the longer-term cost benefits to the issuer. Issues of less than US$1 billion (or the currency equivalent) are unlikely to produce this.

- *Offering technique.* The underwriting syndicate is drawn up so that each investment bank is mandated to handle distribution in a designated territory and issues are launched by the "fixed-price reoffering" technique; the effect of this is to deter outside intermediaries from speculating on the issue and to maximize orderly primary distribution.

- *Issuance costs.* In addition to reducing the cost of the debt to the issuer, the investor benefits from lower transaction costs; there are savings in time and expense of the clearing and settlement of trades; custody costs are also lower because the investor uses a custodian in his or her own market.

- *Benchmarks.* A highly liquid issue by a major international borrower provides a benchmark against which other international issues may be compared and priced.

There have been few issuers of global bonds to date which have successfully emulated the World Bank. The Canadian power utilities have launched global issues denominated in Canadian dollars; however, a large proportion of these issues have been sold back into Canada, thus defeating the purpose of the exercise. Other borrowers launched issues for amounts which were too small. Some large U.S. private sector multinational corporations are potential issuers but, unlike the World Bank, are not exempted from registration of their issue with the SEC. In order to avoid the delay, these borrowers have resorted to a standard Eurobond issue launched simultaneously with a U.S. private placement, which together make an international issue rather than a global bond.

In addition to a substantial finance requirement and homogeneous credit perception, borrowers must have a program of regular issuance to reap the full benefit of a broader investor base. Presently, few issuers other than the World Bank qualify on these counts. A sovereign borrower such as Italy has the continuing large finance requirement but the perception of the name is weaker in the United States than in the Eurobond market. European supranationals have smaller requirements and are relatively unknown in the U.S. domestic markets. Few private sector corporations have the credit standing and the worldwide visibility. Moreover, a finance requirement of this order is likely to arise in the event of an acquisition which could then affect their credit perception.

In the short term, the global bond market is likely to remain a one-issuer market whom it serves well.* The cost benefits achieved by the World Bank should in due course attract other international names (particularly those

---

* Following a successful series of U.S. dollar global bonds, the World Bank has launched a global Euro-yen issue for Y250 billion, the largest issue ever in this sector to date. The European Investment Bank has launched a global Australian dollar issue of A$400 million, which was placed simultaneously in the Euromarkets and in the Australian domestic market.

with Yankee bond issues) to their record—such as Electricité de France and the Kingdom of Sweden—as they refinance existing dollar debt. Looking ahead, as monetary convergence in Europe takes form and European domestic bond markets coalesce, opportunities for new structures should arise, notably ECU-denominated issues.

Floating-Rate Notes (FRNs)

FRNs are a medium-term debt instrument similar in structure to fixed-income Eurobonds but for the interest base and interest rate calculation. The coupon rate is reset at prespecified regular intervals, normally 3 or 6 months and, occasionally, 1 year. The coupon comprises a money market rate (e.g., the London Interbank Offered or Bid Rate for 6-month deposits—LIBOR or LIBID*) plus a margin which may be positive or, in the case of stronger credits, negative. Eurodollar FRNs are priced off a Eurodollar LIBOR or LIBID base. Sterling LIBOR is used for sterling FRNs and PIBOR (Paris), or FIBOR (Frankfurt) for French franc or Deutsche mark-denominated FRNs, respectively.

Interest is calculated as in *Euro-money market* interest calculations, that is, the number of calendar days elapsed in a year of 12×30-day months[†] and paid in arrears at the end of the relevant interest period. Interest is usually subject to a minimum rate as yield protection for investors and set arbitrarily by reference to the prevailing structure of interest rates and the minimum rate on the previous issue.

FRN issues usually carry a prepayment option for the issuer, which may start as early as the first anniversary. This is a key feature for bank issuers for flexibility of management of their international treasury. Amortization schedules are rare and generally take the form of serial redemption, which is similar to amortization schemes on a syndicated bank loan.

Issuers launch FRN issues because they combine the lower pricing[‡] of a bank loan; the potentially broader investor base of a bond market; and larger amounts and longer maturities than the fixed-income market. Investors are attracted to FRNs because the periodic resetting of the coupon in line with current short-term money market rates offers the strongest protection of capital in times of uncertain interest rates. In times of rising interest rates, the coupon reset mechanism offers an enhanced yield. Conversely, there is less potential for capital gain than on fixed-rate issues.

The first issue of FRNs was for US$125 million and was launched in 1970 by ENEL, the Italian State electricity utility under the guarantee of the

---

* The mean of the LIBOR and LIBID or LIMEAN is also used.

† On Sterling FRNs, the year of 365 days is used.

‡ Assuming a positive or rising yield curve.

Republic. The innovation had an immediate appeal for international banks active in the Eurodollar money markets, and these were to become major issuers of and investors in U.S. dollar FRNs over the following 16 years. Their motivation was to secure longer-term matched floating-rate funding for loan portfolios, most of which are denominated in U.S. dollars. Banks were also major buyers of FRNs because they could be match-funded and, under the then capital adequacy rules, treated in many countries as short-term assets and thus attract a lower capital requirement.* In 1982 the LDC debt crisis all but closed the market in syndicated bank lending and the demand from financial institutions for high-quality tradeable floating-rate assets became acute.

The supply of paper was further affected during this period by the advent of swaps, which added a major new complexion to the market. Whereas the cost of an FRN issue was generally above LIBOR, swaps enabled banks to launch fixed-rate issues in U.S. dollars or other currencies which, combined with currency and interest rate swaps, produced medium-term funding in U.S. dollars at a cost well below LIBOR.† This scheme was used extensively by borrowers hitherto active in the FRN market, in particular, banks (whose operating margins were under pressure) and sovereign borrowers, both of whom prepaid their outstanding FRN issues.

The continuing demand for floating-rate paper, in the context of a shortage of supply, led to a sharp contraction in margins on new issues, which eventually became negative. This paved the way for innovations offering more attractive spreads (e.g., undated, or perpetual, FRNs). By 1986 perpetual FRNs (or "perpetuals") accounted for more than a tenth of FRNs outstanding. However, investor demand for undated paper was finite and the continuing stream of new issues eventually led to a saturation of the market in the autumn of 1986. Market makers marked down their prices to discourage selling; however, other aggressive market makers took the opportunity to sell short. As prices collapsed, market makers withdrew and liquidity in perpetuals disappeared altogether. The crisis spilled over into the standard FRN market where the number of liquid issues fell in 1987 from 200 to 60.

Financial institutions by then were adept at generating an acceptable profit margin on a portfolio of FRNs in relation to their funding cost but the absence of liquidity presented an obstacle for a revival of the market. As interest rates rose in 1988, demand for floating-rate assets resumed but, in the context of weak liquidity, margins came under threat once again. The continuing pressure to generate higher operating margins and the search

* These rules have since changed: FRN holdings are now treated under BIS rules as medium-term assets and attract a weighting of 0–100 percent against capital funds, depending on the credit risk. The most popular FRNs are those issued by banks themselves, which attract only a 20 percent BIS capital weighting on bank investors balance sheets.

† Albeit without the flexibility of early repayment of an FRN issue.

for quality of risk combined to encourage the import from the United States of asset-backed floating-rate securities (see next section). These offer both the quality of credit (AAA rating) and yields not available on unsecured risk of equal rating. Banks and corporate treasury departments were soon drawn to this market, which broadened to include issues denominated in sterling. The FRN market recovered its former position in 1990 but has since fallen out of vogue again.

For the future, investor demand is likely to come from banks and institutions, and the problem will stem from the shortage of issuers. Traditional FRN issuers such as sovereign governments have lesser borrowing requirements while banks are well versed in securing medium-term funding through fixed-rate issues combined with swaps, where shorter maturities are now common in many currency sectors. Where the requirement is very large or the maturity in excess of 15 years, FRN issues nevertheless remain an efficient instrument with an appeal for sovereign borrowers funding a balance of payments deficit or banks raising junior debt.

Variations on the scheme of a floating-rate stream of interest payments have focused on the following possibilities:

- changing the interest base to a fixed-income base (FRN convertibles, drop-lock FRNs)

- separating the frequency of interest payment from the base interest period (mismatch FRNs)

- extending the maturities (longer-dated and perpetual FRNs)

- varying the margin in response to investor demand (VRNs)

Convertible and Drop-Lock FRNs.   Convertible FRNs were introduced to the Eurobond market in 1979 by Manufacturers Hanover and offered the investor an option to convert its FRN at any time over a number of years into fixed-rate bonds at a coupon rate set at the time of launch.

The FRN is priced on standard terms but the fixed rate of interest triggered by conversion is lower than on a fixed-rate offering (at the time of launch). When three-quarters of the issue is converted, the issuer may declare the conversion of the remaining 25 percent. If the FRN is not converted, it remains an FRN until its scheduled maturity. In all other respects, the instrument is similar to a standard FRN issue.

As in partly paid bonds, convertible FRNs are launched in conditions of poor (or even closed) fixed-rate bond markets, high interest rate levels, and an expectation of falling rates. Issuers benefit from (1) the lower funding costs related to short-term money market rates and (2) a fixed rate of funds following conversion lower than would have applied to a straight bond. Investors receive the benefit of high short-term rates plus the option of locking in to a better yield when short-term rates have fallen below the fixed coupon rate on the converted bond.

The convertible feature of the instrument is in effect an option which gains value as yields fall below the conversion rate. This increase in value is reflected in the price of the FRN and the investor, rather than convert, may sell and realize a capital gain.

Convertible FRNs, while giving investors an option to convert, left issuers powerless to manage the interest base of their funding except to declare 100 percent conversion when 75 percent of the issue was converted. An option for the issuer to convert was clearly unpalatable to investors and a compromise was devised in the form of the drop-lock FRN. The drop-lock FRN's conversion was triggered independently of both issuer or investors, when money market rates fell to a certain prespecified level, at which point the FRN converted into a fixed-income bond. The drawback to this structure was that short-term rates fell more quickly than medium- or long-term rates and the coupon level triggered on conversion tended to be lower than current market medium- or long-term yields which lagged short-term rates. On conversion, therefore, the bond price was marked down, leading to a temporary capital loss. The trigger mechanism was then changed as a function of the level of yield on independent medium-term securities. This presented the further difficulty of the choice of security. For want of a benchmark Eurobond issue, reference was made to U.S. Treasury Bonds which, as an instrument of the domestic U.S. capital markets have a market behavior independent to that of U.S. dollar-denominated Eurobonds. For this reason issues with this structure did not meet with wide acceptance and for want of an acceptable reference Eurobond, the instrument has fallen into disuse.

Mismatch FRNs. Mismatch FRNs refix or change their coupons more frequently than they actually pay interest to the noteholders. The concept was introduced by Citicorp in 1979 and used in many FRN issues in the early 1980s. Mismatch FRNs draw on the bank investors' practice of funding their holdings of standard FRNs (which typically had 6-month interest periods), with deposits of a shorter life, say, of 3- or 1-month maturity and, assuming an upwards sloping yield curve, at a lower rate. Thus, the funding of the holding was mismatched and the mismatch created a funding risk. If the level of interest rates rose substantially during any 6-month interest period, the bank which mismatched its FRN holding could find its funding costs exceeding the FRN coupon payment.

The terms and conditions—including interest payment frequency—of a mismatch FRN are those of a standard FRN issue except for the calculation of interest. A typical mismatch FRN issue would pay interest every six months. The coupon would be a 6-month LIBOR rate but would apply for the first month only of the current 6-month interest payment period. At the end of the first month, the coupon would be reset on the basis of the then prevailing 6-month LIBOR rate and apply for the second month only; it would then be reset again in each successive month throughout the

6-month period. The interest payment at the end of the six months would be equal to the sum of the interest accrued in each successive month at the respective 6-month LIBOR rates.

For investors, mismatch FRNs offered two attractions. First, the funding period and the interest period were now reset at the same intervals. Assuming that, during the interest period, each 6-month LIBOR rate was higher than 1-month LIBOR (i.e., a *positive* yield curve) the investor was assured of a systematic treasury profit. However, in exchange for this benefit, the investor received a lower margin. Second, issues were launched at a time when the yield curve was sloping steeply upwards, indicating an anticipation of a higher trend in rates. With rates rising, a frequent refix was welcome.

In practice, the Eurodollar yield curve was not always positive and, from time to time, investors funded a 1-month LIBOR at a higher rate than the 6-month LIBOR level applicable to the particular month. Later issues contained "parachute" clauses, which provided for the interest period to revert to six months when the yield curve became negative. Another drawback lay in the high price of the bonds which was calculated, in the standard manner, on the assumption of a flat yield curve, a condition that was hardly ever verified. Issuers benefited from the low margins and, by avoiding the risk of a significant change in coupon level every six or three months, were able to achieve an average 6-month LIBOR cost often lower than on a standard FRN issue. However, the issue was time-consuming to manage and other issue structures, comprising a fixed-rate issue and a swap, provided more cost-effective financings.

Perpetual FRNs and Variable Rate Notes (VRNs). In meeting the requirements of capital adequacy regulations, many international banks, whose profitability had been upset by large provisions against LDC debt, found themselves unable to raise equity to strengthen their capital base. The strong demand for tradeable floating-rate paper at this time emboldened issuing houses to propose to them FRN issues without final maturity and whose subordinated status would qualify the financing with bank regulators as "primary capital" for the purposes of capital adequacy.

The perpetual FRN has no maturity date. Issuers have a call option to prepay but investors, at least in early issues, have no right of repayment at any time except in the standard case of the imposition of withholding tax on interest payments. Following the 1986 crisis, investment banks, in an attempt to restore liquidity in the market, structured new issues with investor put options or options to exchange their undated paper for bond with a finite maturity.

Perpetual FRNs have subordinated status and in some cases junior subordinated status, so as to rank as close as possible to equity and in contrast to the unsubordinated status of other Eurobonds. As a quasi-equity instrument, they qualify as capital, and, for the purposes of capital adequacy, are treated as equity. Logically, nonpayment of interest is not an event of default in instances where the borrower passes its dividend. As compensation for these risks the investor receives a margin of ⅜ percent (over LIBOR) or more.

The concept was first launched in 1980 by Citicorp and the market opened in 1984 with an issue by National Westminster Bank. Over the following two years, the volume of outstanding issues rose to US$17 billion, principally by international banks and a few corporates. By 1986, investor demand, always limited, was saturated and by then issuing houses had accumulated large positions resulting from unsold underwriting commitments. In the wake of the collapse of the market (see previous), sellers of positions whose price was heavily marked down realized large losses, and remaining holders were left with even larger losses on paper which were only partially recovered in subsequent repackagings. The collapse of the perpetual FRN market rebounded on the much larger standard FRN market of US$155 billion which saw little activity during the ensuing 18 months. Issues of perpetual FRNs have resumed, but issues are now structured to offer greater flexibility for investors to manage the maturity of their holding, through put options or exchanges.

Variable-rate notes were devised in 1988 in an attempt to bring liquidity back to the FRN market. The structure is similar to that of an FRN except for the margin component of the coupon, which is negotiated for each interest period through bids from investors—in theory reflecting market conditions and the borrower's credit more accurately. VRNs have been issued with 10- and 15-year maturities; however, their most notable application is in the perpetual FRN sector.

The terms and conditions of VRNs are as in a standard FRN issue except for the coupon which draws on the Euro-note and Euro-commercial paper markets for its pricing mechanism, and is set as a function of bids received by the lead manager from investors on the outstanding paper for each interest period. The lead manager then determines a rate, which is agreed by the investors who may either retain their holding at the agreed rate or sell it back to the lead manager at par, thus providing investors full protection of their capital. If no bids are received or if the rate is not agreed, then the VRN converts to a standard FRN. Certain perpetual VRNs gave the investor the choice between a perpetual FRN with a fixed margin, say of 75 basis points (the "default margin") over LIBOR or conversion into a 5-year note on a much lower margin. The investor had a further option to convert back from a 5-year note to a perpetual VRN. This was known as a *flip-flop* structure.

Failing agreement on the rate, the investor had a standard FRN on his hands and relied on the market to provide liquidity in the conventional way. In the case of perpetuals, liquidity was doubtful since the number of market makers in perpetual FRNs was very small. In addition, the default margin, although superficially attractive, was fixed and generally lower than the margin obtained over LIBOR by buying old perpetual FRNs in the secondary market. The price of the asset therefore fell to a level in line with other outstanding perpetual FRNs and the investor suffered a capital loss.

Capped FRNs and Minimax FRNs. Toward the mid-1980s the intense demand for floating-rate paper gave issuing houses the scope to devise standard FRN structures with interest rate hedging instruments attached, such as caps and collars.

A cap is an agreement between two intermediaries in the money markets whereby the first agrees to compensate the second in the event that interest rates exceed a certain level on prescribed future dates. Compensation is equal to the difference between the cap rate and the actual interest rate on a certain sum. In return for this protection, or hedge, the second party pays a fee to the first at the outset of the agreement.

Capped FRNs comprise an FRN and a cap which effectively puts a maximum rate of interest on the financing. The issuer enters into the cap agreement with the investors in the FRN who were compensated for their risk by a higher margin. Minimax FRNs provided both a maximum and a minimum interest rate, or collar, thus prescribing a fixed range within which the coupon could fluctuate and giving the investor some protection against lower interest rates. The issuers in either case were generally financial institutions with a requirement to fund assets with a LIBOR-related interest base and for whom the hedging benefit of caps and collars offered no attraction. On the other hand, long-dated hedges are much in demand from corporate borrowers and consequently the hedges were sold by the issuer at the time of launch and the proceeds applied in reducing the cost of the issue.

Capped and minimax FRNs were generally launched in a climate of falling interest rates and, at the time, the margins were considered sufficient reward for the interest rate risks associated with the hedge. However, as interest rates rose in 1986, market sentiment changed and the margins appeared inadequate. Dollar-denominated capped FRNs, a sector where coupon rates fluctuated considerably, fell from grace. In sectors with more stable interest rates, such as the Deutsche mark, capped FRNs have had a sustained acceptance.

Private Placements

Private offerings of debt, or private placements, are bond issues placed with a single or small number of investors. These have found favor with borrowers because of the advantages of discretion, and with investors because of their tailor-made character. Private placements have been arranged in the Eurobond market since the late 1960s to cater to international investors in Switzerland, the monetary authorities of oil-producing countries in the Middle East, and institutional investors in the United States. The major impetus to private placements, however, came in the 1980s when the development of the swaps and derivatives markets coincided with growing surpluses of institutional liquidity in Japan. By the end of the decade, Japanese institutional investors had become the principal providers of funds at an estimated rate of US$50 billion of new debt private placements every year.

The structure of a private placement is close to that of a public issue. The traditional distinction is that the bonds are not listed though, technically, they are still tradeable. Even this distinction disappears in some placements which are listed to satisfy investor criteria and therefore qualify as public offerings. (Conversely, some public issues with a limited number of investors are disguised private placements.) The maturity range of 3–12 years is similar to that of many public bond markets, depending on the currency sector. Issue sizes are in the range of US$50–US$200 million (equivalent) but individual transactions of as much as US$1 billion have been arranged.

Aside from the small number of investors, a private placement is distinguished by:

- the absence of undertaking to make a secondary market
- a yield premium of 20 to 40 basis points in relation to a comparable public issue to compensate for the lack of liquidity
- the absence of primary distribution and hence no underwriting fees or selling concessions
- generally no listing and hence a saving in time and expense in satisfying listing requirements
- shorter documentation and less onerous covenants than on a public issue

Complex structures lead to confusion and militate against liquidity in the public bond markets, but they are ideally suited to the private placement market. Indeed, in the private market, it is common for placements to be initiated by investors who specify their desired structure. The requirements of the Japanese life companies, for example, have produced a variety of structures designed to maximize current yield, including:

- Dual currency financings, for example paying interest in Australian dollars and principal in yen
- High-coupon, high-issue price and redemption at par
- step-up financings, whereby the coupon is artificially low for an initial period, after which the coupon rises sharply to replace the coupon on maturing bond assets
- stock-index-linked, where repayment is linked to the performance of an index, or currency-option-linked, where the option is likewise embedded in the repayment

The majority of financings nonetheless have a plain vanilla structure whose only complication is the addition of a currency and/or interest rate swap into the end currency of exposure. Placements arranged in the United States, Switzerland, or Germany follow this pattern almost exclusively.

Borrowers prefer private placements to public offerings for several reasons:

- *Avoidance of publicity.* A borrower may require additional finance at the same time as the public financing; a private placement reduces the risk for a frequent issuer of saturating the public markets; a private placement may also be cost-attractive and the issuer may wish to keep the structure confidential.

- *A lower cost of funds.* For less well-known or infrequent borrowers in the Eurobond market, a private placement avoids the expenses of investor relations, due diligence audits, prospectus, and other listing requirements and underwriting fees.

- *Legal or regulatory obstacles.* A U.K. company may not wish to incur the (greater) expense of a prospectus on the scale required by the U.K. Companies Act; private U.K. companies may not launch public issues at all.

The principal category of issuer is sovereign borrowers; many European governments (e.g., Finland, Iceland) have contracted a significant portion of their external debt in this way. The governments of Canada, Australia, of countries in Southeast Asia, government agencies such as the Foreign Trade Banks of Bulgaria, and Russia are also known to have arranged significant volumes of debt finance in this form. International commercial banks have also used private placements extensively to raise capital funds by way of subordinated debt. Leveraged buy-out finance has occasionally been arranged in this way for similar reasons of discretion.

Investors in international private placements are essentially institutional and the principal investor markets are onshore, that is, in the domestic bond markets. The principal providers of funds in the five-year period to 1991 have been Japanese institutions, including life insurance companies, the Post Office, leasing companies, and the large city and small regional banks. The most active among these are the life companies which are ranked according to the current yield on their assets and are continuously seeking to improve on yields found in the domestic market. Many found the key to realizing their ambitions in the international capital markets which, by means of vast array of currency and interest rate swap markets, currency options, and commodity and stock-index-linked repayment structures, enabled these institutions successfully to arbitrage their domestic market through highly structured and individual private placements.

- The institutions first specify their maturity, redemption currency, and coupon criteria, and the structure of a private placement is exactly tailored to these specifications.

- Many transactions are specifically designed to hedge a long-term risk, and liquidity is not a concern; investments are generally held to maturity and match funded.

- Under Japanese accounting rules, private placements do not have to be revalued or *marked to market* for periodic reporting purposes, unlike holdings of public bonds.

- Access to the swap markets enable investors to manage continuously the currency and interest mix of their portfolios to optimize current income. Indeed, the swap markets are so liquid that they offer a substitute for poor liquidity in the public Eurobond markets.

Private placements were an ideal asset for the life companies and demand increased rapidly in the late 1980s. These institutions, however, are subject to limits on their holdings of international assets. To circumvent these regulations, Japanese leasing companies, whose international operations are less regulated, have been introduced in the structures of placements to intermediate between the life companies and the borrower. Institutions, such as banks, with long-term deposits have also been significant providers of funds. For those with the intention of holding until maturity, private placements offer an immediate yield pickup over holdings of public bonds for a similar quality risk. In the early 1990s, the funding costs of leasing companies and institutional investors rose, and the high margins attained on private placements came under threat and, recently, the Japanese private placement market has slowed considerably. Japanese institutional investors, while still major net investors, have generally scaled down overseas investment since the end of 1990 in favor of domestic public issues.

The other significant domestic market for international private placements is the United States, where Eurobond primary placements are permitted as private placements to avoid the registration requirement under the Securities Act of 1933 for a public offering. The private placement exemption stipulates that the bonds are placed:

- with a limited number of sophisticated investors
- with access to information of a quality similar to that of a prospectus for a public offering
- purchasing the bonds as principals without possibility of resale except by registration

The principal investors are insurance companies and mutual funds which, like their Japanese counterparts, are subject to limits on their international exposure known as the *basket* restriction. The scale of demand from domestic borrowers and the basket limits on foreign exposure led to low demand for placements by overseas borrowers, and volumes of placement have been significantly smaller than in Japan.

Insurance companies, which make up the bulk of the investors typically "buy and hold" to maturity to reap the benefit of the premium in yield in relation to public bonds. These institutions have become the principal source of long-term funds, serving the full spectrum of rated and unrated borrowers,* and have less concern for the liquidity of their investments. By contrast, the other main category of investors—the mutual funds—looks for tradeability of their assets,† and their appetite for private placements was therefore confined to shorter-term high-grade investments. In 1989, the U.S. securities regulations on private placements were amended by the so-called Rule 144A, which relaxes the requirement of registration as a condition of resale. This rule was intended to free up balance sheet space of investors hitherto prevented from investing in nontradeable private placements and thereby open up a limited secondary market. This was intended to narrow down differential in yields against public bonds and lead to a lower cost of funds to borrowers. In practice, despite a launch in a poor economic climate and technical problems in setting up electronic systems, the volume of "144A" placements has grown steadily to roughly 14 percent of the market. Borrowers must be rated and investors are required to be managing at least $100 million in securities. Although somewhat restrictive, these criteria have served to attract investors traditionally focused on the public markets. A secondary market is gradually developing, particularly in highly rated placements. Mutual funds, however, are still wary of entering the market until it offers genuine liquidity. To overcome this problem, investment banks have intermediated between the issuer and the investors by subscribing themselves to the placement in full, only to resell it immediately to their private placement clientele with an undertaking to make a market. In their effect, these private placements are being fully underwritten and are public issues in all but name.

Elsewhere, the principal providers of funds are from countries such as Switzerland and West Germany which have a strong savings industry and low and stable interest rates. The low volatility of bond prices makes for less active trading and a greater willingness to hold to maturity. Private placement markets have operated in both countries for many years and traditionally have been significant sources of funds.

The arrangers of international private placements include major investment banks such as Bankers Trust, CS First Boston, Morgan Stanley, and Swiss Bank Corporation. In Japan, leading securities houses such as Nomura, Daiwa, and Yamaichi are major intermediaries, but they are rivaled by the commercial banks such as Bank of Tokyo and the life insurance companies themselves, many of whom have developed direct relationships with borrowers. For the arrangers, there are reduced fees but there is no underwriting risk. Mandates for private placements are awarded by investors and fulfilled when market conditions allow investors' yield objec-

---

* In 1991 the industry's trade association, the National Association of Insurance Commissioners held that borrowers rated lower than BBB should not be considered as investment grade. This has not ruled out lesser-rated issuers, but has effectively made the cost prohibitive. Nor does it rule out unrated borrowers for whom a placement is priced on its own merits.

† Mutual funds deal with retail investors who may redeem their investment at any time.

tives to match the borrower's target cost-of-funds. Unlike the public bond markets, arrangers cannot lose money on private placements which have become a relatively lucrative source of revenue with arrangement fees ranging from ¾–1½ percent for more complex deals.

Euro-Medium-term Notes

While a public issue is effective in raising large amounts in a single transaction, it rarely matches the precise funding requirement of the issuer or the investment criteria of individual investors. Medium-term notes (or MTNs) were first introduced in the U.S. domestic capital markets in an attempt to overcome these drawbacks by combining the maturity range and the tailor-made structure of a private placement with the speed of issuance of a commercial paper program. Like private placements, MTNs are investor-driven but, through the provision of small denominations, may be offered to a wider investor audience. Investors specify the amount, the rate, maturity, and repayment structure which is then proposed by a dealer to the issuer under a prearranged program of continuous issuance. Thus, an investor can hold notes in a wide range of maturities and yields issued by the same borrower under the same program. MTNs are tradeable but not listed. The program is normally for an indeterminate period and the only limitation is the maximum amount which may be outstanding at any one time.

The flexibility of MTN programs had considerable appeal to U.S. borrowers such as GMAC and Ford who were the first to issue MTNs in 1977 in the U.S. domestic market as a means of match-funding their receivables on their car loans. The U.S. market presently offers the largest pool of liquidity with MTNs outstanding in excess of US$400 billion (1991). However, only a small proportion of U.S. domestic MTN paper is placed outside the United States.

The instrument was adapted to the Euromarket in bearer form and the Euro-medium-term note (E-MTNs) market emerged in 1984. Outstandings grew to US$350 million in 1986, US$4.8 billion in 1988 and to US$34 billion in 1991. Historically, E-MTNs were issued in the form of floating-rate notes and interest was similarly calculated on a Euro-money market basis; however, E-MTN programs now provide for the issuance of notes in fixed-, floating-, or zero-coupon form. The documentation is negotiated at the outset on a once-and-for-all basis and presently permits issuance of plain debt or more complex structures tailored to investor requirements. This provides the issuer the maximum flexibility in terms of structure, amount, maturity, and timing to optimize the matching of investor criteria.

Like its U.S. counterpart, Euro-medium-term notes combine features of public issues, commercial paper, and private placements:

Maturities:	Maturities are specified by investors. The most common maturities are in a range of 1–5 years, but 10 years has also

been seen. One quarter of outstandings are in the range of 0–2 years and 80 percent in the range 0–5 years. The average maturity is rising as the market broadens.

Amount:	Individual investments in notes are normally in the range of US$5–$20 million.
Interest:	E-MTNs are interest bearing and interest is calculated on the same basis of the fixed-, floating-, or zero-coupon Eurobond it emulates.
Currency:	E-MTN programs were originally denominated in U.S. dollars but are presently issued in 14 Euro-currencies. By giving the investor the opportunity to specify precise currency, coupon, and maturity criteria, the E-MTN has proved an ideal instrument for multicurrency bond portfolios. The Eurobond market rarely offers a precise maturity and coupon match and dealing in small amounts of bonds is time-consuming and relatively expensive.
Offering procedure:	E-MTN issues are investor-led and therefore no need arises for an issue to be underwritten. Instead, MTN paper is offered continuously through individual intermediaries acting as dealers or through a group of intermediaries acting as a tender panel. Recently, some major borrowers such as Swedish Export Kredit have used their programs to issue large amounts in one transaction and, in such instances, the issue has been fully underwritten. These financings are virtual Eurobond issues with the added benefit of a lower cost of funds and no further documentation.
Secondary market quotation:	The secondary market price is expressed as a percentage of the PAR value.
Fees:	There are no underwriting fees (except for large scale issues—see previous). Instead the issuer is charged a placement fee of the order of 5 basis points per 6 months of maturity.

Borrowers prominent in the Eurobond market were initially skeptical of the liquidity of MTNs and the market got off to a slow start because of their reluctance to arrange programs. Presently there are over 130 E-MTN programs in place, including:

- sovereign governments raising foreign currency for balance of payments purposes under multicurrency E-MTN programs with a limit denominated in U.S. dollars: the Kingdom of Belgium (US$2 billion), the Kingdom of Spain (US$1 billion)

- European government export agencies: Oesterreichische Kontrollbank (US$300 million), Swedish Export Credit (US$1.5 billion and ECU 2 billion)

- European corporates and banks raising U.S. dollars for North American operations: BP America Inc. (US$1 billion), ALSK-CGER North America (US$500 million), Petrofina Delaware (US$500 million)

- banks and corporates raising local currency: Amro Bank (Dutch Fl500 million), Mass Transit Railway (HK$2 billion)

- United States corporates setting up E-MTN programs to complement their domestic program: Ford Motor Credit (US$2 billion), RJR Nabisco (US$500 million)

The E-MTN market is now established, witness the broad range of existing issuers; however, many borrowers have yet to arrange programs. Euro-investors are historically less receptive to corporate names with an A or AA rating which have had to turn instead to the U.S. market. Other issuers are deterred by the incremental yield expectation of 10–20 basis points over Eurobonds. There are also technical reasons which inhibit an issue: over 40 percent of outstandings are swapped into floating-rate dollars and the target cost of funds of issuers, defined in terms of margin *below* LIBOR, may not be achievable as U.S. dollar interest rate swap spreads narrow. Borrowers, on the other hand, with a requirement for U.S. dollars and eligible to tap the U.S. market (i.e., with an AA rating or an SEC registration) will opt for the U.S. MTN market for its greater depth, size, flexibility, and liquidity. Presently the dearth of issuers is encouraging the market to open up to lesser-rated names and the process is facilitated where the borrower has already established an MTN program in the United States.

The dominant categories of investors are central banks (37 percent), followed by fund managers (34 percent), other financial institutions (22 percent), and corporates (7 percent).* Fund managers and financial institutions in turn conceal substantial Swiss- and German-based retail funds which account for 50 percent of all investors. Investor demand is considered to outstrip supply but at the higher end of the credit spectrum only. Euro-investors are typically risk-averse and look for a premium in yield to compensate for lesser-quality risk and poor liquidity.

E-MTNs as tailor-made instruments are, like private placements, intended to be bought and held to maturity. Yet liquidity has been a recurring problem in the development of the market. Initial attempts to interest Eurobond investors were frustrated: professional investors typically trade their holdings to manage the average maturity of their portfolio and were concerned about the small number of market makers. Few accepted that the traditional market model of a large number of market makers was not essential, and that a small number of large houses who were prepared to commit their resources would meet the need. However, this model of U.S.-style liquidity has gradually prevailed and the investor market has become more established. Many

* Source: Merrill Lynch International & Co.

dealers argue, too, that whereas the average Eurobond market maker has little commitment to the issuer, the E-MTN dealer has a continuous relationship with issuer and investors and is likely to be more committed to both.

Recently, the search for liquidity and the need to attract investors more attuned to the public markets led a number of issuers to use their E-MTN programs quite legitimately to launch large-size fully underwritten issues. In yet another experiment, several issuers have also written into the documentation of their program the ability to issue into the U.S. private placement market with the option of resale under Rule 144A. By demonstrating that a program can offer access to more markets and at less cost in documentation and commissions, E-MTN programs are likely to become more popular with issuers. The ability to issue at short notice, moreover, also opens up the potential to seize windows of market opportunity which are denied in the Eurobond market, where the sheer size of a financing can make the structuring (to include swaps and derivative features) more time-consuming. Thus, while a public bond issue is a natural resort for a large widely distributed financing, E-MTN program offers the versatility of a multioption issuance facility, which makes it an important financing tool.

Mortgage-backed and Asset-backed Securities*

Securitization is the process by which pools of financial assets are packaged, underwritten, and sold in the form of securities. The securities themselves are collateralized by, and derive their revenue from, the cash flows generated by the underlying assets. The financing structures adopted are typically designed to ensure that the securities are nonrecourse and can also ensure that the overall transaction is granted off-balance-sheet status.

The general effect of securitization is twofold. From the originator or issuer's viewpoint it removes assets from the balance sheet, freeing up capital for reinvestment while retaining the revenue stream from the securitized assets in the form of fee income. At the same time, the process transfers funding risk from the originating institution to a new and different group of investors and usually enables precise match-funding of the assets to maturity. By virtue of its nonrecourse nature it removes the commercial and financial risk on the securitized assets entirely from the issuer.

The technique was developed in the United States in response to specific inefficiencies in the funding of U.S. residential mortgages. These were largely a result of the funding mismatch which had historically been underwritten by the home loans industry, and of the lack of availability of suitable long-term funding within the individual states. The first securitizations were completed in the early 1970s when the U.S. Government National Mortgage Association (GNMA, or Ginnie Mac) began to issue mortgage

---

* This section has been contributed by Ken G. Cox.

pass-through certificates. Other agencies such as the Federal Home Loan Mortgage Corporation (FHLMC, or Freddie Mac) and the Federal National Mortgage Association (FNMA, or Fannie Mae) promptly followed suit and the U.S. market then rapidly developed beyond agency-related transactions into the private sector. Total outstandings of mortgage-backed securities were US$1.2 trillion in 1991.

The market in the United States has moved on since the early days of residential mortgage securitization. Commercial mortgages, credit cards, auto and truck receivables, lease receivables, healthcare and other trade receivables, and even yacht loans have all been securitized. Although dwarfed by the size of the securitized mortgage market, total outstandings of securities backed by other assets amounted to US$155 billion in 1991.

Asset securitization in the Euromarkets is at a very different stage of development, although there are many signs that the market will follow a pattern very similar to the U.S. one. For the moment, the European securitization market is dominated by the U.K. mortgage-backed securities (MBS) industry, discussed in more detail in the next section. The other European markets for the financing of mortgages and other asset-backed loans are less well developed and, individually, offer less scope for the adoption of securitization techniques. However, the development of a single European market for financial services will undoubtedly throw up other opportunities; securitization techniques might be used to smooth out market anomalies by the transfer of capital and funds to the markets and for the products where they are most required.

Development of the
U.K. MBS Market

The floating-rate, long-term nature of the U.K. mortgage industry, together with the appetite of the domestic and international investing community for sterling FRNs, led to the development of the sterling mortgage-backed FRN as the most commonly used form of security. The FRN structure enabled the cash flows of the underlying mortgages to be most closely matched to the required frequency of interest payments to investors; and the use of three-month sterling Libor as a benchmark clearly mirrored most closely the historic level of mortgage rates in the United Kingdom. From the issuer's point of view, too, there was already a proven and deep market in building society FRNs upon which to build.

The first public issue of mortgage-backed securities in the United Kingdom, a £50 million floating-rate note issue, was launched in January 1985 by a vehicle company called Mortgage Intermediary Note Issuer (No. I)—Amsterdam B.V. (Mini). The company was formed to fund mortgages originated by Bank of America. Other mortgage lenders that might have been in a position to follow Bank of America at that time did not. It was left to the new mortgage lenders, led by National Home Loans (NHL) to pick up the threads over two years later with what is widely acknowledged to be the issue that led the way to the £8 billion market of today. The Mortgage Corporation (TMC) and the Household Mortgage Corporation (HMC), fellow new lenders, swiftly followed NHL with issues. Others have responded quickly to the opportunities offered by this new market and a number of mortgage lending arms of foreign banks, and two of the U.K. clearing banks have joined the ranks of issuers.

It is estimated that a total of £16–18 billion of U.K. mortgages have now been securitized in both the public and private markets. About 9.4 percent of new mortgage lending was securitized in 1991. Most of the paper was initially placed with banks, which saw the FRNs as a lucrative, secure and transferable alternative to their traditional investments. Certainly, by comparison with other instruments in the market and considering their high (AA or AAA) rating and level of collateral, they were priced very generously indeed. This was to compensate for the perceived lack of liquidity in the market and relative complexity. The investor base has broadened significantly from the early days. There is now wide placement in the domestic U.K. institutional and corporate marketplace. Offshore institutions, too, have contributed extensively to both primary and secondary market investment demand. By U.K. capital market standards the growth has been dramatic. Figure 2-1 highlights the cumulative new issue volume in the Eurosterling mortgage-backed FRN market since 1987. The annual volume of new issues peaked at just over £3 billion in 1988 and reached £2.3 billion in 1991. This level of growth is quite remarkable for any U.K.

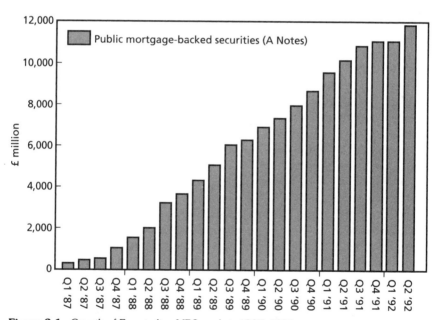

Figure 2-1. Growth of Eurosterling MBS market, 1987–1991.

market that is effectively only six years old and has continued despite the well-publicized problems in the U.K. housing market during 1990, 1991, and 1992.

Structural, Tax, and Accounting Considerations. The structures and ownership of the special purpose issuing vehicles (SPV) themselves is a complex subject and is largely derived from the necessity to comply with guidelines set out by a number of regulatory bodies, including the Bank of England and the Building Societies' Commission. Additionally, in order to achieve full off-balance-sheet treatment, the requirements of the Accounting Standards Board and provisions of the Companies Act must be strictly adhered to as regards the exercise of control over the financing vehicle's activities. Because of the need to adopt an arms-length structure in order to accommodate these regulatory requirements, the whole question of the extraction of profit and fees is also a complex and lengthy one. Finally, in each overall structure, the original lender will usually take care to ensure compliance with the Secondary Mortgage Market Working Group's (SMMWG) code of practice, which seeks to ensure that the interests of the individual mortgagor are not overlooked in the whole securitization process.

In simplified form, Figure 2-2 illustrates the nature of the transaction. The most common structure is to establish a limited liability company or SPV which has the capacity to purchase assets, borrow money, and give security for the borrowings. For the banks, the key element of this method

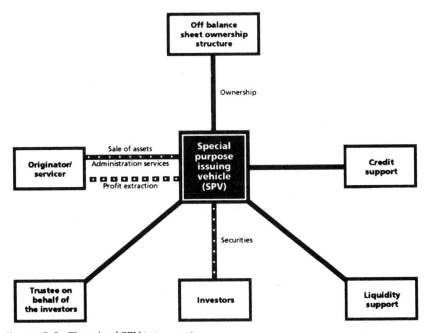

Figure 2-2. The role of SPV in transactions.

The Principal Medium-Term Euro-Debt Instruments

is the limitation on the liability of the owners of the vehicle company for its debts, thus enabling nonrecourse financings. The position for corporate originators is slightly different. It is likely that the Accounting Standards Board will oblige them not just to limit their exposure to the risks of a vehicle but also to forgo all returns from it, other than a servicing fee. For those entities subject to the Bank of England regulations, ultimate ownership in the shares of the SPV has generally been vested in a discretionary charitable trust. An independent trustee is required to monitor the asset pool and act on behalf of the investors in relation to matters relating to their security interests.

Day-to-day administration of the assets themselves will normally be carried out under a long-term contract by the originating or issuing entity itself, using its normal business procedures. As mortgages redeem, the redemption proceeds are passed through to the investors on interest payment dates by way of a pro rata reduction in the nominal amount of the outstanding securities or drawing by lot. Various mechanisms are used to permit substitution of new mortgages into the pool and further advances on existing mortgages in the pool. In order to obtain the required AAA rating status, it is necessary to provide credit enhancement to the pool of mortgages themselves. This may be through the provision of a pool insurance policy covering all losses of principal and interest on the mortgages in the pool up to a limit agreed by the rating agent(s) (but usually in the region of 7–10 percent of the principal amount). This pool insurance should be written by an AAA-rated insurance company or by a lesser-rated institution with appropriate reinsurance. Alternatively, the issuer can arrange for the placement of an equivalent amount of subordinated or junior notes, which will, in effect, provide the same cushion against loss. In this case, £107–110 million of mortgages provide the cash flows and collateral to service 100 million of senior notes, the 7–10 million junior notes receiving payment on a subordinated basis. Finally, in order to ensure that payments of principal and interest are made on a timely basis, liquidity facilities are provided by suitably rated financial institutions in order to cover the risk of delayed payment resulting from administrative delays or errors in dealing with regular mortgage payments or arrears and defaults on individual mortgages. As can be envisaged, the final structure is inevitably fairly complex and involves a number of third parties. For this reason securitization transactions often result in difficult commercial, regulatory, legal, and taxation issues, which require careful handling. The securities that finally emerge, however, are invariably of the highest credit quality and with minimal event risk. As an illustration of a past transaction, Figure 2-3 is a diagrammatic representation of the Barclays Bank issue in mid-1989.

Pricing Considerations. For the time being, mortgage-backed securities carry relatively high margins. Issuers and market participants alike believe that, since these carry the highest credit ratings, they are priced unfavorably compared with that achievable by building societies in the

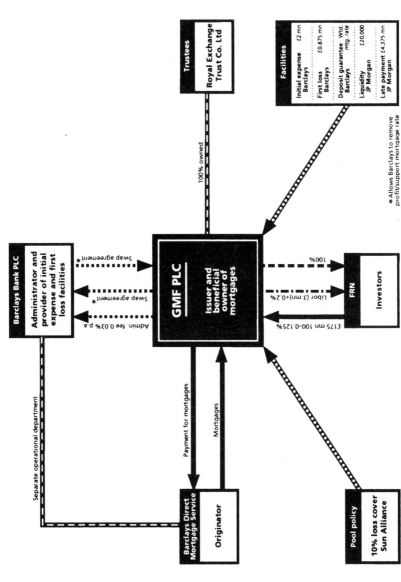

Summary terms and conditions

Amount:	£175 mn
S&P/Moody's Rating:	AAA/Aaa
Maturity:[†]	June 2019
Redemptions:	Pro rata/purchase & cancellation
Expected average life:	6.2 yrs
Margin:	0.2%, Step up 0.5% (June 1999 or max, £17.5 mn O/S)
Coupon base:	3-month £ Libor, payable 3-monthly
Issue price:	100%
Commissions:	0.125%
Further advances:	None within pool
Substitutions:	100% to June 1992
Launch date:	May 30, 1989
Issue date:	June 30, 1989

▬▬▬	Principal & collateral movements at issue
▬ ▬ ▬	Interest movements
▬▬ ▬▬	Principal movements at maturity
▪▪▪▪▪▪▪	Interest support agreements
▭▭▭▭	Ownership
▦▦▦▦	Credit enhancement
●●●●●●	Administration fee

[†] Issue may be called if principal amount is less than £17.5 mn or after June 1992

Figure 2-3. Gracechurch Mortgage Finance plc (£175 million mortgage-backed floating-rate notes due 2019). (Source: Baring Brothers & Co., Ltd.)

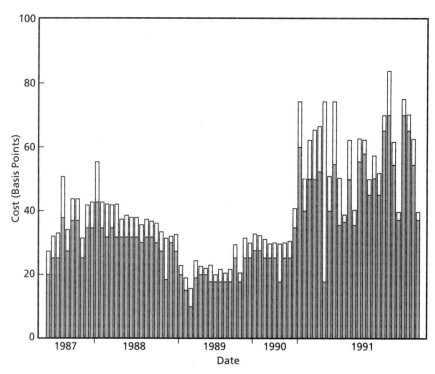

Figure 2-4. Mortgage-backed securities—historical launch spread analysis. (Source: Baring Brothers & Co., Ltd.)

FRN market for unsecured, unrated, transactions. Figure 2-4 shows the historical launch spreads of all the issues to date. This is broken down into the margin and the front-end fees amortized over the estimated average life of the issue. The chart shows the classic pricing development of a new product in the securities markets. The earliest transactions carried margins of 25 and 20 basis points, and it appeared that these would suffice. However, participants rapidly found that the flow of issues was greater than the capacity of the investing community and that lead managers and investors required significantly higher margins in order to compensate for illiquidity in the market and lack of placement. Margins were soon pushed up to 30 basis points and beyond in 1987. Subsequently, they gradually declined, over a period of intense issuance activity, to margins of 18 basis points and a front-end fee in the 15–30 basis-points range by 1989. As concerns about the risks of the underlying assets grew, margins increased to their current (mid-1992) levels of 40 to 60 basis points. This increase also reflected the Bank of England's announcement in January 1992 that, from January 1993, mortgage-backed securities would be 100 percent weighted for BIS purposes, rather than 50 percent weighted as now.

Chapter Two

Investor Considerations. Although trading yields on mortgage-backed securities have declined considerably from the 20 basis point highs, their yields are still some 10 basis points above building society paper. There are two main reasons for this. First, the issuing entities are typically special purpose vehicles and, as such, the investor will acquire their paper only if the investor fully understands and is seeking to buy mortgage-backed securities. This rules out those investors that buy only easily recognized names. Second, there is undoubtedly some uncertainty about the average life of these issues (upon which all estimates of the returns to the investor are based). Inevitably, with a market as young as this, there is no hard demonstrable evidence that the average lives of any of these portfolios will in fact perform in the way their originators have suggested. So the investing community demands an additional price in compensation for the uncertainty and possible mechanical disadvantages of dealing with complex amortizing issues. There is little doubt that liquidity in the market has improved substantially since the early days. Nevertheless, there is currently comparatively little trading going on in the mortgage-backed area. This may be due to the fact that many investors in the earlier issues are sitting on assets with a very attractive margin and so have no interest in switching or selling.

Alternative Structures. Issuers have tried a number of different techniques to make mortgage-backed securities more attractive to investors. Since the earliest days of pool insurance, still part of the staple diet, the Household Mortgage Corporation and National Home Loans, in particular, have developed the senior/junior market, and there is now a healthy, if specialized, appetite for subordinated mortgage-backed securities. HMC and others have also tapped the fixed-rate sterling markets through a sophisticated structure. This provides the issuer with the opportunity to take advantage of particularly attractive swap opportunities to raise funds at levels well below those offered elsewhere. NHL has, among its various innovations, turned to the offshore markets and has established a U.S. domestic commercial paper program ultimately backed by U.K. mortgages.

The Bank of England's recent relaxation of its "five-year rule" on the issuance of sterling securities has encouraged the issuance of short-dated mortgage-backed paper. With plenty of liquidity at both the short and very long ends of the maturity spectrum, we have seen the development of sterling "slow pay/fast pay" tranched issues.

Other Assets and the Outlook for the Markets

What of other securitizable assets? For several years now, there has been considerable discussion about the potential for securitizing assets other than residential first mortgages. For most of that time, issues have taken place but, until recently, they have almost always been Euromarket securitizations of U.S. assets, usually credit card receivables. It is only in the last 12 months that European nonresidential first mortgage assets have been securitized with any frequency. Recent transactions have included securitizations of residential second mortgages, trade receivables, car loans, and leases. It remains to be seen whether this burst of activity will be sustained. Certainly, there are reasons why it should be. As banks experience credit problems globally, so their desire to lend decreases. Companies and financial institutions have responded to this by raising a higher proportion of their debt finance in the capital markets. While this is relatively straightforward for highly rated corporate credits, many medium-sized companies and financial institutions cannot do so easily. Their only means of accessing the capital markets is via a securitization in which investors take risks on segregated, carefully selected and monitored pools of assets rather than the corporate covenant. Specific considerations apply to two asset classes.

The securitization of commercial property has been the focus of considerable activity since the mid-1980s. Then, a considerable amount of work was done on the securitization of equity in commercial properties. Only one issue was launched, however, led jointly by Barings and Goldman Sachs. As property values declined in 1989, 1990, and 1991, the emphasis shifted to debt securitization as borrowers have sought to reduce their dependence on the banking markets. While the U.K. domestic debenture market provides institutional finance, it does so only on relatively rigid terms. Issuers see a Euromarket securitization as a means of raising finance on more flexible terms. Two such issues have been undertaken so far.

Export Credit-backed receivables have also been securitized. The first such issue was in 1984 and in recent years the Export Credits Guarantee Department has been a regular issuer via Guaranteed Export Finance Corporation, a funding vehicle.

The securitization markets are less developed in continental Europe than in the United Kingdom. Growth has, however, been rapid, particularly in France, Spain, Italy, and Sweden which have also seen issues. As in the United Kingdom, a need on the part of corporates and financial institutions has been the main motivation.

The outlook is somewhat uncertain. Certainly the more ambitious plans for the growth of the securitization markets in the United Kingdom and Europe have not been realized as the problems of recession have taken hold. However, in many cases, the recognition of those very problems is forcing numerous financial institutions and corporates to reassess their traditional methods of raising both debt and equity, and will lead to a wider embracing of securitization. While, therefore, at the time of writing, new issuance activity may be rather slow, there is a great deal of development work going on which will lend a new impetus to the markets in late 1992 and 1993.

Market Aspects

An MBS issue is normally syndicated and traded under the usual AIBD conventions.

The *syndication policy* to date of those houses involved in the MBS market has been to "pre-place" a large proportion of each issue prior to the assembly of a final syndicate. A number of recent developments has led to a concentration of distribution in the hands of a few houses that are active and long-term players in the MBS market. This has resulted in the "dealer" approach adopted by TMC for its PIMBS* program. This approach has had the effect of encouraging the development of new investors by the "dealer" houses and will ultimately lead to greater liquidity, which will be beneficial to the MBS market as a whole.

Secondary market trading is undertaken, despite the issue's listing on a stock exchange, in an over-the-counter market (trades are effected by telephone to one of a number of market participants). Prices are quoted "clean" (that is, net of accrued interest—the net proceeds of the trade are subsequently calculated taking this into account) as a percentage of the nominal amount of the issue; and they disregard any redemptions of the notes/bonds that may have taken place. Prices are determined by a number of factors, including the creditworthiness of the issuer, current market conditions, the issue's rating, and the liquidity of the individual issue (in particular its size and seasoning). In addition, for FRNs the price takes into account the relationship between the issue's current coupon and prevailing money market interest rates until the next coupon fixing date. Once a price has been agreed and a trade struck, settlement is conducted through one of the recognized clearing systems for a value date (as is standard in the Eurobond market) seven calendar days from the trade date. If an investor does not have an account with one of the recognized clearing systems, a number of institutions offer delivery and collection services, which are cost-efficient and can save the investor the time and additional expense involved in individually arranging the settlement of trades in the Euromarkets. As part of this service, most institutions also offer custodian services, which involve their holding in safe custody, for a fee, an investor's securities.

MBS denominations can vary considerably, but most of them to date are available in either £10,000 or £100,000 amounts.

Net proceeds calculations are undertaken subsequent to a trade and take into consideration any accrued interest (that is, interest earned but not yet due and payable, as stated in the AIBD rules under Section 220). Accrued interest is calculated differently in various international markets according to the method of calculating the days in a year. The conventions that apply to sterling MBS are as follows.

* Program for Issuance of Mortgage Backed Securities.

1. Accrued interest on sterling MBS FRNs is calculated on the basis of actual days from, and including the day following, the due date of the last paid interest, or the day following the day from which interest is to accrue for a new issue, up to and including the value date of the transaction, divided by 365 days (366 days in a leap year). However, no accrued interest is due when the value date of the transaction coincides with an interest payment date and the buyer does not acquire that coupon. For example, if £500,000 of an MBS FRN issue with a current coupon of 14 percent (including a 0.1875 percent margin over three-month LIBOR at 13.8125 percent), payable for the period June 10 to September 11, is traded for value on July 18 at a price of 101, there are 38 days of accrued interest (consisting of 20 days remaining in June and 18 days in July). The net proceeds for this transaction would therefore be:

$$£500,000 \times \left[\frac{101 + 14 \times 38}{365} \right] \div 100$$

$$= £500,000 \times 1.02457534247$$

$$= £512,287.67$$

2. Accrued interest on MBS fixed-rate bonds is calculated from, and including, the day following the due date of the last paid coupon, or the day from which interest is to accrue for a new issue up to and including the value date of the transaction. A month is counted as 30 days and interest to a value date on the 31st calendar day of a month is the same as to the first calendar day of the following month. As with MBS FRNs, no accrued interest is due in the case where the value date of a transaction coincides with a coupon payment date and the buyer does not acquire that coupon. For example, if £500,000 of an MBS fixed-rate bond issue with a coupon of 11 percent, and paying interest on July 1, is traded for value August 29 at a price of 99.5, there are 58 days of accrued interest consisting of the remaining 29 days of July and 29 days in August. (It must be noted that if the bonds were traded for value August 31, there would be 60 days of accrued interest, just as if the value date was in fact September 1.) The net proceeds for this transaction (that is, for 58 days accrued interest) would therefore be:

$$£500,000 \times \left[99.5 + \frac{11 \times 58}{360} \right] \div 100$$

$$= 500,000 \times 1.012722222$$

$$= 506,361.11$$

Yield calculations are the standard methods of measuring the return a security earns on the price at which it was purchased. Different methods are used in the calculation of FRN and fixed-rate bond returns, as follows.

1. The standard yardstick for the measurement of the relative value of FRNs is the "discounted margin" calculation, which assumes that the index, three-month LIBOR in most cases remains constant throughout the life of the issue. (It is worth noting that it is current market practice to assume future LIBOR rates of 11 percent.) Many participants in the MBS market assume that an MBS FRN is a bullet FRN, with a maturity equal to the average life of the issue. While this is the simplest method of calculating a discounted margin (an HP-12C or AIBD calculator can be used) and gives a rough guide, in practice differences can result of up to 0.03 percent compared with calculating it on a cash flow basis. In calculating the discounted margin on a cash flow basis, a slight modification to the "standard" calculation is required, in that the interest on the MBS FRNs should be calculated on the basis of a declining balance and the investor receiving principal payments before final maturity. Account should also be taken of any step-up in the interest margin, which is one of the reasons why discounted margins to maturity tend to be greater than discounted margins to call (see Table 2-4).

2. The standard yardstick for the measurement of the relative value of fixed-rate bonds is the "AIBD yield" calculation, which assumes that the coupon payments are reinvested at the same yield. As the two fixed-rate MBS issues currently in the market have bullet maturities (that is, they have no early redemption features), this calculation can be undertaken on the same basis as normal fixed-rate Eurobonds (using an HP-12C or AIBD calculator). However, if a fixed-rate MBS issue is launched in the future with early redemption features and/or a step-up in the coupon, a modification will be required to the AIBD yield calculation and, for precision, it should be calculated on a cash flow basis (see Table 2-4).

Average lives are a measure of the weighted average maturity of the issue, taking into account a number of factors, including the following:

- an assumed constant repayment rate (CRR) based on the prepayment characteristics of the underlying mortgage pool and the issuer's historical experience, if any
- an assumed default rate based on the characteristics of the underlying mortgage pool and the issuer's historical experience, if any
- the likelihood of a call option being exercised by the issuer
- an assumed rate at which prepayments are either increased or decreased by further advances to existing mortgagors, depending on the funding method used
- any substitution period allowed

Table 2-4. MBS Market Calculations

MBS FRN discounted margin (declining balance method)

$$(P+A) \times [1 + \left[\frac{(1+DM)}{100} \times \frac{d}{365}\right] - C] \times SF = (Ia + Qm_1) \times h \times \sum_{i=1}^{n_1} \frac{IAO \times (1-r)^{(i+k)}}{(1+j)^i}$$

$$+ (Ia + Qm_2) \times h \times \sum_{i=n_1+1}^{n} \frac{IAO \times (1-r)^{i+k}}{(1+j)^i}$$

$$+ \sum_{i=0}^{n-1} (IAO \times 100) \times \frac{(1-r)^{i+k}}{(1+j)^i}$$

$$+ (IAO \times 100) \times \frac{(1-r)^{n+k}}{(1+j)^n}$$

Where:
- P = price
- A = accrued interest
- I = index rate for period up to next coupon date
- Qm_1 = initial quoted margin
- Qm_2 = step-up quoted margin
- d = days to next coupon date
- C = value of next coupon payment
- DM = discounted margin

$$h = \frac{365.25}{365} \times \frac{1}{f}$$

- f = number of coupon periods from settlement date to maturity date
- n_1 = number of coupon periods from settlement date until the step-up quoted margin date
- IAO = initial amount outstanding
- k = number of coupon periods from issue date to settlement date
- r = effective compound redemption rate per coupon period

$$j = \frac{(Ia + DM) \times h}{100}$$

- SF = $IAO \times (1-r)^k$
- Ia = assumed index rate from the next coupon date

This calculation may be summarized in HP-12C keystrokes as follows:

1. Enter the average life of the issue, multiplied by 4
2. Press "n"
3. Enter the discount rate (usually the medium-term government bond rate) divided by 4
4. Press "i"
5. Enter "O"
6. Press "FV"
7. Enter the price of the FRN (as a discount or premium to par so that a price of 98 becomes a discount of 2)
8. Press "PV"

9. Press "PMT"
10. Multiply by 4 by pressing "4" and then "x"
11. Input the margin
12. Add 10 and 11 by pressing "+"

MBS fixed-rate yield to maturity (annually compounded AIBD method)

$$MP = \frac{1}{f} \sum_{i=1}^{fn} \left[\frac{C}{(1 + r/f)^i} \right] \frac{P}{(1 + r/f)} \, fn$$

Where: MP = market price
C = coupon payment per annum
f = number of coupon payments per annum
r = yield to maturity
P = principal value
n = number of years to maturity

MBS FRN average life (declining balance method)

$$AL = \frac{1}{f} \sum_{i=1}^{n} \left[\frac{RA_i \times i}{RA_i} \right] - \frac{d_a}{y}$$

Where: AL = average life
RA_1 = amount redeemed at coupon dates
n = number of coupon/redemption dates
f = number of coupon payments per annum
d_a = number of days from last coupon date to last settlement date
y = days in year

It must be remembered that the expected average lives published in MBS prospectuses on the launch of an issue are assumptions of the average life at issue. Clearly, for an MBS issue that has been outstanding for some time, the average life today will be less than the average life at launch.

3
Calculations of Value

Fundamentals of Compound Interest*

Compound interest is fundamental to the solution of financial problems and the evaluation of securities, yet surprisingly among those working in the securities industry, few have much grasp of the subject. This chapter aims therefore to set out the principles and worked examples of the basic calculations of value used in the evaluation and pricing of Eurobonds.

Definitions

Let i = interest rate (expressed in decimals rather than as a percentage), or yield level

v = the discount factor and is expressed as $\dfrac{1}{(1 + i)}$

So if $i = 0.09$

then $v = \dfrac{1}{1 + 0.09}$

n = number of periods to final maturity; these may be annual, semiannual, quarterly, or monthly periods

PV = present value or present market value of the bond

FV = future value or market value at a future date

The cash flow of a bond is similar to that of an annuity, i.e., a finite regular stream of level payments. The symbol a_n = the present value of an annuity with a payment of 1 for n periods starting at the end of the first period.

* Contributed by Robert Chillcott.

Compound Interest. An initial sum or principal of US$1 invested for one period at a rate of interest i per period becomes $\$1 \times (1 + i)$ at the end of the period. The same principal sum at the end of the second period becomes

$$[\$1 \times (1 + i)] \times (1 + i)$$

or

$$\$1 \, (1 + i)^2$$

And, at the end of n periods, the principal sum has become $\$1 \, (1 + i)^n$.

Conversely, if the future principal amount (or FV) is known together with the number of periods and the rate of interest, then the initial sum (or PV) can be calculated by discounting back as follows:

Let the future principal amount at the end of n periods be US$ FPA, then $PV = FPA \times v^n$.

In our notation v is the symbol for $1/(1 + i)$.

From the example, let FPA = US$1 $(1 + i)^n$; then,

$$PV = \$1 \, (1 + i)^n \times \left[\frac{1}{(1 + i)} \right]^n$$
$$= 1$$

Calculating PV from FV and v is called *discounting* and v is the *discount factor.*

A good approach to beginning to work out a problem in compound interest is to set out an *equation of value.* On the left hand side, we write PV, or the present value, at a specified date. On the right hand side, we write the stream of future interest, capital, and other payments (if any) and then write the relevant discounting factor (e.g., v, v^2, etc.) against *each* item of future income.

Example: Calculate the present value of a fixed rate bond paying an 8 percent annual coupon with a 10-year maturity and repayment at 100 percent. Today's yield level is 9 percent.

The cash flow of the bond is as follows:

End of year	Payment
0	+PV
1	−8
2	−8
3	−8
4	−8
5	−8
6	−8
7	−8
8	−8
9	−8
10	108

Note: The payments preceded by a negative sign denote outgoings while payments with a plus sign denote an incoming amount. The cash flow shown here is written from the point of view of the issuer; the reverse would apply from the point of view of the investor who lays out cash to buy the bond and thereafter receives interest payments and principal repayment.

To calculate *PV* or the present value of this stream of payments, we calculate the present value of each payment. This can be summarized as:

$$PV = (8 \times v) + (8 \times v^2) + (8 \times v^3) + (8 \times v^4) + (8 \times v^5)$$
$$+ (8 \times v^6) + (8 \times v^7) = (8 \times v^8) + (8 \times v^9) + (108 \times v^{10})$$

or in abbreviated form

$$PV = 8 \ (v + v^2 + v^3 \ldots + v^{10}) + 100 . v^{10}$$

The yield level, *i*, is 9 percent or 0.09, therefore

$$v = \frac{1}{1 + 0.09}$$
$$= 0.91743$$

and,

$$v^2 = \left[\frac{1}{1.09} \right]^2$$
$$= 0.84168$$
$$v^3 = 0.77218$$
$$v^4 = 0.70843$$
$$v^5 = 0.64993$$
$$v^6 = 0.59627$$
$$v^7 = 0.54703$$
$$v^8 = 0.50187$$
$$v^9 = 0.46043$$
$$v^{10} = 0.42241$$

Let the sum of $v^1 + v^2 + v^3 + v^4 + v^5 + \ldots v^{10} = a_{10}$

then, $a_{10} = 0.91743 + 0.84168 + \ldots 0.42241$
$$= 6.41766$$

Therefore the present value of the coupon payments at 8 percent is:

$$8 \times a_{10} = 51.34$$

The present value of the principal repayment is:

$$100 \times v^{10} = 42.24$$

Thus the *PV* of all the stream of payments is:

$$51.34 + 42.24 = 93.58$$

A bond is a stream of payments and the present value of the bond is the present value of the stream of interest and principal payments discounted at today's interest rate or yield level. The present value is the current value of the bond in the market.

Manual calculations may be abridged by using the HP-12C which is programmed to solve for *PV*. Using the terms of the example given, key in as follows: $i = 9$, $n = 10$, *FV* = −100,* *PMT* = −8, and solve for *PV* to obtain 93.58.

---

* Payments are viewed from the issuer's standpoint; payments of interest and repayments of principal are outgoings and are therefore input into the HP-12C with a negative sign, for example, 100, CHS, FV.

Author's note: The Hewlett-Packard calculator HP-12C has been popular in the financial industry for many years. It is neat, powerful, and cheap. The owner's handbook and problem-solving guide that comes with every new machine contains many practical examples of compound interest problems and warrants careful study.

Exercises

1. (*a*) Work out longhand the present value (or current market price) of a fixed-income (straight) bond with an annual coupon of 5 percent, a maturity of 7 years and repayment at 100 percent. Today's yield level is 10 percent. (*b*) Afterwards, check your result by using the HP-12C.

2. Using the HP-12C, work out the present value of a straight bond with an annual coupon of 10 percent, a maturity of 5 years, redemption at 100 percent. Assume a yield level of 5 percent.

3. A fixed-income bond has an annual coupon of 8 percent, and a final maturity of 9 years. The issuer has the option to repay after 2 years (call) and investors have the option to request repayment (put) after 5 years. Repayment in all cases is at 100 percent. Using the HP-12C, work out the *PV* to the call, the put, and the final maturity when:

$$(1) \quad i = 7\%$$
$$\text{and (2)} \quad i = 9\%$$

If you are (*a*) the issuer or (*b*) an investor would you exercise your option in case (1), case (2), or neither? For the purpose of the exercise, assume that yield levels remain unchanged.

Solutions

1. (*a*) *Manual:*

$$v = \frac{1}{1 + 0.1}$$

$$= 0.9091$$

$$v^2 = \left[\frac{1}{1 + 0.1} \right]^2$$

$$= 0.8264$$

$$v^3 = 0.7513$$
$$v^4 = 0.6830$$
$$v^5 = 0.6209$$
$$v^6 = 0.5645$$
$$v^7 = 0.5132$$

$$a = v + v^2 + v^3 + v^4 + v^5 + v^6 + v^7$$
$$= 4.8684$$

Present value of interest payments:

$$PV = 5 \times 4.8684$$
$$= 24.34$$

Present value of terminal payment:

$$PV = 100 \times 0.5132$$
$$= 51.32$$

Therefore the present value of the bond is:

$$PV = 24.34 + 51.32$$
$$= 75.66$$

(b) *Using the HP12C:*   Key in as follows:

$i = 10$
Annual coupon or PMT $= -5$
Maturity (seven *annual* periods) or $n = 7$
Repayment (or future value) $= -100$

Solve for PV by keying in PV, which shows up in the display as 75.6579.

2. Key in the HP-12C as follows:

$n = 5$
$i = 5$
$FV = -100$
Annual coupon/$PMT = -10$

Solve for PV, which shows as 121.6474.

3. (1) $i = 7\%$

Key in the HP-12C as follows:

$FV = -100$
$i = 7$
$PMT = -8$

To calculate the present value to call date,

$$n = 2 \text{ (annual periods)}$$

and solving for PV, the display shows 101.8080.

To calculate PV to put date, key in:

$n = 5$

and solving for PV, the display shows 104.100.

To calculate PV to maturity, key in

$n = 9$

and solving for PV, the display shows 106.5152.

(2) $i = 9\%$

Key in:

$i = 9$
$n = 2$

and, solving for PV, derive PV to call date of 98.2408. Then key in:

$n = 5$

and solving for PV, derive PV to put date of 96.1103. Key in:

$n = 9$

and solving for PV to maturity, display shows 94.0047.

The issuer would call the issue if i were 7 percent but not if i were 9 percent. If the present value of the bond to call date is above par and remains so at the call date, the issuer should repay because he could refinance more cheaply. (*Note:* the issuer might not take this course if his or her credit rating had declined—which would increase the cost of a new issue—and account would have to be taken of expenses which reduce the cost saving of a refinancing).

The investor would exercise his put option if $i = 9\%$. He realizes a capital gain (100 − 96.1103) and reinvests the proceeds of redemption (at 100 percent) at the same yield (or, in effect, a higher yield for his original outlay). He would not exercise his option if $i = 7\%$ and/or the bonds were trading above par unless the credit of the issuer had deteriorated.

Current Yield or Dividend Yield

The current yield on a bond is the ratio of the coupon of the bond to its current price. Thus, a bond with a price of 95 percent and a coupon of 13 percent has a current yield of:

$$\frac{13}{95} \times 100 = 13.6842\%$$

Redemption Yield

A straight bond has an annual coupon of 8 percent, a market price (or present value) of 75 percent, a maturity of 10 years and redemption is at par or 100 percent.

Recalling the equation of value on p. 66, the summary equation of value may be written as follows:

$$75 = (8 \times a_{10}) + (100 \times v^{10})$$

The only unknown in the equation is i, which is calculated by a process known as *iteration*. To do this manually is a lengthy process and using the HP-12C is quicker.

In general, if we know four out of the five values n, i, PV, PMT, FV, then the HP-12C will calculate the remaining value.

In the case just presented, key in:

$n = 10$
$PV = 75$
$PMT = -8$
$FV = -100$

and solving for i, the display shows 12.519 percent.

If the yield level is high in relation to the redemption yield of other Eurobonds of comparable credit and maturity, the bond would attract buyers and the price would then be marked up until the yield fell to the level of other bonds.

The Yield Curve*

Analysis of a bond market as a whole, rather than the evaluation of individual issues, can be carried out by the use of the yield curve concept. In order

* Contributed by Lawrence de V. Wragg.

to derive a yield curve, a group of homogeneous debt securities (that is to say, issued by either the same borrower or by borrowers with as nearly identical credit standing as possible) with differing maturities is identified. At a given moment, the yield to redemption is calculated for each security. From what has been said earlier, it will by now be clear that comparison of like with like is essential, and appropriate adjustments are effected if comparisons are to be made between bonds of different coupon frequency, or with different maturity arrangements.

The resulting maturity yields, expressed as percentages per annum, are then plotted on a graph with life to maturity on the horizontal or x-axis, and yield to maturity on the vertical or y-axis. Although the y-axis is normally linear (of uniform scale at all of its points) the x-axis is normally plotted on a logarithmic scale, with diminishing amounts of space given to the longer maturity periods in order to depict more clearly the proportionate effect of yield changes.

A typical yield curve is shown in Figure 3-1. The securities involved have been taken from the U.K. gilt-edged market, in order to satisfy the test of homogeneity of issuers (in this case, the U.K. government).

The normal slope of the curve when the market is in equilibrium is positive—yields rise as maturity lengthens; and long-term interest rates are higher than short-term interest rates. In these conditions, investors are receiving higher remuneration for forgoing immediate consumption and for the increased risks associated with longer-term investments.

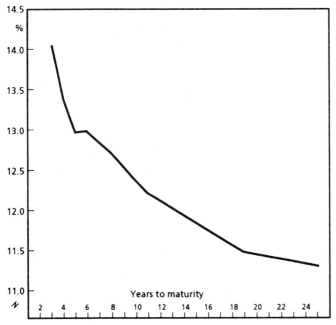

Figure 3-1. Par yield curve for U.K. government gilts (semiannual yield, March 28, 1990). (*Source: Datastream.*)

The degree of slope is significant: the gradient steepens when the market expects a general rise in interest rates, and therefore sells holdings of longer-dated bonds (thereby forcing the price down and the yield up) in favor of short-term instruments or money market deposits (tending to depress short-term interest rates at the same time). By doing so, the risk of capital loss on the longer-dated holdings is eliminated, and the investor is well placed to reinvest in the longer-dated bonds after the expected increase in yields has taken place.

When market sentiment is the converse, and short-term interest rates are expected to fall, then the slope of the yield curve reverses and becomes inverse (or negative), with long-term rates being higher than short-term rates. This is caused by investors buying longer-dated securities in order to receive the higher return available (and possibly before there is a general fall in longer-term rates, too), thereby driving the price of longer-dated bonds up and their yields down. At the same time, funds are likely to have been removed from the money markets, driving up short-term interest rates, and exacerbating this effect.

A generally flat yield curve appears when short-term and long-term interest rates are at much the same levels, suggesting that investors are—for the time being—indifferent to maturity risk.

A further alternative arises where the yield curve has one or more bulges (or "humps") of relatively high yield, with lower yields on either side. There is normally a technical explanation for such phenomena, such as oversupply of bonds in a particular maturity band (say, as a result of a glut of new issues or a major issue of bonds by a government), or by investors actively seeking bonds of a particular maturity in a thin market, which will drive the price up and the yield down in relation to the rest of the market.

A yield curve is of necessity a "best fit" average of the individual yields, so the individual bond yields may well lie above or below the line when it is drawn. This gives a preliminary indication as to whether a particular issue has a relatively high or low yield (and hence low or high price from an investor's viewpoint) in relation to its market. Points standing above the curve may be considered as high-yielding (cheap), and those below as low-yielding (dear). Where there are two bonds with similar maturities (and similar credit standing as a result of the criteria applied earlier), then a switch—selling the low-yielding bond, and buying the high-yielding bond in its place—will enhance the return of a bond portfolio without increasing risk or maturity. Switching of this nature on any scale will tend to have an arbitraging effect, and to even out the anomalies between different issues.

A development of the two-dimensional yield curve is the yield surface, where the third axis is provided by size of coupon, thereby segmenting the market into bonds with low, medium, and high coupons. The greatest relevance of this technique, best developed by institutions investing in the U.K. gilt market, is where tax considerations are important in the evaluation of the yield in the hands of the investor. Where tax regimes distinguish between income and capital gains, taxing income more heavily than capital gains, then investment in low-coupon bonds will (all things being equal) increase the proportion of return to be derived from income (the coupon) in relation to capital (the discount to the investor), and hence increase the after-tax yield to the investor. This in turn has an effect on the market's valuation of such bonds, and leads to distortions in the yield surface. As before, the surface is an average and individual bond issues tend to lie above or below it, thereby giving the investor an indication of their relative price.

Semiannual Yields

Many bonds, such as issues in the U.S. domestic market by foreign issuers (termed *Yankees*), pay interest twice yearly or semiannually.

Let us consider a bond as follows:

Coupon = 8% per annum payable semiannually

Price = 75%

Final maturity = 10 years

Redemption price = 100%

What is the Redemption Yield? A maturity of 10 years and semiannual interest periods produces $2 \times 10 = 20$ periods. The coupon of 8 percent per annum is equivalent to 4 percent per period of 6 months. Thus the equation of value may be written as follows:

$$75 = (4 \times a_{20}) + (100 \times v^{20})$$

Using the HP-12C, key in:

$n = 20$
$PV = 75$
$PMT = -4$
$FV = -100$

and solving for i, the display shows 6.2184 percent.

Thus on a bond which pays 4 percent every six months, the redemption yield at a price of 75 is 6.2184 percent. Note that this yield only relates to periods of a length of six months. The same yield can be expressed in terms of 12-month periods or $6.2184 \times 2 = 12.4368\%$ "semiannual."

What Is the Relationship between Annual and Semiannual Yields? A comparison of two bonds illustrates the question.

Bond A	Bond B
Coupon: 8% per annum annual bond	Coupon: 8% p.a. semiannual
Price: 75%	Price: 75%
Maturity: 10 years	Maturity: 10 years
Redemption yield: 12.519% annual	Redemption yield: 12.4368% semiannual

Calculations of Value

Bond A pays interest once per year and is said to have a redemption yield of 12.519 percent per annum (annual bond). Bond B pays interest twice per year and is said to have a redemption yield of 12.437% per annum (semi-annual bond).

Expressed in this way, the two bonds are not comparable. However, the redemption yield of Bond A may be expressed in semiannual terms and that of Bond B in annual terms.

Notation

Let i = per annum redemption yield on a bond paying interest annually
si = per annum redemption yield on a bond paying interest semiannually
$si/2$ = six-monthly redemption yield on a bond paying interest semi-annually

Then to derive a formula to convert semiannual to annual yield, we write again an equation of value as follows:

$$\left(1 + \frac{si}{2}\right)^2 = 1 + i$$

$$i = \left(1 + \frac{si}{2}\right)^2 - 1$$

and to convert annual to semiannual:

$$si = (\sqrt{(i+1)} - 1) \times 2$$

and to express i or si as a percentage multiply by 100.

To express the redemption yield of Bond A in semiannual terms:

$$si = \left[\sqrt{\left\{\left(\frac{12.519}{100}\right) + 1\right\}} - 1\right] \times 2$$

$$= 0.1215$$
$$\text{or } 12.15\%$$

Thus Bond A has a lower redemption yield (semiannual) to that of Bond B (12.4368 percent). This makes sense if one considers that all other terms being the same, the interest on Bond B is reinvested every six months as opposed to only every twelve months on Bond A.

Compounding

Compounding calculations are best understood and achieved by equations of value which express the interest and principal payment calculated in two different ways.

Recalling the definition of *si* given previously, the value of the principal of US$1 at the end of six months is:

$$1\left(1 + \frac{si}{2}\right)$$

Let us take as an example an interest rate of 10 percent per annum compounded monthly. The interest rate for one month will be:

$$\frac{10}{100} \times \frac{1}{12} \text{ monthly}$$

and the future value of US$1 at the end of one month is:

$$1\left[1 + \left(\frac{10}{100} \times \frac{1}{12}\right)\right]$$

The future value of US$1 at the end of six months is:

$$FV = 1\left[1 + \left(\frac{10}{100} \times \frac{1}{12}\right)\right]^6$$

To calculate the equivalent annual interest rate compounded six-monthly, we write:

$$FV = 1\left[1 + \left(\frac{10}{100} \times \frac{1}{12}\right)\right]^6 = 1\left(1 + \frac{si}{2}\right)$$

and solving for *si:*

$$\frac{si}{2} + 1 = \left[1 + \left(\frac{10}{100} \times \frac{1}{12}\right)\right]^6$$

$$si = \left[\left(1 + \frac{1}{1200}\right)^6 - 1\right] \times 2$$

$$= 0.1021$$
$$\text{or } 10.21\%$$

Exercise: What is the equivalent annual coupon on a bond that pays interest at 8 percent per annum, payable quarterly? Think of the equation of value.

Solution: Let the principal amount be US$1 and *i* the annual coupon. Then the future value at the end of the year is simply expressed as $1 + i$.

A bond paying 8 percent per annum payable quarterly pays interest at ¾ or 2 percent per quarter, and at the end of a year the principal value of the bond may be expressed as:

$$\left(1 + \frac{2}{100}\right)^4$$

We then set out the equation of value as follows:

$$\left(1 + \frac{2}{100}\right)^4 = 1 + i$$
$$i = (1.02)^4 - 1$$
$$= 0.08243$$
$$\text{or } 8.243\%$$

Fractional Periods

To calculate the price of a bond in the course of a year, we:

1. calculate the price at the last interest payment date

2. compound forward from that price

Let us consider a bond with an 8 percent per annum coupon payable annually, 9⅔ years to maturity and a current yield of 9 percent.

Given annual payment, the bond, at the last interest payment date, would have had a remaining maturity of 10 years. Using the HP-12C, key in:

$n = 10$
$i = 9$
$PMT = -8$
$FV = -100$

and solving for PV, the display shows 93.5823 or the value as of the last interest payment date.

The bond has currently 9⅔ years remaining life so ⅓ year has elapsed since the last interest payment date at which the value of the bond was calculated. The present value of the bond can then be treated as investment of 93.5823 for one-third of a year at a rate equal to the current yield level. Thus,

$$PV = 93.5823\left(1 + \frac{9}{100}\right)^{⅓}$$
$$= 93.5823 \times 1.029142$$
$$= 96.30952$$
$$= 96.31$$

An alternative method of calculating the price is to calculate the present value of the principal and accrued interest separately. Starting with this principal, we key in:

$n = 9.66666666$ (accuracy requires a sufficient number of decimal places: these are accepted by the HP-12C after keying in STO, and then EEX, when a small c appears in the display):
$i = 9$

$$PMT = -8$$
$$FV = -100$$

and solving for *PV,* the display shows 88.756.

We then *add* the present value of the coupon payment due in two-thirds of a year. This implies *discounting* the coupon amount at the current yield level of $i = 9$ for a period of two-thirds of a year. Setting the equation of value:

$$PVI = 8 \times \left(\frac{1}{1 + 0.09} \right)^{\frac{2}{3}}$$

$$= 7.553339$$

The sum of both present values amounts to:

$$88.756 + 7.553339 = 96.309$$

Internal Rate of Return

There is no difference between i, the interest rate or yield referred to so far, and the internal rate of return (IRR). In cases where cash flows are at regular intervals but of irregular amounts, it is common to refer to the applicable valuation rate of interest as the *internal rate of return.*

Example: What is the IRR of a company generating the following profits on a capital investment of US$1 million?

End of year	Profit	
1	−US$60,000	
2	US$50,000	
3	US$100,000	
4	US$200,000	
5	US$1,100,000	(including repayment of capital)

There are six items of cash flow which are entered in the HP-12C as follows:

Keystrokes	Display	
f CLEAR REG	0.00	Clears financial and storage registers
1,000,000 CHS g CFo	−1,000,000	Initial capital (with a minus sign to indicate a negative cash flow)
60,000 CHS g CFj	−60,000	First-year loss (with a minus sign to indicate a negative cash flow)
50,000 g CFj	50,000	Second-year profit
100,000 g CFj	100,000	Third-year profit
200,000 g CFj	200,000	Fourth-year profit
1,100,000 g CFj	1,100,000	Fifth-year profit and repayment of capital
f IRR	7.136	IRR

Exercise: Calculate the IRR for the following cash flows:

Initial outlay:	US$500,000
Income at end of year 1:	−US$100,000
Income at end of year 2:	US$75,000
Income at end of year 3:	US$150,000
Repayment at end of year 4:	US$700,000

Solution

Keystrokes	Display	
f CLEAR REG	0.00	
500,000 CHS g CFo	−500,000	(a minus sign is required because this is the initial outlay)
100,000 CHS g CFj	−100,000	(a minus sign indicates the first year's result was a loss or another outflow)
75,000 g CFj	75,000	
150,000 g CFj	150,000	
700,000 g CFj	700,000	
f IRR	13.194	

Thus the internal rate of return of the cash flow is 13.194 percent.

Average Life of Bond Issues with Sinking Funds

This notion is best illustrated by an example as follows:

A bond with a ten-year final maturity has a sinking fund which redeems one-fifth ($\frac{1}{5}$) of the original issue amount each year starting on the sixth anniversary of the issue. What is the average life of the issue?

The amortization schedule is set out as follows:

End of year	Amortization
1	0
2	0
3	0
4	0
5	0
6	× 20% = 120
7	× 20% = 140
8	× 20% = 160
9	× 20% = 180
10	× 20% = 200
	800

Dividing the sum by 100 percent, we obtain a result of 8 years.

Another method of calculation is based on fractions rather than percentage amortization, as follows:

$$\text{Average Life} = \left(\frac{1}{5} \times 6\right) + \left(\frac{1}{5} \times 7\right) + \left(\frac{1}{5} \times 8\right) + \left(\frac{1}{5} \times 9\right) + \left(\frac{1}{5} \times 10\right)$$

$$= \frac{1}{5} \times (6 + 7 + 8 + 9 + 10) = 8 \text{ years}$$

Yield to Average Life*

Where a bond has a mandatory redemption schedule, the yield to maturity is meaningless to the investor and the borrower, because there is a material probability that any one bond will be drawn at random on one of the redemption dates. As a result, the measure of yield to average life is used which takes account of these probabilities. Thus in the example given, the calculation of the yield to average life would be performed using a value of 8 for n.

Exercise: What is the average life of a bond with a ten-year final maturity and a sinking fund which redeems one-fifth ($\frac{1}{5}$) of the original issue amount each year starting on the sixth anniversary of the issue?

Given a coupon of 7 percent and a price of 92, what is the yield to average life?

Solution

$$\text{Average life} = \frac{1}{5} \times (6 + 7 + 8 + 9 + 10)$$

$$= 8 \text{ years}$$

For yield to average life, use the HP-12C and key in:

$n = 8$
$PV = 92$
$PMT = -7$
$FV = -100$

solving for $i = 8.4141\%$

Accrued Interest

The section on compound interest explained how the present value or purchase price of a bond reflects the value of the future stream of payments discounted at current yield levels. When the purchase is made in the course of an interest period, the purchase price paid to the seller is augmented by the amount of accrued interest since the last interest payment date on the bond up to date of settlement.

* Contributed by Lawrence de V. Wragg.

Fixed-Rate Bonds. Accrued interest is calculated in accordance with the following formula:

$$\text{Nominal amount} \times \frac{\text{coupon}}{100} \times \frac{\text{accrual period}}{360}$$

where:

- "accrual period" is the number of days between the last interest payment date and settlement date. (*Note:* the maximum number of days in any month by convention is 30 days; a full month of February also counts as 30 days.
- interest accrues up to settlement date, regardless of trade date.
- nominal amount is the face amount of the bonds purchased.

Example: What is the settlement amount of the following bond?

Market price:	93.58%
Coupon:	7%
Last coupon date:	31 January 1989
Settlement date:	25 February 1989
Nominal amount of purchase:	US$1,000,000
Accrual period:	25 days
Accrued interest:	$\text{US\$1,000,000} \times \frac{7}{100} \times \frac{25}{360}$
Principal amount:	$\text{US\$1,000,000} \times \frac{93.58}{100}$
Settlement amount:	$\text{US\$1,000,000} \left[\frac{93.58}{100} + \left(\frac{7}{100} \times \frac{25}{360} \right) \right] = \text{US\$940,661.11}$

Floating-Rate Bonds. Accrued interest is calculated in accordance with a similar formula:

$$\text{Nominal amount} \times \frac{\text{coupon}}{100} \times \frac{\text{days elapsed}}{360}$$

FRN accrual calculations are based on money market calculations whereby the term *days elapsed* refers to the actual number of calendar days over a 360-day year.

Example: Calculate the settlement proceeds for the following FRN purchase:

Market price:	97.25%
Current coupon:	9%
Last coupon payment date:	2 February 1989
Settlement date:	25 May 1989

Nominal amount of purchase:	US$3,000,000
Accrual period:	$26 + 31 + 30 + 25 = 112$
Accrued interest:	$\text{US\$3,000,000} \times \dfrac{9}{100} \times \dfrac{112}{360}$
Principal amount:	$\text{US\$3,000,000} \times \dfrac{97.25}{100}$
Settlement amount:	$\text{US\$3,000,000} \left[\dfrac{97.25}{100} + \left(\dfrac{9}{100} \times \dfrac{112}{360} \right) \right] = \text{US\$3,001,500}$

FRN Margin Calculations

The yield evaluation of an FRN is expressed in terms of a margin over LIBOR. There are two calculations of this margin: the simple margin and the effective margin.

Simple Margin. The simple margin is a widely used measure but does not use compound interest and is therefore not "correct." It provides quick results and, for low interest rates with prices close to par, the simple margin as at the date of a new issue or roll-over date is close to the effective margin.

> **Example:** Calculate the simple margin on an FRN issue with a final maturity of 10 years, a margin of 0.25 percent over LIBOR and a price of 98 percent.
>
> $$\text{Simple margin} = 0.25 + \left[\left(100 - 98 \right) \frac{1}{10} \right]$$
> $$= 0.25 + 0.20$$
> $$= 0.45$$
>
> The discount from par—in this case two percentage points—is divided by the number of years to maturity and the result added to the basic margin to give the simple margin.

Effective Margin. The method of calculation of the effective margin over LIBOR provided by an FRN issue depends on whether it is: (1) a new issue or an existing issue on an interest payment or roll-over date (when there is a quick way of calculating the result), or (2) a normal secondary market issue or a mismatch FRN. For a normal secondary market issue, it is necessary to use a program.

Calculation of an Effective Margin (Compound or True Margin)
at New Issue or Roll-over Date

Given a new issue, as in the last example, we need to make two assumptions:

Assumption 1: The FRN pays 0.25 percent over one-year LIBOR so that there are ten interest periods.

Assumption 2: $i = 10$ percent.

Note: i needs only to be approximate and has the value of the current interest rate for the roll-over period of the FRN. Thus interest rates are assumed to be a nominal 10 percent for a one-year period.

Then, using the HP-12C, key in:

$i = 10$
$n = 10$
$PV = -2$
$FV = 0$

and, solving for *PMT,* the display shows 0.325491.

$$\text{The effective margin} = 0.25 + 0.325491$$
$$= 0.5755.$$

The essence of the calculation is that the discount is converted into an annuity.

Example: Calculate the simple and effective margin of a new FRN issue with a final maturity of ten years, a margin over 0.125 percent over three-month LIBOR and a price of 97 percent. Assume *i* is 10 percent.

The simple margin is calculated as follows:

$$\text{Simple margin} = 0.125 + \left(100 - 97 \right) \frac{1}{10}$$

$$= 0.125 + \frac{3}{10}$$

$$= 0.425$$

To calculate the effective margin, we calculate first the interest rate for a three-month period or $\frac{10}{4} = 2.5$. Then, using the HP-12 C, key in:

$n = 40$ (4 interest periods per year for 10 years)
$i = 2.5\%$ (annual yield divided by the number of periods per year)
$PV = -3$
$FV = 0$

and, solving for *PMT,* the display shows 0.110509. However, this figure applies to a quarterly period and for equivalent annual figure, this should be multiplied by 4 to derive 0.478035.

$$\text{Effective margin} = 0.125 + 0.478035$$
$$= 0.603035$$

Calculation of the Margin on an FRN Issue Trading in the Secondary Market

Here it is necessary to use a program which may be written into a personal computer for general use in a dealing room or equally into an HP-12C. (*Note:* The program memory on an HP-12C is limited to 99 program lines and the FRN margin program for the HP-12C requires 74 lines. Entering the program will delete any prior program and leave little room for other programs.)

Chillcott's Program for FRN Margins

(f)	P/R	37	–
(f)	PRGM	38	STO 4
1	RCL 5	39	RCL i
2	RCL 0	40	1
3	(g) DYS	41	%
4	RCL 2	42	1
5	÷	43	+
6	RCL 4	44	RCL 2
7	×	45	y
8	RCL 9	46	RCL 8
9	+	47	×
10	STO 8	48	CHS
11	RCL 5	49	RCL 5
12	RCL 1	50	+
13	(g) DYS	51	RCL 6
14	RCL 2	52	×
15	÷	53	RCL 4
16	RCL 4	54	÷
17	×	55	STO 9
18	1	56	RCL 3
19	0	57	+
20	0	58	RCL 7
21	+	59	+
22	STO 5	60	RCL 6
23	RCL 0	61	÷
24	RCL 1	62	STO 1
25	(g) DYS	63	RCL i
26	RCL 2	64	–
27	÷	65	f3
28	RCL 6	66	(f) RND
29	×	67	(g) x = 0
30	STO 2	68	(g) GTO 72
31	f9	69	RCL i
32	1	70	STO i
33	*PMT*	71	(g) GTO 31
34	*PV*	72	RCL 9
35	CHS	73	RCL7
36	1	74	+
		(f)	P/R

To enter the program, clear the HP-12C of existing programs and key in as just indicated starting with:

(f) P/R	00 -	appears in display
(f) PRGM	00 - PRGM	appears in display
RCL 5	01 - 45 5	appears in display
RCL 0	02 - 45 0	appears in display
etc.		

To calculate the margin of an FRN on the HP-12C using the program, key in as follows:

Settlement date	then press STO 0
Next interest date	STO 1 ***
360 for US$ issues or 365 for £ issues	STO 2 ***
LIBOR for unexpired portion of current interest period	STO 3
Coupon (inclusive of margin)	STO 4 ***
Last interest date	STO 5
Number of coupons in a year (normally 2 or 4)	STO 6
Fixed margin	STO 7
Clean price (i.e., without accrued interest)	STO 9
Starting estimate of i	i
Number of coupon payments from last payment date to maturity	n
Then press	R/S

After running for several seconds, the effective margin will be displayed.

Notes

1. The HP-12C provides two choices of format for entering dates: either day, month, and year or month, day, and year. To select day, month, and year, enter g D.MY. before you start entering the variables.

2. *** The values in these stores are changed while running the program and should be re-entered for each run.

Example: You are selling bonds in an FRN issue by Bankers Trust Company with a final maturity date of 11 March 2000. Interest is 0.0625 percent over three-month LIBOR. The current price is 98. The last interest payment date was 13 December 1988. The next interest payment date is 13 March 1989. LIBOR for the unexpired portion of the current interest period is 9.375 percent. The current coupon is 9 percent (inclusive of margin). Settlement date on the sale is 27 February 1989.

Begin by calculating the number of periods: 11 years at 4 periods per year plus the current period gives a value for n of 45.

The value of i need only be a guess since iteration is then used in the calculation. If yield levels are 10 percent annual, then for three months $i = 2.5$ percent.

Using the HP-12C, key in as follows:

Keystrokes	Display	
f FIN, f REG	0.00	clears registers
27.021989 STO 0	27.021989	
13.031989 STO 1	13.031989	
360 STO 2	360	
9.375 STO 3	9.375	
9.0 STO 4	9.0	
13.121988 STO 5	13.121988	
4 STO 6	4.00	
0.0625 STO 7	0.0625	
98.00 STO 9	98.00	
2.5 i	2.5	
45 n	45	
R/S	0.365	

The effective margin is thus 0.365 percent.

Exercises: What is the effective margin on the following U.S. dollar FRN issues?

1. National Westminster Bank, due 18 April 2005

Next interest payment date:	21 April 1989
LIBOR for unexpired portion:	9.4375%
Current coupon:	8.5%
Last interest date:	21 October 1988
Interest:	0.0625% over 6-month LIBOR
Price:	97.5
Settlement date:	27 February 1989

2. Royal Bank of Canada, due 15 July 2005

Next interest payment date:	28 February 1989
LIBOR:	9.375%
Coupon:	9%
Last interest payment date:	31 January 1989
Interest:	0.0625% over 6-month LIBOR
Price:	95
Settlement date:	27 February 1989

What is the effective margin on the following Sterling FRN issues?

3. Halifax Building Society, due 24 September 1996

Next interest payment date:	28 February 1989
LIBOR:	13%
Coupon:	13%
Last interest payment date:	31 January 1989
Interest:	0.08% over 1-month LIBOR
Price:	99.90
Settlement date:	27 February 1989

4. Halifax Building Society, due 24 September 1996 "B"

Next interest payment date:	28 March 1989
LIBOR:	13%
Coupon:	12.33%
Last interest payment date:	26 September 1988
Interest:	0.08% over 6-month LIBOR
Price:	99.80
Settlement date:	27 February 1989

5. What is the effective margin on the following U.S. dollar FRN perpetual issue by National Westminster Bank?

Next interest payment date:	14 May 1989
LIBOR:	9.5%
Coupon:	8.875%
Last interest payment date:	14 November 1988
Interest:	⅜% over 6-month LIBOR
Price:	92
Settlement date:	27 February 1989

6. What is the effective margin on the following "mismatch" FRN issue by Credit Commercial de France due 22 March 1997?

LIBOR:	9.5%
Interest payments:	Paid six-monthly
Interest rate and fixing:	6-month LIBID refixed monthly
Price:	99.35
Settlement date:	22 March 1989

Solutions: The program is used for all exercises except the CCF mismatch FRN due 1997.

1. National Westminster Bank, due 2005

$$n = 33 \text{ and } i = 5\% \text{ (guess)}$$

Using the program produces an effective margin of 0.37.

2. Royal Bank of Canada, due 2005

$$n = 198 \text{ and } i = 0.8\%$$

Note: The issue will actually redeem on 31 July 2005 because of interest dates having moved forward because of weekends and holidays.

Using the program produces an effective margin of 0.69.

3. HALIFAX Building Society, due 24 September 1996

$$n = 92$$

Key in 365 in STO 2.

$$i = 1.1\% \text{ (guess)}$$

Using the program produces an effective margin of 0.10.

4. Halifax Building Society "B," due 24 September 1996

$$n = 16$$

Key in 365 in STO 2.

$$i = 1.1\% \text{ (guess)}$$

Using the program produces an effective margin of 0.11.

5. National Westminster Bank Perpetual (Old)

$$n = 9999999999 \text{ and } i = 5\% \text{ (guess)}$$

Using the program produces an effective margin of 1.26 percent.

6. Credit Commercial de France mismatch FRN, due 1997

This FRN is known as a "mismatch" since the refixing of coupons takes place every month although the calculation of those coupons depends on the level of six-month LIBOR on each refix.

The calculation of the effective margin is complex but is built up from four manageable elements:

(a) *The basic margin.* In this case, it is negative at –0.125, since LIBID = LIBOR – 0.125%.

(b) *The discount to par.* The price is 99.35 percent therefore the discount from par is 0.65 percent. This can be translated into a margin over LIBOR in the same way that a new issue is handled. Using the HP-12C, we key in:

$PV = 0.65$
$i = 4.75$
$n = 16$
$FV = $ nil

and, solving for *PMT*, we derive –0.059. After changing the sign, the result is multiplied by 2 to derive an equivalent annual rate of 0.12.

(c) *The compounding cost.* If a holding in the issue is match-funded, then one-month funds will be borrowed each period. However, the issue only pays interest every six months: 9.5 percent per annum paid six-monthly is translated into an equivalent monthly rate as follows:

■ Convert the annual rate into a six-monthly rate by dividing by 2:

$$\frac{9.5}{2} = 4.75$$

■ Then, setting down the equation of value:

$$1 + \frac{4.75}{100} = (1 + z)^6$$

$$z = \sqrt[6]{(1.0475)} - 1$$
$$= 0.007764$$

This is the monthly rate paid monthly and, to convert to an annual rate (paid monthly), multiply by 12 to derive:

$$0.007764 \times 12 = 0.093173$$
$$\text{or } 9.32\%$$

The difference between the two *annual* rates represents the compounding cost:

$$9.50 - 9.32 = 0.18\%$$

(d) *The yield curve.* There is no calculation but an estimate which is subjective. Mismatch FRNs were almost all issued when the yield curve was steeply upward and shortsighted investors were attracted by the apparent good initial yield. This was a supposition which was impossible to sustain throughout the life of the issue, where both positive and negative yield curves could prevail. Assume, therefore, a *flat* yield curve resulting in a NIL estimate.

The effective margin on the mismatch is the sum of these four elements as follows:

Discount:	+0.12
Basic margin:	−0.125
Compounding cost:	−0.18
Yield curve:	0
Effective margin:	−0.185%

This answer shows that if the yield curve were flat throughout the life of the issue, then the return would be 0.185 percent below LIBOR. A prospective purchaser might still buy the bond despite this poor margin if, at the time, a steeply upward yield curve prevailed.

4
The Principal Currencies of Issue in the International Bond Markets

Eurobonds are issued in a variety of currencies and this is a unique feature of the market. Since the abandonment of pegged exchange rates in 1973, currency fluctuation is the greatest concern of many international bond investors but, for professional investors, it is their strongest motivation to deal. Presently, investors have a choice of Eurobonds denominated in 23 currencies.* The wide variety of high- and low-volatility currencies has made it possible to satisfy their diverse bond investment strategies. These can be broadly split into two groups:

- the European currencies with low or controlled fluctuation including (1) the currencies within the EMS which are dominated by the Deutsche mark and fluctuate against each other within a prescribed band; (2) the ECU, a composite currency comprising EMS and EC member state currencies; and (3) the Swiss franc and Austrian schilling, currencies economically tied to the Deutsche mark. Together these constitute approximately a quarter of the international bond issues outstanding.

---

* International investors also invest massively in domestic securities, principally debt securities issued by governments and their agencies in their domestic markets. They also invest in domestic bonds issued by foreign issuers (e.g., Yankee U.S. dollar bonds).

- the freely floating currencies which make up the balance and include the U.S. dollar, the Japanese yen, the Australian and Canadian dollars.

An investment in a Eurobond creates a currency risk for the investor when the currency of denomination is other than the investor's base currency. Many investors seek to minimize their currency risk and, where investment in foreign currency bonds is desirable (or unavoidable), their concern for the safety of their capital directs their choice to low-volatility currencies. On the other hand, the professional investor searches for opportunities to maximize yield and currency gain. He or she may seek out bonds denominated in speculative currencies and will offset the currency risk of the investments through currency hedging strategies. Here, relative yields in different currency sectors for a given maturity is a key factor which influences the choice of currency sector. Thus the high absolute yields on short-dated Australian dollars and sterling bonds in the late 1980s stimulated considerable investor interest, despite the risks of high inflation and currency depreciation.

Issuers are similarly concerned with the currency exposure of their borrowings and select the currency of an issue in the light of several considerations as follows:

- local operations in the country of the currency in which the issue is denominated, or sales in the currency concerned.

- the availability of swaps: where the issue has no commercial reason to be denominated in a foreign currency, the borrower will issue only if a currency swap can be added to the bond issue to neutralize his currency exposure. Many Eurobond issues are now "driven" by the opportunity of a swap whose effect is to create a financing in the borrower's preferred currency, and at a cost that may be significantly below that of an issue in that currency.

  The pricing of swaps relies, as in bond markets, on supply and demand. If swaps out of U.S. dollars into yen produce a positive benefit, a swap in the reverse direction is likely to be uneconomic. Smaller swap markets such as French francs do not offer good liquidity; if a borrower issuer launching an issue in French francs requires funding in another currency, the issue clearly cannot proceed, regardless of investor demand, unless a swap is available.

- issuance controls: occasionally borrowers are "crowded out" from their domestic bond market by the government and have no choice but to issue in foreign currency. Where no swap is available in the borrower's home currency, the choice of currency exposure will be determined by the lowest interest cost and the least potential for appreciation.

The interaction of investor and issuer considerations of yield curve and swap market liquidity determine in the short term the share of individual currency sectors in the Eurobond market. Over a longer period, the trend in shares of each sector reflects the medium-term weakness or strength of each currency. Although western governments have tended in recent years to adopt and maintain similar monetarist policies, their success has been mixed and this is reflected in some measure in the varied performance of different sectors.*

The U.S. Dollar

As will be gathered by now, the Eurobond market is dominated by U.S. dollar-denominated instruments. The reasons for this are found in the history of the currency since World War II. The continued and widespread use of the U.S. dollar as an international reserve asset makes it a natural store of wealth. The supply of off-shore U.S. dollars is self-generating as a result of large reflows of U.S. dollar-denominated interest and principal payments on existing Eurobond issues. More recently, the United States has become a net debtor nation and is likely to remain so for the forseeable future. Concerns about the currency's weakness are, in some measure, assuaged by the knowledge that major creditors such as Japan have an interest in protecting their U.S. dollar investments from depreciation.

From the standpoint of issuers, several factors underlie the importance of Eurodollar bond instruments: First the role of the U.S. dollar as an international reserve asset made it the traditional choice for issues by sovereign borrowers looking to fund balance of payments deficits. Second, the Eurodollar bond market is unregulated, and for many years was the only choice of market for non-dollar-based international borrowers looking to avoid the queues and other quantitative issuance controls in the Swiss franc, Deutsche mark, French franc, and sterling bond markets. Third, the size of the Eurodollar bond market makes it still the first choice for very large-size offerings.[†]

Notwithstanding its pre-eminent role, the share of U.S. dollar sector in the Eurobond market has fallen by 50 percent since 1982. And at the same time as the loss of value of the currency deterred non-dollar-based investors, the growing supply of Eurobonds denominated in other currencies— including composite currencies such as the ECU—enabled investors to diversify and stabilize their currency risk. Issuers, too, were deterred by the chronic U.S. balance of payments and budget deficits in the 1980s which led to high U.S. dollar interest rates. Further, a volatile yield curve shortened the range of maturities which were acceptable to investors and issuers looking for longer-term finance had to resort to other markets.

---

* With the exception of the dollar, which is still the dominant international reserve currency, the shares of the different currency sectors in the new issues markets bears little relation to the shares of these currencies in the international money markets.

[†] The U.S. dollar is no longer the sole choice of currency for balance of payments or other financings in size. The ECU market has gained considerable momentum and presently boasts the largest plain fixed income issue outstanding (see p. 109). Global bond issues for large amounts have also been arranged in Canadian dollars.

Issuers.   Issuers in the Eurodollar bond market include the full range of international borrowers. The most highly rated but least numerous categories of issuer are the supranational and regional development bodies which launch almost exclusively fixed-rate instruments. Foremost among these is the World Bank because of a high credit rating, a regular presence in the new issues markets, liquid issues and, unusually, a continuing technical contribution to the development of the Eurobond market.*

In terms of credit quality, these are followed by some 20 sovereign governments from Europe, Asia, Australasia, and North and Latin America, which have launched mostly fixed-rate issues. Governments like the United Kingdom have launched both fixed- and floating-rate issues, raising very large amounts in a single issue. Austria and Denmark have also launched zero-coupon bonds, whose proceeds are generally swapped for floating-rate dollars. Government agencies, provincial governments, and municipal authorities are a significant category including the Scandinavian export credit agencies from Sweden, Denmark, Finland, and Norway, a dozen French government agencies, and the provincial governments and their agencies in Australia, Canada, and New Zealand.

International banks are the second-largest category of issuer in the Eurodollar bond market and include approximately 200 of the major universal and commercial banks from Europe, North America, Australasia and the Pacific Basin, U.K. merchant banks, and investment banks from Japan, the United States, former Comecon countries, and the Bank of China. Most issues are floating-rate note instruments. They serve to meet medium-term international treasury funding and are intended to match fund U.S. dollar LIBOR-based assets.

The largest category of issuer is the corporate sector, which was established through issues by multinational U.S. corporations such as Amoco, Campbell Soup, Exxon, Ford Motor, and General Electric. Many such issuers have an AA or AAA rating on their domestic debt and all have an international profile which has lent prestige to the market. By contrast, European corporate issuers in the Eurodollar bond market are rare: these have borrowing requirements in domestic or European currencies, and dollar requirements are increasingly raised through short-term commercial paper which offers greater flexibility of treasury management. Corporate issuers in the Eurobond market generally have a substantial scale of operations, an international profile, and extensive U.S. operations or sales markets (Siemens, Volkswagen, Unilever, Philips, Volvo, and ICI). However, the most prolific category of corporate issuer is comprised of some 300 Japanese corporations which rarely meet all these criteria—and often none. With the help of very buoyant stock market conditions and advanta-

---

* The World Bank is directly involved in the development of global bond issues and launched the first issues in 1989. It currently has six global bond issues outstanding for a total of US$9.5 billion.

Table 4-1. Issue Volume and Currency for all Foreign Bonds, 1981–1991

Currency	1984 ($M)	Iss.	1985 ($M)	Iss.	1986 ($M)	Iss.	1987 ($M)	Iss.	1988 ($M)	Iss.	1989 ($M)	Iss.	1990 ($M)	Iss.	1991 ($M)	Iss.
U.S. dollar	4,600.00	18	4,790.00	23	4,290.00	27	6,695.05	34	11,350.00	64	10,072.87	64	11,458.00	51	15,176.35	54
Deutsche mark	—	—	—	—	—	—	—	—	—	—	7.55	1	—	—	58.84	1
ECU	296.30	2	366.06	4	189.00	2	—	—	—	—	208.33	1	—	—	322.57	2
Canadian dollar	75.89	1	73.80	1	407.53	5	277.16	4	117.30	1	—	—	—	—	—	—
Sterling	1,362.88	17	814.10	8	394.45	4	559.76	10	340.69	2	1,144.90	6	252.05	2	89.46	1
Australian dollar	—	—	40.49	1	1,192.23	15	78.43	1	172.63	3	446.53	7	150.85	3	77.42	1
Austrian schilling	41.50	1	52.48	1	84.79	2	57.60	2	242.31	2	314.82	4	496.00	7	330.97	5
Belgian franc	167.06	3	259.65	3	451.79	5	496.88	5	223.57	2	106.13	2	187.54	1	231.87	1
Danish krone	—	—	—	—	—	—	25.22	1	77.54	1	41.79	1	52.34	1	—	—
Dutch guilder	1,251.14	21	1,263.82	21	—	—	—	—	—	—	—	—	—	—	—	—
French franc	—	—	440.00	4	224.11	1	674.78	3	587.69	2	541.61	3	633.68	3	350.13	1
Hong Kong dollar	—	—	270.46	4	51.26	1	312.55	4	75.79	11	115.30	9	140.69	2	64.59	1
Italian lira	—	—	219.04	4	207.68	2	147.10	2	357.36	3	—	—	161.03	1	—	—
Japanese yen	4,822.02	73	5,643.93	62	4,948.75	48	3,362.66	24	6,143.94	41	8,685.68	55	8,442.99	68	5,222.72	37
Luxembourg franc	224.26	32	396.89	63	822.52	88	1,360.05	152	1,556.44	181	1,636.17	200	3,545.18	315	3,114.67	166
New Zealand dollar	—	—	—	—	299.77	5	1,259.59	20	133.72	2	30.83	1	46.61	1	59.58	1
Singapore dollar	—	—	—	—	107.59	2	68.65	2	—	—	—	—	—	—	—	—
Swedish krona	—	—	—	—	42.91	1	—	—	—	—	—	—	—	—	—	—
Swiss franc	12,688.23	364	14,930.01	408	23,087.67	410	23,248.56	406	26,114.35	393	18,680.79	311	23,422.96	369	21,114.50	381
Finnish markka	—	—	—	—	47.76	1	—	—	38.27	1	57.61	1	—	—	49.18	1
Irish punt	—	—	12.83	1	—	—	—	—	—	—	—	—	—	—	50.56	1
Spanish peseta	—	—	—	—	—	—	240.52	3	897.64	9	2,077.03	21	1,673.79	14	2,596.95	21
Portuguese escudo	—	—	—	—	—	—	—	—	34.67	1	90.90	2	309.92	5	603.45	7
Total	25,529.28	532	29,573.56	608	36,849.81	619	38,864.56	673	48,463.91	719	44,258.84	689	50,973.63	843	49,513.81	682

SOURCE: Euromoney Bondware.

Table 4-2. Issue Volume and Currency for All Eurobonds, 1984–1989

Currency	1984 ($M)	Iss.	1985 ($M)	Iss.	1986 ($M)	Iss.	1987 ($M)	Iss
U.S. dollar	61,998.78	486	94,079.39	652	113,134.59	817	56,236.12	4
Deutsche mark	5,919.19	104	10,081.43	138	15,831.69	164	12,958.32	1
ECU	2,742.76	63	6,674.31	124	6,687.29	78	7,439.72	
Canadian dollar	1,983.70	42	2,870.62	54	5,175.90	87	5,747.84	
Sterling	4,272.24	49	5,780.54	61	10,506.00	80	14,486.58	1
Australian dollar	320.90	10	3,096.37	91	3,029.22	90	8,472.34	1
Austrian schilling	—	—	—	—	164.70	2	822.30	
Danish krone	—	—	425.97	17	1,087.31	26	1,332.89	
Dutch guilder	658.66	20	504.71	20	2,465.14	34	1,780.93	
French franc	—	—	1,103.80	21	3,494.27	46	1,479.60	
Hong Kong dollar	63.87	1	—	—	—	—	—	—
Italian lira	—	—	125.36	3	413.75	7	720.43	
Japanese yen	1,129.64	15	6,890.64	78	17,717.62	155	21,757.30	
Kuwaiti dinar	—	—	—	—	7.01	1	374.72	
New Zealand dollar	41.85	3	1,053.18	45	436.67	15	1,233.23	
Norwegian krone	158.27	6	189.01	7	—	—	—	—
Swedish krona	—	—	—	—	—	—	—	—
Finnish markka	—	—	—	—	30.37	1	181.09	
Irish punt	—	—	—	—	—	—	—	—
Spanish peseta	—	—	—	—	—	—	—	—
Portuguese escudo	—	—	—	—	—	—	—	—
Icelandic krona	—	—	—	—	—	—	—	—
Total	79,289.86	799	132,875.33	1,311	180,181.53	1,603	135,023.41	1,

SOURCE: Euromoney Bondware.

geous currency and interest rate swaps out of U.S. dollars into yen, these borrowers launched fixed-rate issues with equity warrants and swaps attached to produce very low-cost yen. The popularity of the scheme with Japanese borrowers has made it the single largest category of instruments in the Eurobond markets until (and even since) the start of the dramatic fall in Japanese stock prices in 1991.

Investors. Investors in Eurodollar instruments include the full spectrum of Eurobond investors, from central banks, government agencies, commercial banks, managed funds, pension funds and insurance companies, and corporates to retail investors. Central banks are major holders of U.S. dollars and invest excess liquidity in U.S. Treasury stock or listed Eurodollar instruments with an AAA rating. Insurance companies and pension funds look for listed instruments but are less concerned with ratings or liquidity. Retail accounts held in nominee and/or discretionary accounts with Swiss banks are also regular buyers of dollar instruments. International investors with dollar cash flows will typically maintain liquid dollar balances and invest some of the

Table 4-2. Issue Volume and Currency for All Eurobonds, 1984–1989 *(Continued)*

1988 ($M)	Iss.	1989 ($M)	Iss.	1989 ($M)	Iss.	1991 ($M)	Iss.
70,917.14	457	119,049.41	558	69,958.54	354	78,744.40	401
22,802.00	183	14,646.70	123	15,510.30	105	17,731.72	144
11,210.71	92	12,231.34	114	17,466.77	79	30,578.68	90
13,030.34	164	11,050.11	109	6,341.94	55	22,482.42	165
23,877.86	132	19,916.72	109	20,645.14	89	26,365.53	128
8,214.42	151	6,658.47	118	5,007.58	95	4,429.72	57
974.94	3	1,231.77	3	1,296.41	9	268.18	4
985.94	23	211.44	5	180.70	4	321.98	7
3,168.54	36	1,954.53	23	1,346.33	10	3,716.26	24
2,504.70	20	4,523.57	46	9,175.13	53	16,543.84	84
—	—	—	—	—	—	—	—
1,529.45	16	3,671.54	31	5,853.21	34	8,997.66	56
15,478.69	204	14,535.56	273	21,364.17	268	34,639.07	210
—	—	—	—	—	—	—	—
692.79	18	692.08	21	527.86	13	325.11	10
—	—	—	—	—	—	104.09	1
78.65	1	1,371.52	25	300.26	5	1,189.46	19
447.18	6	—	—	882.32	15	686.54	12
—	—	74.70	1	—	—	154.66	1
—	—	—	—	—	—	370.73	1
—	—	—	—	—	—	81.96	1
—	—	—	—	—	—	41.40	2
175,913.35	1,506	211,819.46	1,559	175,856.66	1,188	247,773.41	1,417

Table 4-3. Share (%) of Ten Principal Currency Sectors on Total Volume of New Issues of International Debt Securities, 1984–1991

	1984	1985	1986	1987	1988	1989	1990	1991
U.S. dollar	63.54	60.86	54.11	36.19	36.66	50.42	35.89	31.59
Japanese yen	5.68	7.72	10.44	14.45	9.64	9.07	13.14	13.41
ECU	2.64	4.33	3.17	4.28	5.00	4.86	7.70	10.39
Sterling	5.38	4.06	5.02	8.33	10.79	8.22	9.21	8.90
Canadian dollar	1.98	1.81	2.57	3.46	5.86	4.32	2.80	7.56
Swiss franc	12.10	9.19	10.64	13.37	11.64	7.30	10.33	7.10
Deutsche mark	5.65	6.21	7.29	7.45	10.16	5.72	6.84	5.98
French franc	—	0.95	1.71	1.24	1.38	1.98	4.32	5.68
Australian dollar	0.31	1.93	1.95	5.19	3.74	2.77	2.27	1.52
Dutch florin	1.82	1.09	1.14	1.04	1.51	0.76	0.59	1.25
Total	99.10	98.15	98.04	95.00	96.38	95.42	93.09	93.38
Other*	0.90	1.85	1.96	5.00	3.62	4.58	6.91	6.62

* Austrian schilling, Belgian franc,[†] Danish krone, Hong Kong dollar, Norwegian krone, Italian lira, Luxembourg franc,[†] New Zealand dollar, Singapore dollar,[†] Kuwaiti dinar, Swedish krona, Finnish markka, Irish punt, Spanish peseta, Portuguese escudo.

[†] Foreign bond market only.

SOURCE: Euromoney Bondware.

excess liquidity in dollar bonds. As the dollar weakened throughout the 1980s, the proportion of dollar holdings declined. Investors diversified their currency exposure and professional investors speculated against the U.S. dollars by buying Euro-DM, yen, ECU, and even sterling bonds. Better U.S. trade figures over 1988–1989 resulted in renewed demand for dollar bonds and the resumption of Eurodollar bond issuance. In the medium term, renewed confidence in the currency will release considerable latent demand for dollar-denominated instruments which will prevail so long as the dollar remains the prime international reserve currency.

Instruments and Issuance Terms. The Eurodollar bond market is the principal unregulated bond market worldwide. There is no restriction on amount, maturity, form, interest base, denomination, or status, and the depth of the market makes it ideal to launch large-scale offerings and to test new instruments:

- The Eurodollar bond market offers the complete range of medium-term bond instruments including fixed-, floating-, or zero-coupon bonds, and fixed-income bonds with debt warrants attached; equity-related dollar instruments include convertibles and fixed-income bonds with equity warrants attached.

- The market caters to large amounts, subject to credit and perception (for example, the US$2 billion 9% percent bonds due 1999 by the Republic of Italy and US$4 billion FRN issue due 1996 by the United Kingdom). Maximum issue size is gradually increasing in response to the demand for more liquid issues, while the minimum issue size, to ensure liquidity, is not less than US$250 million.

- The range of maturities for fixed income bonds is 7–12 years*; Longer maturities are seen in the US$ FRN market, where approximately 60 issues have no final maturity.

- Issues are generally in bearer form, but registered form is standard practice for global U.S. dollar fixed-rate issues (for example, the US$2 billion 8% percent due 1995 by the World Bank).

- Fixed-rate dollar issues are normally unsecured; however, many floating-rate issues are secured or collateralized on the assets which they fund (see Chapter 2).

Issuance Procedure. London is the leading center for new issues of Eurodollar bond, although they may be launched from any major interna-

---

* Maturities of 15 years were offered prior to the decoupling of the dollar from the gold standard but, since 1973, the longest common maturity has been 10 years. The exceptions are the supranational agencies such as the European Investment Bank and the World Bank, which have issued fixed-rate dollar Eurobonds with 30-year maturities.

tional financial center. The U.K. capital has a larger population of issuing houses than Paris, Frankfurt, or Zurich, which tend to confine themselves to issues denominated in the respective local currency. Eurodollar issues, wherever issued, are launched at the discretion of the lead manager without notification to any official or regulatory body and subject only to market conditions.

Syndicate and distribution arrangements are at the discretion of the lead manager. Pricing was traditionally left open until the syndicate was formed; this is now rarely found except in international equity issues. Instead, an issuing house will typically offer to buy the full amount of the issue from the borrower at a fixed price, simultaneously lay off his underwriting risk on the members of his underwriting syndicate, and sell the issue into the market. It is common for several issues to be launched simultaneously and normally this does not present a problem. Where large-size issues are concerned, issuing houses participating in the issue will have been informally notified beforehand. Guidelines on syndicate practice are set by the International Primary Markets Association, a voluntary organization which was founded by the London leading Eurobond issuing houses to establish and enforce standards of practice in the primary market, which apply to most currency sectors.

Public Eurodollar issues are listed on the London or Luxembourg stock exchanges.* Documentation conforms to the practices of the industry (see Chapter 12).

The Deutsche Mark

With the backing of a strong external economy and consistently low inflation, the Deutsche mark has offered stability and a relatively low-interest rate structure. These features have made it the principal currency of issue in the international bond markets after the U.S. dollar. Foreign issuers have launched DM bond issues because of low absolute debt service costs, low interest rate volatility, and predictable currency exposure. The supranational institutions and development banks who seek the lowest service costs are prominent issuers. Investors have found a reliable store of wealth in Deutsche mark bonds; and aggressive U.S. dollar-based investors have relied on the stability of the currency to speculate against the weakness of the dollar by investing short term in Deutsche mark instruments.

Foreign borrowers were first admitted to the Deutsche mark capital markets in 1958 but the international DM bond market found its impetus in 1964 when a coupon (or withholding) tax was first levied on interest payments to nonresidents. Bond issues by non-German borrowers were exempted and, in response to the growing demand for tax-free Deutsche

---

* *Not* New York where any issue has to conform inter alios with the registration requirements of the U.S. Securities Act of 1933.

mark bonds, the volume of issues by non-German borrowers grew rapidly. The coupon tax was abolished in 1984, introduced once more in 1989 at a lower rate, again with the exemption of Euro-DM bonds issued by non-German domiciled borrowers. It was abolished again the same year. However, proposals for its reintroduction are presently under study: this would provide for the tax to be withheld not by the borrower but by the paying agent, and foreign investors would be exempt.

Issuers.　The largest category of issuer is that of the international regional development agencies, the European supranationals agencies, and the European Community and its agencies. Other international borrowers include Western sovereign governments, government agencies acting as a vehicle to raise foreign currency for their national Treasury, private sector corporates issuing straight fixed-rate debt, and Japanese borrowers issuing fixed-rate bonds with equity warrants attached. German banks and private sector corporates have issued extensively in Euro-DM through offshore finance vehicles to circumvent federal withholding tax regulations. Non-German commercial banks are infrequent borrowers and issue floating-rate notes for medium-term local treasury funding.

Investors.　Germany offers the most extensive network of retail banking and savings institutions in continental western Europe. Although retail investors are not sophisticated, they have a high propensity to save and are heavily marketed on issues of financial instruments by the financial intermediaries. The placement of a Deutsche mark issue in the German retail investor market is therefore a decisive factor in the success of the issue. The stability of the investor base and the strong distribution system ensure a high degree of firm placement and are the principal attractions of the Deutsche mark bond market to issuers.

This stability is also an attraction to the growing population of foreign institutional investors. Historically, foreign demand for Euro-DM instruments was largely determined by the withholding tax applicable to income from domestic bonds. At times when withholding taxes are not in force, domestic bonds are on the same tax footing as Euro-DM instruments, and the interest of international investors in the Euro-DM bond market revolves around the following factors:

- yield differentials in relation to those offered in the more liquid domestic bond market
- speculative demand from institutional investors taking a defensive but temporary stance against the U.S. dollar
- permanent currency diversification into Deutsche mark instruments as Germany consolidates its position as the leading economic power in Europe

International institutional investors dealing in Euro-DM securities conduct their business offshore to avoid the stock market turnover tax applicable in the Federal Republic to secondary market trades in securities with nonbank institutions. This is particularly the case with DM floating-rate notes where the incidence of the tax can reduce the yield from a positive to a negative margin. The tax was, however, abolished with effect from 1 January 1990.

Instruments and Issuance Terms.   The majority of Euro-DM issues are standard fixed-rate bonds. Domestic retail investors are conservative, familiar with plain fixed-rate instruments, and very substantial in number. Issues are tailored to their preference and rarely come adorned with innovative structures seen in other currency sectors. Earlier restrictions on issue size and issue price have been relaxed. The requirement of a minimum maturity of two years has also been abolished, except for bank issuers. There is no maximum maturity and the depth of the market in fixed-rate instruments has allowed for maturities of as long as 30 years.

Other instruments include the following:

- *floating-rate notes*   These have been allowed since 1985 and are priced generally off the Frankfurt Interbank deposit rate in Deutsche marks (DM FIBOR). Call options hitherto proscribed until after four years, are now allowed after two years. Issue sizes have reached DM1 billion and over.*

- *zero-coupon bonds*   The World Bank has issued a 30-year zero-coupon Deutche mark bond and two sovereign governments have issued Deutsche mark "zeros" which were swapped into floating-rate funds; some two dozen serial zero-coupon issues have been launched by Euro-DM securities, a special purpose borrower, and secured on Schuldschein instruments issued by a federal government agency which could not benefit from the tax regime of zero-coupon bonds, had it been issued in its own name.

- *equity-warrant-linked issues*   These have been issued mostly by Japanese and, to a lesser extent, Swiss and German corporates. Issuers from other European countries are rare. DM convertibles are few in number and have been issued mainly by Japanese names.

- *private placements*   The DM private placement market is substantial. Placements are similar in most respects to a public bond issue, apart from the listing which is replaced by an official over-the-counter listing on what is termed the *geregelter Markt*. Occasionally private placements are listed on the Luxembourg stock exchange to enable the stock to qualify

---

* Domestic floating-rate issues for Staatsbank, the former central bank of the East German republic, have been launched in sizes of DM2–6 billion.

as investment-grade with institutional investors. Fixed-rate private placements usually carry ⅛ percent higher coupon to compensate for the theoretical absence of liquidity but lower issuance fees and a nominal listing fee. An unofficial limit on maturity of seven years still applies.

Issuance Procedure. The control of capital exports by foreign borrowers, hitherto exercised by a queuing system, was abolished in 1989. The only reporting requirement is to notify the terms and conditions of the issue to the Bundesbank within two days of launch. An important element of control, however, remains in place as regards the management of the issue. The Bundesbank requires issues by international borrowers to be lead-managed in Germany, a stipulation which blurs the distinction between the foreign and Euro-DM bond markets. This is the "anchoring" principle historically justified by the control of capital movements and now serving to keep DM bond issuance within national borders. Management groups, formally made up only of banks of German origin, now admit of non-German institutions* which have incorporated subsidiary issuing houses entitling them to lead or co-manage Deutsche mark issues in Germany. At present, the rule is less rigidly enforced and management groups of Euro-DM issues may now include the parent institutions, instead of the German subsidiary, as co-managers. The advent of the single European market will, anyway, see such requirements being phased out as from 1993.

The documentation of new issues (prospectus, syndicate agreements, etc.) comprises fewer items and is generally shorter than for new issues launched in London. Underwriting and subscription agreements are combined in a single agreement, and the agreement among managers takes the form of a short letter. The choice of governing law, hitherto only German law, may now be elected by the issuer.[†]

Issues were traditionally required to be listed on one of the regional German stock exchanges, and at a cost of ½ percent flat of the issue. The listing is *sponsored* by the lead manager who shares responsibility for the prospectus with the borrower (unlike London listings where the prospectus is the responsibility of the issuer alone). After many years of lobbying, Deutsche mark Eurobond issues may now be listed at much lower cost abroad (for example, in Luxembourg).

The concept of a trustee is more limited under German law than it is under English law issues. The lead manager usually acts as trustee itself with a duty to verify the issuer's compliance with undertakings. Where events of default are triggered, bondholders have recourse only to the issuer. Paying agents need not be German banks.

---

* Foreign banks have been allowed to feature in a subsidiary bracket of underwriters for some years.

[†] This has paved the way for issuers like the Republic of Italy, who hitherto refused to accept German law, to issue DM-denominated Eurobonds.

Euro-DM securities transactions are cleared principally through the German clearing system, Effektengiro but also through Euroclear and Cedel. Stock is held with depositaries known as *Kassenvereine* which are located throughout Germany.

The Swiss Franc

There is no Swiss franc Eurobond market and international borrowers have access to what is for all intents and purposes a domestic market only. Issues in Swiss francs may not be launched outside Switzerland and international banks may not lead-manage, co-manage or underwrite issues by foreign borrowers except through subsidiaries incorporated in Switzerland.* The Swiss franc foreign bond market is nonetheless a key market for international borrowers because of the following features:

- a substantial retail investor base of domestic and foreign clients within the networks of the five main commercial banks (see following)
- massive discretionary funds managed by the commercial and private banks for the account of foreign investors
- a stable political and economic environment
- low real interest rates
- an historically strong currency, though under some pressure for the last four years from the weak trade and capital accounts on the balance of payments

The market has benefited since 1980 from deregulation affecting product range, the range of instruments and issuance procedure in order to compete with, and have reciprocity of access to, competitor bond markets, both domestic and international.

Issuers. The Swiss franc foreign bond markets have attracted the full range of highly rated international borrowers including supranational institutions looking for low debt service costs such as the World Bank and the EEC, sovereign governments (Kingdom of Sweden, the Republic of Austria), government agencies (Electricite de France, Hydro Quebec), international banks (Creditanstalt Bankverein, Citicorp), and corporate borrowers (Philip Morris and many Japanese names).

In 1985, the rule which required that only indigenous Swiss banks could launch Swiss franc issues was finally relaxed, and foreign-owned Swiss banks

---

* The logic of this restrictive practice is similar to that in Germany which is to retain control over capital flows. It also has a fiscal purpose which is to conserve the revenue from stamp duty which is applicable to all securities transactions.

at last were able to form underwriting syndicates and launch issues. Subsequently, these houses brought many unrated foreign companies to the Swiss franc bond market. These were attracted by the relatively low absolute cost of funds and, moreover, the small increase in coupon that they had to pay in relation to issues by high-quality names. Many such companies suffered in the aftermath of the 1987 stock markets crash and even more so later in the wake of the more generalized recession which affected most of Western Europe and the United States. Issuers in several instances, in particular property companies in the U.K., Australia, and Canada, have defaulted on their debt service payments. These defaults have tarnished the image of the Swiss franc bond market which is now considered to have its own category of junk (rather than high-yielding) bonds.

Investors. Demand for Swiss franc debt securities issued by foreign issuers is assured by the discriminatory treatment of domestic bonds on which a 35 percent withholding tax is applied, regardless of the holder. As in other foreign bond markets, the principal placement of Swiss foreign bonds is the Swiss domestic market, including traditional institutional and retail investors. Among the institutional investors are the Swiss financial institutions which act in a nominee or discretionary capacity on behalf of domestic and, above all, foreign clients. Bank secrecy rules make it difficult to gauge the extent of custom or the currency spread of foreign-owned portfolios. It is clear, however, that international investors have been long-term holders of Swiss franc bonds. Their main criterion of investment was safety of capital rather than income, the abscence of which was compensated by the steady appreciation of the Swiss franc against the dollar and sterling until the late 1980s. It is notable in fact that total investor returns[*] on debt instruments are maximized in low coupon/low inflation currencies. International demand for Swiss franc bonds also arises from speculation against the U.S. dollar and from short-term arbitrage operations between the German, Austrian, and Swiss franc fixed-rate bond markets.

Instruments. Straight debt instruments accessible to foreign borrowers are classified into public fixed-rate bonds (*bonds*) and private fixed-rate placements (*notes*).

There are no rules governing issue sizes or maturities and amounts, the choice of which is largely determined by the fixed costs which apply to all issues. The larger the issue and the longer the maturity, the smaller the increment in all-in cost. Thus bonds are generally issued in amounts of CHF 20 million and upwards. The maturity range is 8–12 years but longer maturities of 15 and 20 years are offered subject to market conditions.

---

[*] Total investor return is made up of (1) coupon income, (2) capital appreciation, and (3) currency appreciation.

Interest payments are annual and calculated on the same basis as fixed-rate Eurobonds of 12 times 30-day months and a year of 360 days. Securities are in bearer form. There is no withholding tax on foreign bonds which carry a prepayment option in the event of imposition of withholding tax.

Notes may be issued in amounts of CHF 10 million and with no upper limit. The maturity range is 3–7 years and a maximum of 10 years. All other features are virtually identical to those of a public bond, with the exception of the listing. Notes are placed through the banking system to institutions and retail investors. A placing memorandum is required describing the issue and issuer in summary form only and the lack of disclosure requirements are one of the main attractions of this instrument. However, following a series of defaults by borrowers, disclosure standards are being tightened.

Equity-linked Issues. Convertibles and equity-warrant-linked debt issues—in bond and note form—account for more than 30 percent of Swiss franc issues by foreign borrowers. As in the case of most dollar-equity warrant issues, the proceeds are swapped for low-cost yen. In the case of Swiss franc-denominated equity warrant issues, the swaps have produced yen at a negative interest rate. Swiss franc convertibles have also been issued by Japanese corporate borrowers for the low interest cost and low foreign exchange risk.

Dual Currency Issues. These combine Swiss franc interest payments and principal repayment in another—weaker—currency, traditionally U.S. dollars. The advantage to the issuer is a saving in coupon charges in relation to U.S. dollar coupons. The investor, however, has a currency risk on the principal repayment in relation to a standard Swiss franc bond issue and the weakness of the U.S. dollar in the 1980s has diminished the popularity of this instrument.

Other Instruments. The Swiss franc bond markets have also offered zero-coupon bonds, floating-rate notes, and perpetual FRNs issued by public offering only.

Issuance Procedure. Issuance procedure in the Swiss franc bond markets has been a subject of controversy. Until recently issues of *bonds* were conducted by *fixed syndicates* of banks which had to be domiciled in Switzerland. There were four main syndicates whose members agreed to rules and restrictions on their activity in return for a guaranteed invitation into deals launched by other syndicate members. The principal syndicate which historically comprised the three largest Swiss banks—Credit Suise, Swiss Bank Corporation, and Union Bank of Switzerland—was expanded in 1988 to include the three principal German banks acting through their Swiss subsidiaries. This syndicate was so powerful as to dominate new issues of bonds by foreign borrowers, with a market share in excess of 75 percent. The smaller Swiss banks and foreign banks felt disadvantaged in their solicitation of mandates and pressure mounted to abolish the fixed syndicate structure. This eventually came about in 1991; however, the move, if anything, strengthened the control of the big Swiss banks over their new issues business. Although there is a greater degree of competition, the competition has manifested itself in more aggressive pricing and hence a greater underwriting risk, in which the smaller banks feel unable to participate. The smaller banks, especially Japanese houses, are in any event excluded from the underwriting syndicates on the grounds of insufficient placement. The resulting change of structure in the industry is likely to follow the pattern of the Eurobond market, where new issues are dominated by a small group of well-capitalized houses.

Issues are offered through public subscription, publicized by advertisement in the financial press, and listed on several of the five regional stock exchanges.* Documentation requirements include a full prospectus. Syndicates of *note issues* are put together on an ad hoc basis but, here too, the principal Swiss institutions command a major share of the market.

The requirement for authorization from the Swiss national bank for the export of capital is common to all issues by foreign borrowers, but is rarely withheld. Legal documentation is straightforward, comprising a subscription (or note purchase) agreement and a paying agency agreement. Agreements are governed by Swiss law. Federal and cantonal taxes are levied on new issues at a rate of 0.315 percent of the principal amount.

Bonds are traded principally over-the-counter between market makers and to a small extent on the exchanges. Trades are cleared on the Swiss clearing system, SEGA, and through Euroclear and Cedel. Notes are traded over-the-counter by intermediaries who act as market makers.

The Secondary Market.   The secondary market in Swiss foreign bonds is conducted exclusively in Switzerland, in parallel with practice in the primary market. The environment of exceptionally stable interest rates makes for less trading and stamp duty, which is levied on all securities transactions, reduces the incentive to trade even further. A further complication is the absence of a liquid market in government issues which would provide a benchmark for pricing purposes and a hedging instrument for trading other Swiss franc-denominated issues. All these factors make for a weak supply of paper in the secondary market. The Swiss banks, which have long campaigned for the abolition of stamp duty, claim it is also losing them new issues business to the Euro-DM and ECU bond markets.

In 1991 Swiss Bank Corporation launched an SFr600 million 10-year issue for the World Bank with the intention that it should serve as a benchmark for the market. A further novelty was the provision for the bonds not only to be placed but, exceptionally, to be traded in London as well as Switzerland with a view to promoting liquidity. SBC launched another simi-

* The number of stock exchanges is to be reduced from five to two to include Geneva and Zurich.

lar issue for the European Investment Bank which provides for further issues of fungible bonds. These moves have been criticized and it has been argued that liquidity is not vital in a bond market which caters principally to end-investors. It seems probable, however, that such moves will hasten the opening up of the Swiss Franc bond market to international competition and to enable it to resume a leading role.

The Gray Market.   A gray market in new issues was launched in 1984 by Citicorp and Chemical Bank in an attempt to provide a more continuous market assessment of price and more widespread access to paper. The move was successful and challenged the established Swiss banks which otherwise enjoyed control over their issues. The gray market makers were joined by American Express in 1987 (Amtrade) and in 1988 by Credit Suisse itself, operating out of Zug to avoid the prohibition on gray market trading in Zurich. Union Bank of Switzerland and Swiss Bank Corporation followed suit, and trade out of Geneva and Zug, respectively. The big three Swiss now dominate the gray market at the expense of its authors who have withdrawn, leaving Shearson Lehman as the significant major foreign participant.

The Euro-Yen

The Euro-yen bond market offers the same attractions to investors of low inflation and a low and stable interest rate structure as its Deutsche mark and Swiss franc counterparts. The currency is underpinned by massive external trade surpluses but, unlike the Deutsche mark, its appreciation is not subject to the restraint of arrangements such as the European Monetary System. Thus international investors are particularly attracted to Euro-yen instruments. Conversely, international issuers are generally averse to currency exposure in yen and the flow of new issues has been largely subject to the liquidity of the swaps market or, in effect, the demand for yen of Japanese financial intermediaries. While issuance volume dropped steadily over the period 1987–1989, the restrictive monetary policy from December 1989 of the Bank of Japan* led to higher interest rates and renewed interest on the part of international investors. Higher yen yields and the availability of swaps led to a sharp growth in new issues in Euro-yen and the sector achieved second place after the U.S. dollar in 1991. The key features of the Euro-yen bond market may thus be summarized as follows:

- the strength of the currency and an expectation of appreciation which was often realized

- the wide range of credit and geographical risk on offer

* Under its new Governor Mieno appointed December 1989.

- the relative ease of access for Euro-investors, by contrast to the Japanese domestic bond market
- activity in the new issues market dependent largely on the availability of currency swaps out of yen

Issuers. The Euro-yen bond market has been tapped by the full range of international borrowers including supranational agencies (the World Bank, European Community, EIB), sovereign governments (New Zealand, Sweden), government agencies (Société Nationale des Chemins de Fer Francais, Ente Nazionale dal' Elettricita), international commercial banks (e.g., Credit Lyonnais, Bayerische Landesbank), and private sector corporations (e.g., General Motors, Procter & Gamble). Aside from supranational agencies and sovereign governments, most non-Japanese borrowers have sought to swap the proceeds of their issues out of yen into a secondary currency of exposure.

Issuance in Euro-yen by Japanese corporations is limited. These borrowers have issued in the foreign and Eurobond markets principally in order to circumvent restrictive practices and issuance regulations in the domestic yen market.* Their issues are denominated for principally in U.S. dollars or Swiss francs and swapped into yen at a lower cost than an issue in Euro-yen.† With few exceptions, Japanese financial institutions have refrained from

---

* Some liberalization took place in 1989 in the form of competitive bidding for mandates and shelf registration; however, new issue procedures in the domestic capital market, which are modeled on U.S. practice, are lengthy and expensive. In particular, issuers must retain and remunerate a bank which serves to advise the issuer and to act as Trustee for the investors. Competitive bidding, however, had drawbacks inasmuch as it led to below-market pricing of new issues; underwriters then protected themselves against loss through excessive underwriting commissions. A breakthrough to defeat this practice was finally achieved when Morgan Stanley Japan, as co-lead manager of a domestic issue for Nippon Telegraph and Telephone, introduced the primary distribution technique used in the Euromarkets of a fixed price reoffering.

† Japanese corporates found an even cheaper source of yen funding by attaching equity warrants to their fixed-rate Eurodollar and Swiss franc bond issues. The warrants gave the investor a medium-term option to buy equity stock of the issuer at a price which was likely to be soon realized or exceeded in the stock market, thereby generating a profit on exercise. The inclusion of the warrants in the issue structure allowed for below-market coupons on the bond issue whose proceeds were then swapped for yen at a low—or even negative—all-in cost.

As it happened, stock market expectations, far from being fulfilled, were seriously frustrated after 1990 and the exercise price of the warrants in the case of most issues is well above the current market price of the stock. Some US$160 billion equivalent of such issues are due for redemption over the period 1992–1994. The redemption payment is now unlikely to be met from the subscription to new equity by warrant holders, and the Japanese corporations concerned are having to find the repayment from other sources or refinance. The Japanese government, aware of the problem, has relaxed restrictions on corporate issues in the domestic bond market and is encouraging changes in issuance practice. As a result domestic bond issuance by Japanese corporations has risen. Some Eurobond issuers may repay out of cash flow; however, most will have to refinance. Without the benefit of buoyant stock market conditions, an equity warrant structure is no longer appropriate. Borrowers whose maturing Eurobonds may not be refinanced in the domestic market are then likely to have recourse to Swiss franc or Eurodollar issues—subject to bond and swap market conditions—and also the Euro-yen bond market where they are better known to investors.

funding in Euro-yen altogether, whether through an issue in Euro-yen or in another currency with a swap into Euro-yen. Such financings effectively circumvent the strict regulation of issuance by Japanese financial institutions in the domestic bond markets.

The Japanese Ministry of Finance (MoF) requires all issuers in the Euro-yen bond market to be rated by a recognized rating agency. Historically, a minimum rating of single A was sought but this requirement is now relaxed.

Investors. International investors in Euro-yen bonds are essentially institutional. Few of these are natural holders of yen and, given the comparatively low coupon income on Euro-yen instruments, most look to currency appreciation to enhance the return on their investment. This policy has paid off during the decline of the U.S. dollar in the currency markets. Conversely, the subsequent appreciation of the dollar at the expense of the yen (among other major currencies) has led to a dwindling in foreign demand for Euro-yen instruments. Since 1989, tight monetary policy in Japan has caused yields on yen bonds to rise and has attracted renewed offshore demand.

International investors in Euro-yen bonds are not in the majority and, on the whole, Euro-yen bonds have a low weighting in international investors' portfolios. This may appear surprising at first sight, given that international investor interest is mainly currency driven. On the other hand, the majority of international investors are still U.S. dollar-based and treat their yen exposure in the same way as that in Deutsche mark, or the Swiss franc (i.e., as diversification and temporary refuge from the dollar). Some longer-term yen holdings may be affected by adding a currency swap; however, yen/U.S. dollar swaps have, if anything, entailed a loss rather than a gain in margin.

Domestic Japanese placement of public Euro-issues is subject to a 90-day sales embargo or *seasoning period* similar to that operating in the United States.* This has not in any way inhibited domestic investors which traditionally accounted directly or indirectly for the greater part of the placement of a Euro-yen issue. Investor demand from within Japan is essentially from institutions which accept both Japanese and international names. Placement in Japan of Euro-yen issues by Japanese borrowers was historically subject to a 50 percent limit, but this guideline has been relaxed.

Issuance terms. Issuance terms (e.g., maturity, calls, denominations, withholding tax, clearing) on Euro-yen Eurobonds are unregulated and standard practice on Eurobond issues is applied. Maturities are commonly in the range of 5–9 years, but issues of 12, 15, and 20 years have been offered on fixed income bonds. Issues sizes, originally small (yen 10 billion or US$75 million), have risen sharply. In the spring of 1992, The Kingdom of Spain launched an issue of yen 125 billion (US$960 million). Listing is

---

* This rule was relaxed in the case of the World Bank yen global bond described later.

in London or Luxembourg and English law is commonly used to govern documentation.

In 1992 the World Bank launched a global issue of yen250 billion (US$1.92 billion).* This is the largest Euro-yen issue to date and was structured on similar lines to the World Bank's global Eurodollar issues. The bonds are in registered form and the issue is listed in Luxembourg. Interest is payable semiannually, free of withholding tax; the 90-day seasoning rule was relaxed. Pricing, for the first time on a Euro-yen issue, used the "Pricing Discovery Process" practiced in the domestic Japanese market and was fixed at 19 basis points below the yield on Japanese Government Bond (JGB) number 129, a domestic bond—thus emulating practice in the Eurodollar bond market; however, the fee structure was based on Eurobond practice, thus avoiding the lead commission fee structure of the domestic Japanese bond market.

Instruments.   A full range of Euro-yen instruments has been issued including fixed-rate bonds, FRNs, zero-coupon bonds, a bond warrant linked issue, yen/U.S. dollar dual currency issues, convertibles, and stock-index linked issues. Medium-term notes have also been sanctioned by the MoF. (Other categories of Yen bond include the foreign public bond or "Samurai" bond market and the domestic private placement or "Shibosai"—see "Private Placements" in Chapter 2). The predominantly domestic institutional placement of Euro-yen instruments led to a decline in the volume of public issues in the late 1980s in favor of domestic private placements, which accounted for the overwhelming majority of yen debt financings by international borrowers. These have the advantage of being tailor-made to the hedging and cash flow requirements of investors and are placed with no more than 1–3 institutions. Liquidity is not required since the investors' intention is typically to hold to maturity, and the scale of individual investments can be very large, up to US$1 billion. Aside from these factors and the absence of listing, the design of the financing is identical to that of a public issue. Yen domestic private placements are invariably swapped because of (1) the requirement of international borrowers for exposure in third currencies and (2) the unlikely acceptance by borrowers of exposure to tailor-made investor features such as stock-indexed linked redemption. Recently the Japanese private placement market has slowed due to the rise in domestic corporate issuance and a general retrenchment from overseas investment and/or foreign names over the early 1990s.

Issuance Procedure.   Lead managers are required to file powers of attorney and a mandate from the issuer with MoF. This requirement aside, issuance procedure is unregulated and identical to that of a Eurodollar issue. Underwriting, syndication, and primary distribution follow standard

* See "Global Bonds" in Chapter 2.

Eurobond practice. There is no requirement of a Japanese lead manager, but non-Japanese lead managers must have offices in Tokyo.

The Pound Sterling

Until 1972, international borrowers of sterling could launch issues only in the domestic sterling (or Bulldog) market, which was small and confined to sovereign government names. The Euro-sterling bond market opened that year but then closed again until 1977, by which time the external perception of the U.K. had radically changed to that of a major oil producer. Exchange controls were abolished in 1979, capital exports were freed up and, by 1982, the Euro-sterling bond market had reached £1.2 billion.

In the second half of the 1980s, sterling lost its attraction as a petro-currency but sterling bonds continued to find favor with international investors. The currency was perceived to shadow the Deutsche mark, thanks to high nominal and real interest rates which affect the negative impact of a widening external trade deficit. The volume of sterling Eurobonds outstanding reached £26 billion at the end of 1987. Helped by a liquid swaps market, borrowers (40 percent of whom were non-sterling-based) launched a further £11 billion in 1988 when the market took second place after the U.S. dollar.

By then the U.K. authorities had started a program of Public Sector Debt Repayment which was to have an immediate repercussion on the portfolios of U.K. institutional investors, the main buyers of U.K. government stock. With only a small alternative supply of stock from the domestic private sector (loan stock and debenture markets), U.K. institutions resorted to the Eurobond market to top up their sterling bond portfolios and found a selection of high-quality credit risk and long maturities.

In the autumn of 1990, the United Kingdom joined the wider band of the Exchange Rate Mechanism of the European Monetary System. The implication, as far as the currency is concerned, is that sterling would be allowed to fluctuate no more than 6 percent above or below the central rate at which it joined the System. In due course it was intended that sterling would join the "narrow band" of currencies which may fluctuate no more than 3 percent of their central rates. The cost of keeping sterling within the 6 percent band in the following two years was high. The structural trade deficit of the British economy forced the authorities to maintain interest rates at levels which offered substantial yield differentials in real terms relative to those of other stronger EMS countries. High interest rates compounded the adverse effect of the worldwide recession to produce a severe downturn of activity. Following particularly heavy speculation against sterling in the autumn of 1992, the currency was taken out of the EMS system.

Issuers. The Euro-sterling bond market has played host to the full range of Eurobond issuers including supranational agencies (the World Bank,

EIB); sovereign governments (Republic of Italy, Republic of Austria); government agencies (Hydro-Quebec, Caisse Nationale des Télécommunications); commercial banks (Citicorp, Deutsche Bank); and private-sector corporate borrowers from (1) abroad (e.g., Ford Credit Canada, Ciba-Geigy, Pepsico) and (2) increasingly, the U.K. (e.g., ICI, BP, Rolls Royce, Pilkington, Sainsbury). The participation of foreign issuers, other than banks and supranational borrowers, is predicated on the liquidity and cost-effectiveness of the sterling swap markets.

Investors.   The investor base for the Euro-sterling bond market presently rests on demand from both domestic and international investors. Investors in the domestic market are virtually all institutional and, for many, their exposure to sterling bonds—other than government "gilt-edged" bonds—is of recent date. In the mid 1960s the share of loan and debenture stock in U.K. institutional portfolios was over 15 percent but by the mid-1980s had fallen to below 5 percent. The overall return on fixed-income securities was considered to be relatively unattractive and the composition of U.K. institutional portfolios over the last 30 years has been biased predominantly towards equity stocks. When U.K. institutions could no longer rely on a steady supply of "gilts" to meet their long-term annuity obligations, they invested in Euro-sterling bonds and are now a significant part of the investor market.

The implication of the withdrawal of sterling from the EMS for the Euro-sterling bond market is that international investors are no longer protected from a sudden depreciation of sterling. International issuers on the other hand may welcome the opportunity to borrow at low cost in a depreciating currency, provided that U.K. institutions will buy their paper. It is likely, however, that the U.K. government itself will have a prior call on their appetite for bonds.

Issuance Terms.   The principal attraction to borrowers of the sterling bond markets is the availability of long maturities which are keenly sought by U.K. institutional investors. This feature is offered in the foreign bond markets (Swiss franc, yen Samurai and U.S. dollar Yankee markets) but not in any other Euro-currency sector. Thus British Aerospace and Lucas have launched issues of 25 and 30 years, respectively, targeting this market sector, as have the European Investment Bank and Electricité de France which both launched 20-year issues.

There is no restriction on issue size. British Telecom and Hanson PLC have issues outstanding of £500 million, but the normal range is £150 million. This is small in relation to U.K. government stock issues of £1.5–3 billion and the absence of large very liquid issues acts as a brake on the development of the market.

Euro-sterling bond yields and new-issue pricing are typically expressed in terms of a margin over the offer yield on U.K. government stock of equivalent maturity, similar to the expression of Eurodollar bond yields.

Other issuance terms are standard for Eurobond issues, including annual interest payments, bearer form, London or Luxembourg listing, no withholding tax, Euroclear, and Cedel clearing. Earlier restrictions on minimum maturities, denominations, and investor and/or issuer options of repayment were removed by the Finance Act of 1989.

Instruments.   The Euro-sterling bond market offers the standard range of instruments including fixed-rate issues (including later tranches fungible with earlier offerings), floating-rate notes, zero-coupon bonds, asset-backed securities, convertibles, and equity and bond warrants.

Issuance Procedure.   A queuing system, consisting of prior notification of a new issue to the Bank of England, is no longer in force and issues may be launched at any time without notification to any party. There is, however, a new voluntary queuing system. The requirement remains that a Euro-sterling bond issue be managed in the United Kingdom by a U.K. incorporated institution with the capabilities of an issuing house. In the case of a foreign issuing house, the authorities require reciprocal facilities for managing issues to be given to U.K. banks in the issuing house's country of origin. Underwriting, syndication, and primary distribution follow the standard pattern for Eurobond issues.

The European Currency Unit (ECU)

The ECU is a *composite* or *basket* currency made up of the currencies of the member States of the EEC. The amount of each currency in the ECU is determined by its weighting in the basket and reflects the relative size of the country's economy and its share of trade within the EEC. The ECU was created in 1979 with an initial value identical to that of its predecessor, the European Unit of Account (EUA).* The ECU is a currency in its own right and its value fluctuates as a function of the following:

- the change of *value* of the component currencies: in practice, fluctuation of the component currencies is restricted to within maximum bands under EMS arrangements (EMS members in most part are the same as the countries whose currencies are in the ECU).

- changes to the *weighting* of the component currencies by the EC.

- the introduction of new currencies such as the Spanish peseta and the Portuguese escudo.

---

* The European Unit of Account, unlike the ECU, is *not* a currency but a unit of account whose value may be expressed in different currencies (known as reference currencies which are exclusively EMS currencies).

As a currency, ECUs may be bought or sold against other currencies, bank accounts may be denominated in ECU, and invoices may be rendered and settled in ECU.

The ECU has no country of origin and is in effect an offshore currency. This makes ECU bonds Eurobonds par excellence* The first ECU bond was for the Italian State Telecommunications agency, SOFTE, and launched in 1981. Within 10 years, ECU bonds have come to account for over 12.3 percent of new issues of Eurobonds, and the volume of ECU bonds outstanding is about US$80 billion.

The underlying impetus to this growth has been the growing perception of the ECU among international investors as the future single currency of continental Europe. The Treaty of Maastricht, whose signatories include the twelve Member States of the European Community, contemplates monetary union within the Community by 1999. The Treaty relies for the achievement of a single currency in particular on the will of the signatories to implement policies for the convergence of national interest rates, interest rate stability, and currency stability. Major technical details such as the irrevocable composition of the ECU remain outstanding and will not be addressed until 1994.†

Issuers. Frequent borrowers of ECU in the Eurobond market include the European supranational institutions (the European Community, EIB, ECSC, Eurofima), European governments (Belgium, Denmark, Italy, Ireland, Portugal, and the United Kingdom) and their agencies (Crédit Foncier de France). Outside the EEC, the full spectrum of borrowers has tapped the ECU bond market including the World Bank, sovereign borrowers (such as Iceland and New Zealand), government agencies (such as Hydro Quebec and New South Wales Treasury), commercial banks (such as Dai-Ichi Kangyo Bank and Royal Bank of Canada), and private sector corporate borrowers (including Nestlé, R. J. Reynolds, Walt Disney). Most issues by non-European corporate borrowers are driven by the availability

---

* This said, not all ECU bond issues are international issues. The Republic of France and the Kingdom of Denmark have targeted ECU issues at their domestic bond markets, making these domestic issues in all but the choice of currency. Other borrowers have targeted ECU issues at the domestic market of third countries, making these in effect "foreign" (and not Eurobond) issues.

† *Author's note:* The path to a single currency is not straightforward. At the time of writing, the ratification by the Member States of the Maastricht Treaty is not complete and was upset by its rejection by Denmark in a referendum in the summer of 1992. Most governments of the Member States have attempted to implement policies of economic convergence, however the cost of setting interest rates in relation to Deutsche mark yields in terms of low growth and rising unemployment is proving unsustainable, notably in the United Kingdom. These developments, coming at a time of continuing low growth worldwide, have caused the professional ECU bond investor to query the likelihood of a uniform application of a single currency throughout the Community. The political will for a single currency in other countries such as France and the Benelux is undiminished and, it is thought, could lead to attempts to introduce monetary union in two stages. This would raise a question mark about the future of the ECU as a currency basket comprising one stable and several weaker currencies.

of swaps. On the other hand, European issuers, and in particular sovereign issuers, retain their ECU exposure.

Investors. With no domestic investor base, the appeal of the ECU bond market has shifted between different investor market sectors as a function of currency appreciation and yield. In the first five years of its life, the performance of the currency has shown the highest correlation to the Dutch guilder, sterling, and the Deutsche mark and the least correlation to the U.S. dollar. The ECU bond market over this period has offered better yields than guilder or Deutsche mark Eurobonds and has served as a refuge from Eurodollar bonds during periods of dollar weakness. Thus, substantial holders of U.S. dollar instruments, such as Japanese and Swiss investors, switched part of their bond portfolio into ECU bonds. As their perception of the ECU as the European currency became stronger, the portfolio allocation to ECU bonds became permanent and the volume of new issues put the ECU among the top six-place currencies in Eurobond league tables. This same perception has had a novel effect in Europe, and notably in Denmark, where the latest ECU offering by the government provided for a 25 percent domestic tranche. In effect, this is an ECU global bond issue.

Issuance Terms. Issuance terms (maturities, call options, withholding tax) on ECU Eurobonds are unregulated and standard Eurobond practice applies on governing law and jurisdiction, denominations, listing, and clearing. Issue sizes have increased dramatically as international investors, for example from Japan, have come to regard the ECU as a means of spreading their European currency exposure. Belgium has raised ECU1.5 billion, Italy ECU2.5 billion and the United Kingdom ECU2.75 billion in a single issue.

Payment provisions on ECU bonds specify the payment of interest and principal in ECU under a "basket" clause which requires one of the following:

- Payments are made in accordance with the then ruling definition of the ECU (open basket).
- All payments are made in accordance with the definition of the ECU prevailing at the time of launch (closed basket).

Most issues have open-basket clauses. Settlement is made in ECU and the purchase consideration or sale proceeds are bought/sold against a component or other currency. In the event that the ECU were abolished, payments would be made in a component currency.

Pricing an ECU bond issue was for many years complicated by the absence of a benchmark ECU issue—whether by a national government or supranational borrower—and relied on subjective market assessment such as the relative credit risk of the borrower, bond market conditions, and the secondary market performance of existing issues. In 1989 the French government launched a program of ECU-denominated issues targeted at the

French domestic market (Obligation Assimilable du Tresor—OAT). The first issue had a final maturity of 8 years and further issues have been launched (by the French Treasury or by French government agencies) with maturities of 10, 12, 15, 20, and 30 years. These issues are serving as benchmarks for ECU issues generally and provide a full and homogeneous ECU bond yield curve.

Instruments. The ECU has been used to issue straight bonds, zero-coupon bonds, FRNs, convertible bonds, equity-warrant- and bond-warrant-linked debt issues. ECU FRNs are priced by reference to a margin over/under the ECU interbank offered rate and funded through ECU deposits in the usual manner—though the ECU deposit market does not have the depth of its U.S. dollar counterpart.

Issuance Procedure. Issuance procedure is unregulated and identical to that of a Eurodollar issue. An unofficial queue agreed informally by the lead managers ensures an orderly new issuance market. Underwriting, syndication, and primary distribution follow standard Eurobond practice.

The Canadian Dollar

The Euro-Canadian dollar (Can$) bond market serves primarily as an international bond market for Canadian indigenous borrowers and Canadian subsidiaries of foreign corporations. The market has come about largely because investors regard the currency as linked to the U.S. dollar while offering a substantial premium in yield—of as much as 100–150 basis points in relation to U.S. dollar bonds. The appreciation of the Canadian dollar in the mid-1980s against the U.S. dollar helped to stimulate significant institutional interest in the Euro-Can$ bond market and provide greater depth to the market. New borrowers, including leading international Eurobond issuers were attracted and the availability of currency swaps enabled them to tap the market. The consolidation of the sector* which followed is a classic example of the successful development of a Eurobond market.

Issuers. The principal motivation of Canadian borrowers to issue Eurobonds is one of cost: the yields on Euro-Can$ issues are historically lower than on domestic issues for comparable borrowers. For Canadian private sector names, domestic issues are also more time-consuming. Issuance procedure is modeled on U.S. practice which requires registration of the issue with the provincial securities commission and extensive disclosure of the business and financial condition of the borrower. Canadian Federal Crown corporations such as Export Development Corporation and Federal

---

* Achieving fifth place in 1991 with total issuance of Can$22.5 billion.

Business Development Bank are prohibited from borrowing in the domestic bond markets altogether.

International borrowers are also prominent in the Euro-Can$ bond market and include the full range of Eurobond issuers, namely:

- supranational institutions (EIB, World Bank)
- sovereign governments (New Zealand, Kingdom of Sweden)
- government agencies (Australian Industrial Development Corporation, Crédit d'Equipement des Petites et Moyennes Entreprises)
- international commercial Banks (Banque Nationale de Paris, Bank of Tokyo)
- private sector corporations (Michelin, McDonalds)

While private sector corporations may have local operations to finance, the government borrowers and international banks have little natural demand for Canadian dollars. The issues of the latter borrowers are therefore invariably predicated on a swap out of Canadian dollars and the issue serves essentially as a vehicle for funding cheaper than what direct access to the bond market of the target currency would provide.

Investors. The international investor market in Can$ bonds has traditionally been associated with Benelux retail markets. But recently it has attracted growing numbers of institutional investors who have brought substantial new placement, larger-size orders, and greater liquidity. Low inflation and confidence in the currency also make them loyal investors with large appetites. It is estimated that more than 50 percent of large global bond issues issued by the provincial power utilities have been placed with European and Far Eastern investors.

Canadian investors—both retail and institutional—have a 10 percent ceiling imposed on their holdings of debt (or equity) issued (1) in foreign currency or (2) by non-Canadian entities. However Euro-Canadian dollars are not considered as foreign currency and the domestic Canadian investor market is a frequent participant in Euro-Can$ issues, often complementing international investors whose yield criteria on individual issues may diverge from their own.

Issuance Terms. International borrowers have no restriction on issuance terms. Canadian corporate borrowers are required under Canadian law to issue in maturities of not less than five years and one day, regardless of currency. The gathering momentum of the market has allowed issue sizes to increase dramatically. In 1991, a series of large global issues for amounts in excess of Can$1 billion were launched by the power utilities, Quebec Hydro and Ontario Hydro. The range of maturities has also been extended and there are currently fixed-rate issues of Can$1.25 billion and Can$1.1 billion, each with a final maturity of 30 years. A zero-coupon bond issued by Ontario Hydro has a maturity of 40 years.

Instruments. The range of Euro-Can$ instruments includes principally fixed-rate bonds and a small number of zero-coupon bonds, bond-warrant-linked issues, convertibles, and gold-linked issues. There are no LIBOR-based floating-rate note issues since the Euro-Can$ interbank deposit market is not considered to have sufficient depth. Issuer interest is also lacking since currency and interest rate swaps against fixed-rate Can$ issues have tended to produce U.S. dollar funding at well above LIBOR.

Issuance Procedure. Issuance procedure is unregulated and not subject to any restriction. In particular, there is no requirement of a Canadian lead manager. Underwriting, syndication, and primary distribution follow standard Eurodollar bond issue practice. However, Canadian investment banks are normally included in the management group of an issue to ensure coverage of the Canadian investor market.

The Australian Dollar

The decline in interest rates in the United States, Japan, and West Germany in the mid-1980s led Eurobond investors to search for new sectors offering higher coupon income. The Australian economy was characterized in the second half of the 1980s by high current account deficits, a gross external debt approaching 40 percent of GDP, and high inflation. These factors were reflected in a volatile currency and nominal interest rates and bond yields among the highest in the international bond markets—at times as much as 10 percent higher than comparable yield levels in low-coupon currency sectors. International retail investors, looking for incremental rather than alternative investments, put to one side their traditional concern for safety of capital and bought heavily for yield into Australian dollar (A$) denominated issues. International issuers attracted by an active and highly cost-effective swaps market flocked to the Euro-Australian dollar bond market which flourished to seventh place in volume in 1987.

Issuance volume trailed off in 1989 and, by 1991, had reached half its peak level. Australian dollar yields started to fall, the shape of the yield curve reversed and by 1992 became steeply positive. Retail investors, accustomed to high yields and short maturities, were deterred by the exigence of longer maturities to achieve a lesser yield and withdrew from the market. These have been replaced to some extent by institutional investors whose investment criteria enabled them to accept longer maturities; however, the difficulty of finding long-term swaps out of Australian dollars precluded many issuers from coming to the market. Efforts to develop the market have focused on new issues which are placed both internationally and in the domestic bond market, i.e., a global A$ bond issue. These issues have yet to achieve a satisfactory degree of liquidity in the domestic market and have tended to be sold back into the international market.

Issuers. The sector is dominated by international issuers which by association have confirmed the A$ sector as an established Eurobond market. Issues have been launched by the full range of borrowers, including supranational institutions (such as the World Bank, EIB), sovereigns (Austria, Sweden), government agencies (Eksportfinans), and corporate names (BMW, British Petroleum, General Electric). By far the largest category of issuer is the international banks which, in addition to the issue, contract currency swaps to convert their exposure from Australian dollars into U.S. dollars at an end cost well under their normal U.S. dollar interbank funding rates. German banks in particular have issued extensively in this market and used their branch networks to distribute their issues. Australian issuers have included the public authorities (such as AIDC, Tasmanian Public Finance, New South Wales Treasury), commercial banks (National Australia Bank, Commercial Bank of Australia), and a few corporate names (such as CSR).

Investors. Since early 1986, significant international interest in A$ bonds came from the Benelux and Germany where retail and institutional investors were prepared to tolerate the greater volatility of the currency in return for an attractive interest differential in relation to domestic securities. Recognizing that such investors are name conscious, issuing houses offered added reassurance by launching issues from household names well known to investors in Germany.

The firm monetarist policies of the early 1990s helped stabilize the currency, reduce inflation, and eventually produce a positive yield curve. They also eliminated the speculative interest of the currency to international retail investors, who started to withdraw from the market. International institutions on the other hand, attracted by the stronger yield differential (albeit in longer maturities) in relation to bonds denominated in EMS currencies, have become major investors in both domestic government bonds which offer liquidity and in Euro-A$ instruments which suffer no withholding tax. The effort to promote liquidity by launching larger-size issues has led to the design of global A$ bond issues which clearly also target domestic Australian institutions.

Issuance Terms. Issuance terms in the A$ bond market (maturity, calls, denominations, withholding tax, clearing) are unregulated, and standard practice on Eurobond issues is applied. Listing is in London, Luxembourg, Amsterdam, or Frankfurt, and English law is commonly used to govern documentation.

The yield curve of the Australian dollar government bond market was for many years flat to negative and discouraged issues of more than 7 years final maturity. However with a positive yield curve, maturities are being offered of 10 and 15 years. The more liquid maturities on swaps are still in the range of 4–7 years and the absence of longer-term maturities is braking the flow of medium-term bond issues.

Issue sizes at first low have gradually increased to US$250 million equivalent.

Instruments.   Fixed-rate issues account for the majority of offerings. The volatility of the currency has created opportunities for currency option and futures-linked redemption against the Deutsche mark and the U.S. dollar. High nominal yields have led to a number of zero-coupon issues. A handful of FRNs have been launched on the base of Australian bank bill rates. Equity-related issuance includes a dozen convertibles.

Issuance Procedure.   Issuance procedure is unregulated and not subject to market restriction. Issues may be launched at any time and there is no requirement of an Australian lead manager. Underwriting, syndication, and primary distribution follow standard Eurobond practice.

The French Franc

The French domestic bond market has for many years been the preserve of the French Treasury, and French financial institutions and international borrowers seeking to issue medium-term French francs (FFr) securities have recourse only to the Euro-FFr bond market. Access has been intermittent because of currency crises occasioned by political and economic events. The Euro-FFr bond market opened in 1967, only to close in the wake of the May 1968 upheaval. In 1972, the market reopened and there followed 22 offerings until 1976, when the market closed again. It reopened in 1978 but closed from 1982–1984 under the new socialist administration. It opened again in 1985 and has remained open since. In 1990, the French franc sector gained momentum to achieve eighth place in international bond issuance in 1991 with total issuance of US$16.8 billion. A framework of exchange control regulations, which remained in force throughout the 1980s, is now abolished.

As the economy stabilized in the course of the 1980s, the government favored the expansion of the domestic bond market, partly for political reasons, to raise the profile of Paris as a financial center, but also to provide an alternative source of funding to French borrowers. French commercial banks, which served as traditional providers of funds, tended to be highly geared and the growth of their higher-margin lending was increasingly constrained by Cooke capital adequacy ratios.

The rules on minimum maturity of domestic bond issues by corporations which protected access to the domestic bond market by the French Treasury and financial institutions have now been relaxed and many French corporations—which hitherto had no access to either domestic or international bond markets for want of suitable rating and profile—now have a new source of funding available to them. Major borrowers however are likely to continue to prefer the Eurobond market because of the lower cost of funds for an equal maturity.*

Issuers. The market has been tapped by the full spectrum of international borrowers, including European supranational institutions (such as EIB, Euratom), sovereign governments (Sweden, Denmark, Finland), government agencies (Finance for Danish Industry), commercial banks (Deutsche Bank, Commerzbank), and private sector corporate names (Solvay, Electrolux, Gillette Canada). Many issues are swap-driven; however, the proceeds of issues by international banks and private sector corporations are usually retained to finance local investment.

With heavy issuance by the Treasury in the domestic market, the French authorities for many years encouraged other French borrowers to raise their medium-term funding in French francs through the Euro-French franc market. These include primarily government-related borrowers with wholly domestic operations (such as Crédit d'Equipment des Petites et Moyennes Entreprises and Caisse Nationale des Autoroutes), state-owned utilities (Electricité de France, Gaz de France), and government-controlled financial institutions (Crédit National and Crédit Foncier), all of which had already tapped the international bond markets through issues in other currencies. These names launched issues which for many years carried an explicit guarantee of the government. This practice has now ceased. However, these borrowers' subsequent issues still carry AAA ratings and the credit differential is reflected in an attractive differential in yield in relation to state risk. The French private sector corporations could not issue in the domestic market except with a minimum seven-year maturity, and most companies did not have the credit rating or international profile to permit of a Eurobond issue. Thus, only major corporations such as Peugeot, Michelin, Moet Hennessy, and BSN have tapped the Euro-French franc bond market. Together, French issuers account for 40 percent of total issuance in the Euro-French franc sector.

Investors. Placement relied traditionally on French institutional demand—especially unit trusts and money market funds. The main attraction for international investors was currency diversification or as a strategic play against their domestic currency; however, their interest was often transitory or even speculative. In the second half of the 1980s, the stability of the franc within the EMS coupled with high absolute yields and a choice of high-quality credits led to growing international investor interest in Euro-French bonds. At the same time, the government was making considerable

---

* Selling commission structure on domestic issues is fixed regardless of maturity (unlike Eurobond issues); the basis of yield calculations on domestic fixed-rate issues is varied, but generally produces a higher cost of funds than on Euro-issues.

efforts to develop a liquid government bond market in a broad spectrum of maturities and opened up access to international investors. This provided international investors with an essential means of hedging currency and credit exposure and led directly to the participation of growing numbers of permanent investors.

Issuance Terms.   There are no restrictions on issuance terms (maturities, calls or denominations). Issue sizes at launch, at first low, have grown considerably to FFr6 billion.* Many issues have been increased through successive tranches of fungible bonds. Issues are listed in Luxembourg, occasionally Paris, London, and Amsterdam. Standard Eurobond practice applies on other terms including status, withholding tax, and settlement.

Instruments.   Most issues take the form of standard fixed-income instruments. A handful of FRNs have been launched using the Paris Interbank French franc Offered Rate (PIBOR) as interest base. There are four zero-coupon issues and a small number of convertibles and equity-warrant-linked bond issues.

Issuance Procedure.   There is no queue to launch issues but "permission to proceed" is required from the French Treasury. Application is sought by the lead manager which has to be a French bank (i.e., of French origin or a foreign bank with a subsidiary incorporated in France).

The Secondary Currencies

The secondary currency sectors presently account together for less than 8 percent of international bond issuance. These are currencies which are backed by structurally weaker economies (e.g., the lira); where access has been intermittent because of the necessity of exchange control (e.g., the Swedish krona; or where the domestic investor base is too narrow to sustain a liquid market (e.g., New Zealand dollars or Finnish markka).

Borrowers, especially corporate names, launch issues in the minor currencies, where they have local operations to fund. Conversely, parent company treasury requirements may be best served by an issue in a lesser currency with a currency swap which produces a cost advantage over an issue in the home market. Issue sizes tend to be smaller because of the lesser depth of the investor market, and swap markets in the less common Euro-currencies offer a more limited range of maturities and transaction sizes.

The principal secondary currency sectors in 1991 include, in descending order, the Italian lira, the Dutch guilder, the Luxembourg franc,[†] and

---

* The Kingdom of Spain, 9¼ percent 1991–1994.

[†] Foreign bond market only.

the Spanish peseta.* Other minor sectors include the Swedish krona, the Finnish markka, the Portuguese escudo,* the Austrian schilling, the New Zealand dollar, the Danish krone and the Belgian franc.* Each sector remains subject to some degree of restriction on issuance terms or procedure, reflecting exchange controls or regulation of domestic securities' markets. This section will review two of the secondary currencies—the Italian lira and the Spanish peseta.

The Italian Lira. Italy suffers from an exceptional level of public sector debt and has had to maintain high nominal and real interest rates to fund continuing budget deficits. This has led to yield differentials of as much as 5–6 percent in relation to Deutsche mark or Swiss franc bonds. Italy is also a member of the EMS* and the currency has fluctuated within the narrow band since 1990. The stability of the currency and the yield differentials in relation to other currency sectors have combined to attract foreign capital into the domestic bond market and to help offset persistent trade deficits.

In circumstances similar to those prevailing until recently in France, the Italian domestic bond market is the preserve of the government and there is virtually no issuance by Italian (far less foreign) private sector corporations. The government bond market, which is the third largest in the world after the United States and Japan, until 1990 offered mainly floating-rate debt of short maturity. Inflation in effect precluded the issuance of fixed-rate securities with a maturity beyond five years. In 1991, however, the convergence effect of the European currencies benefited lira bonds—and bonds denominated in other European currencies alike—and encouraged the Italian government to issue fixed-rate bonds with seven- and ten-year maturities. This helped to give a broader base to the market and consolidate investor interest from abroad. The Italian domestic government bond market is now sufficiently evolved to serve (like its French, German, or U.S. counterpart) as an efficient means of holding and/or hedging lira debt securities including in particular Euro-lira bonds.

The Euro-lira bond market opened in 1985 with an issue for the European Investment Bank. Other supranational borrowers include the World Bank and the European Community institutions, and together account for over a quarter of all issues. The market has been tapped by some European sovereigns (such as Denmark and Ireland), government agencies (such as Electricité de France and Swedish Export Credit), international banks (such as Deutsche Bank and Société Generale), and international private sector corporations (such as Johnson and Johnson, Nestlé, General Electric Co., and British Gas).† The potentially most significant category of issuers is

* Until the autumn of 1992.

† Euro-lira issues launched by foreign companies to finance their Italian operations route the proceeds of the issue to their Italian subsidiaries via back-to-back loans which are exempt from withholding tax.

comprised of Italian public and private sector corporations themselves. These have been "crowded out" of the domestic bond market by the Italian government, and the Euro-lira bond market is their only source of fixed-rate medium- or long-term lira funds. Italian borrowers include public sector utilities (such as Ferrovie dello Stato and SOFTE—the telecommunications agency), government-owned companies (such as ENEL—the oil major), international banks (such as Mediobanca and IMI), and private sector corporations (such as Olivetti, Ferruzzi, and CIR).

International investors—in particular retail investors from Germany, the Benelux, and Switzerland—were drawn by the substantial yield premium in relation to their respective domestic markets and the relative stability of the currency.

Italian investors generally have no incentive to invest in Eurobonds— whether in lira or in other currencies—as withholding tax is levied by Italian paying agents on interest payments. The exception to this rule is the case of issues by supranational borrowers (of which Italy is a member) where interest may be paid to Italian residents on a gross basis, regardless of currency of denomination.

Instruments include principally fixed-rate bonds, a small number of floating-rate notes and equity-warrant-linked bond issues, and two zero-coupon issues. Issuers must be incorporated outside Italy and issues must be approved by the Italian Treasury and the Bank of Italy as to issue size, terms, and timing. Issue sizes of up to Lit600 billion have been offered in the fixed income sector and Lit500 billion on FRN issues. There are no restrictions on final maturity but, historically, the yield curve imposed a practicable limit of five years on fixed-rate issues.

Recently the stretching of maturities in the government bond market has enabled several Euro-lira bond issues to be offered with 10-year maturities. Maturities on FRN issues have ranged from 8–12 years. Most other issuance terms (including interest payments, call options, repayment schedules, documentation, and listing) conform to standard Eurobond practice.

Issuance procedure requires at least one Italian bank in the senior management group of the issue; otherwise, syndication conforms to standard practice. Selling restrictions apply as regards Italian residents: to avoid registration of the issues with the Italian Stock Exchange supervisory commission, primary sales into Italy are not allowed except to professional institutional investors. Nonetheless, residents may purchase lira (and other) Eurobonds in the secondary market subject to Italian exchange control and withholding taxes. Interest payments on Eurobonds issued by non-Italian issuers and held by Italian residents are subject to standard income tax* withheld by an Italian paying agent appointed to the issue. In practice, the levy of withholding taxes at source discourages all but institutional

* Or at the rate applicable under specific double-taxation agreements.

investors (except for resident holdings of Eurobond issues by supranational borrowers, which as just described, are exempt from Italian withholding tax).

The Spanish Peseta.   In keeping with the relatively early stage of the market's development, international borrowers issuing peseta-denominated bonds have recourse to the Spanish "foreign" bond market only. There is no issuance offshore and permission to launch a peseta issue has to be sought from the Bank of Spain and the Spanish Treasury. In order to protect access of Spanish issuers to the market and to control outflows of capital, the Spanish authorities have also limited the range of international issuers, with rare exceptions, to sovereign and supranational borrowers which make up the so-called "matador" bond market.*

For some years the Spanish authorities have implemented tight monetary policies which were reflected in high nominal interest rates. Spain joined the European monetary system in 1989 and although the peseta fluctuates within the wider band, the currency has gradually acquired a perception of strength. Thus, despite medium-level inflation, peseta bonds have offered high real returns and attractive yield premiums in relation to Canadian dollar, French franc and Danish krone Eurobonds, and a more secure alternative to speculative currency sectors such as the Australian dollar.[†]

The matador bond market was launched in 1987 with a Pta10 billion issue for Eurofima. As an integral part of the domestic bond market, the matador market is governed by its regulations and practices. The Spanish Treasury controls foreign issues by means of a queueing system.

Foreign banks are allowed to lead manage issues; however, many issues are swap-driven and the swaps market remains largely in the control of Spanish banks. There are no limitations on maturities which range between three and ten years. A variety of instruments have been sanctioned including a zero-coupon issue, a stock-indexed-linked redemption feature, and subordinated debt. Issues are listed in Madrid. Matador issues are free of withholding tax.

The future growth of the matador bond market and, in particular, its opening to a broader range of issuers, is dependent on the continuing development of the domestic bond market. Currently, the domestic market is dominated by government securities which offer features designed to foster international interest, including a wide range of maturities, good liquidity through fungible issues, exemption of withholding tax on non-

* There was an attempt to launch offshore peseta-denominated private placements in 1989, but these issues were pulled by the lead managers following pressure from the Spanish authorities.

† Over 11 percent of Spanish government bonds in issue in 1991 were held by foreign investors.

resident holdings, and a nascent derivatives market. By contrast, the corporate sector, which accounts for only 12 percent of the bond market, offers a smaller range of maturities, less secondary market liquidity, and no tax exemption for nonresidents. Clearly, the further development of the domestic bond market is likely to prioritize access of domestic private-sector corporations, while the matador market is likely to remain confined to sovereign and supranational names. The interest in the matador market of foreign banks and private sector corporations with no local operations in Spain will be entirely predicated on the availability of cost-effective swaps.

5
Principal Participants

The Investors

Most public Eurobonds are in bearer form and therefore make no mention of the holder's identity. From the perspective of a borrower or the new issues department of an issuing house, this is not as important as the knowledge of the criteria by which individual investors make their investment decisions. Bond sales desks, which alone maintain direct contact with investors, convey regular feedback on investor appetite for different instruments, maturity, and currency preference and size of trade. This is the vital information on which are based the design and placement of a new issue.

This information also serves to provide a profile of different categories of investors and their investment behavior. Until recently, investment banks active in the Eurobond market have shied away from researching this subject, usually on the grounds of investor anonymity and dispersal but mainly for want of the will to commit the necessary resources. In the late 1980s these banks were proved deficient when research was undertaken by their best customer, the World Bank, on U.S. dollar holdings of international investors. This research revealed a willingness on the part of international institutional investors to hold U.S. Treasury stock or bonds in registered form. If anonymity were no longer a vital criteria, the door would open to launching new issues which could be placed simultaneously in the Eurobond market and in domestic markets such as the United States where registered form is mandatory. These issues, by virtue of being offered to additional (domestic) markets, could be offered in larger size and would be more liquid. This project was realized by the launch in 1989 of the first global bond issue by the World Bank for US$1.5 billion, the largest fixed-rate offering to date in the international bond markets. Global bonds are now a standard structure serving to link the international and domestic bond markets.

Other issuers are following the example of the World Bank and themselves undertaking investor research or education programs. South African borrowers, for example, newly returned to the Eurobond market in 1991 after a prolonged absence, conducted research programs through investor relations consultants who intermediated on their behalf to focus on concerns of image and credit which had a bearing on the pricing of their new issues. This information proved invaluable to identify specific pockets of investor interest and, equally important, investor resistance to the borrowers. As opportunities arise for novel financings or for new categories of borrowers, such as municipal government authorities in Europe, researching the attitudes and the education of bondholders is becoming an essential adjunct to the professional development of new bond markets.

Retail Investors. The canvasing of demand and subsequent placement among retail investors is time-consuming and, because of the numbers of sales people involved, expensive. But retail investors, once won over, tend to remain loyal. They trade little, which makes for firm placement, and in small amounts, which provides better price support and lower volatility in the secondary market. Access to retail placement is thus precious and it is also scarce. Eurobond issuing and trading houses with a genuine retail clientele are, for the most part, the investment banking arms of the large continental European universal banks who sell bond issues through their branch network for retail banking services. These include in particular the German, Swiss, and Benelux banks who sell Eurobonds to both their respective onshore retail clientele—which is largely captive—and to an extensive offshore foreign clientele, which is often passive in the management of its investments.

The growing depth of onshore retail investor markets owes much to the relaxation of foreign exchange controls on portfolio investment in foreign securities. These controls are now abolished in many countries, both in Europe and overseas. The one restraint which has not been relaxed as regards holdings of Eurobonds by onshore investors is the imposition of withholding tax on interest payments. This is not intended to deter investment in Eurobonds so much as to put Eurobonds on the same tax footing as domestic securities. The tax is usually levied by the local paying agent and the investor receives an interest payment net of tax which is paid directly to the authorities by the paying agent.

Retail investors investing from offshore accounts are unaffected by these considerations and, for these, a debt instrument paying interest on a gross basis is an ideal instrument to shelter their wealth. Investors with substantial assets entrust their funds to professional managers in jurisdictions such as Switzerland, Lichtenstein, or Austria, which offer exemption from local taxes and secrecy laws which confer effective immunity to fiscal regulations of countries of origin. These funds are difficult to quantify but considered to be very substantial.

Institutional Investors. Institutional investors are estimated to account for as much as 75 percent of investors in the Eurobond market. While much of their asset allocation and management is satisfied through dealings in domestic securities, the Eurobond market provided a convenient means for currency diversification. In the last five years, the domestic bond markets of many western countries have become more accessible to foreign investors, and domestic government bond markets in particular have become liquid and, as futures contracts are launched, increasingly sophisticated. Far from encroaching on investment in Eurobonds, the interest in domestic government bond markets has, if anything, enhanced the attraction of Eurobonds, the value added of which for these institutions includes (1) a greater selection of high-quality—but higher-yielding—risk, (2) a choice of 22 currencies, (3) a homogeneous instrument, and (4) identical terms of trading, settlement, and custody. The single major drawback of the Eurobond market for these institutions is that most Eurobond issues are of small size and illiquid. While this may not invalidate their choice, it does narrow the selection of issues in which they may trade.

Institutional investors in Eurobonds are often substantial financial institutions and handle large securities portfolios. They deal in larger size and more frequently—the range of transaction size has increased from US$10,000–US$25,000 in the early 1960s to US$500,000–US$5 million today—and at any one time are likely to be serviced by several securities-trading houses. Most institutions have screen-based price information and research facilities and, within the framework of performance targets, devise strategies of varying complexity. They do not rely on securities houses for advice and use these merely to execute orders. Customer loyalty is weaker and securities houses compete to offer ancillary services to retain their customers. The principal categories of institutional investors include the following:

- Central banks are large holders of Eurobonds, typically bonds issued by other governments and their agencies and, in any event, liquid paper with a AAA rating. A self-imposed five-year maturity limit no longer applies.

- Government agencies and international financial institutions invest according to similar criteria.

- Pension funds and insurance companies will accept lower-quality paper to enhance their yield but are usually required to invest in listed and/or rated securities. Insurance companies and pension funds are often subject to special tax regimes in their home country, and the payment of interest gross on Eurobonds makes these an ideal investment. By the same token, however, the bearer form of Eurobonds presents no advantage and is secondary to liquidity and ease of settlement.

- Investment trusts and bond funds are managed by professional investment managers with less regard for high-quality risk or liquidity than the maximization of income or capital growth of their funds. For investment funds, which are often purposely incorporated in tax havens to minimize corporation tax and, in turn, are subscribed to from offshore funds, the absence of withholding tax on Eurobonds makes these again an ideal instrument.

- International banks buy Eurobonds for their own portfolios, in particular, FRNs issued by governments which have a nil risk weighting (or by other banks which carry a 20 percent risk weighting) for capital adequacy purposes.

- Private sector corporations buy Eurobonds as a marginal investment only, since excess liquidity is generally invested in short-term instruments or government securities.

Investor Criteria. The investment criteria of traditional Eurobond investors were narrow and typically confined to high-quality credit and low currency exposure. Many investors, both retail and institutional, still invest according to these criteria but, as the range of instruments, hedging techniques, and currency sectors has developed, investor criteria have also evolved and broadened from prudential strategy to outright speculation. The basic elements of a strategy for investment in Eurobonds include the following:

- *Quality of credit.* The preference for high-quality names is a practical choice of investors, often made at the cost of a sacrifice in yield. But it is by no means universal. In the late 1980s, the criteria of quality of credit was often ignored as investors subscribed eagerly to issues by luxury retail brand names which have a strong international profile but a weak credit which was compensated by a generous yield.

- *Liquidity.* After quality of credit, this is the foremost criteria of most active investors in public issues. The poor liquidity of many Eurobond issues is a severely limiting factor on the appeal of the Eurobond market and recently borrowers and issuing houses have concerted themselves to promote better liquidity by increasing the size of existing issues by adding new tranches of fungible paper and by launching large-scale global bond issues whose distribution spans offshore and domestic markets. Where investors buy and hold to maturity, clearly liquidity is of less concern— but important nonetheless to put a value on holdings of bonds from time to time.

- *Issuer perception.* This is a nebulous concept because it is subjective and few investors hold the same perception of an issuer or its outstanding issues. Nonetheless, it is the tool of traders and investors alike, and influences their inclination to deal. Thus the high rating and liquidity of issues of the World Bank, coupled with a strong international profile, make for very favorable perception of the borrower. But quality of perception, like quality of credit, has also been safely ignored: this was the case with numerous Eurobond issues by medium-sized Japanese and U.K. corporations with no rating or international business and which were successfully placed with their respective domestic investors. Yet another instance, an extreme case, is that of issues by special-purpose borrowers with no profile at all, which serve to refinance existing holdings of financial assets or are linked to the assets which they fund, such as mortgage-backed FRN issues, and which are targeted and placed with financial institutions.

- *Currency risk.* International investors prefer strong currencies with low inflation and low interest rates to weaker currency sectors with high inflation and volatile interest rates. Investors in Australian dollar and, to a lesser extent, Italian lira issues have ignored currency risk in favor of high coupon income. This group includes retail investors in Germany for whom these are marginal investments.

- *Currency diversification.* With access to Eurobonds denominated in 22 currencies, the market provides a unique means of currency risk diversification for investors with both narrow and speculative currency strategies.

- *Transparency of dealings, ease of execution and settlement.* These criteria are hallmarks of an established market and came relatively late to the Eurobond market. Three-quarters of secondary market trading in Eurobonds is transacted in London and between intermediaries direct rather than through the Stock Exchange. Trading relied essentially on screen-based price information which was not always accurate and, hence, deals were not always struck at the best price. Presently Eurobond orders, regardless of currency or instrument, are executed according to standardized procedures and systems instituted by the market's trade association, the International Securities Market Association (ISMA), formerly known as the Association of International Bond Dealers (AIBD). The London Eurobond trading houses have installed an automated trade confirmation system, TRAX, devised by ISMA, which confirms, matches, and reports all trades within minutes to ISMA, which is therefore able to monitor prices at which Eurobond trades are struck.

  Clearing is assured by the clearing houses, Euroclear and Cedel, and issuing and trading houses are invariably members of one or both systems.

- *Variety of instruments.* The major domestic bond markets offer a wide range of instruments and many of these have been adopted by the Eurobond markets. The international capital markets have also made a contribution in the form of derivatives, such as currency and interest swaps, and access to futures and options markets which have provided Eurobond investors the means for yield enhancement and yield and currency exposure management not afforded by any domestic market.

The Issuers

Issuers in the Eurobond market, unlike investors, are visible and, for the most part, familiar to international and/or domestic investors. This visibility is promoted through periodic press reports, market comment, and issue ratings, and creates a public image which is an essential attribute of an issuer in a public market. While image may be secondary in relation to a technical and financial analysis, its importance should not be underrated in the context of an international market where investors are remote and few have the resources to perform a credit analysis. Thus, issues backed by strong credit but a low public image have encountered an indifferent reception and have performed poorly in the secondary market. Syndicate desks which are conscious of this problem insist on a "roadshow" to introduce the borrower to institutional investors, the financial press, and other issuing houses. By contrast, issues by corporates owning brand names well known in retail markets have successfully relied on their strong public image to overcome the drawbacks of smaller size of operation and/or weaker credit.

The public image of the issuer, however, is no substitute for the quality of the issuer's credit. Investors generally look for strong credit and rely on credit ratings, which measure the ability of the issuer to service a specific issue, to introduce different degrees of risk into their portfolio. As a yardstick, traditional Eurobond issuers have had to demonstrate, in terms of quality of credit risk, a balance sheet and profit and loss account strong enough to (1) preserve debt equity ratios at an acceptable level, (2) service the incremental debt out of cash flow, and (3) support the issue of bonds in unsecured form.

These credit criteria and the need for an international profile has clearly narrowed the range of borrowers eligible to issue Eurobonds. The principal categories, which will be reviewed shortly, are sovereign governments and their agencies, supranational bodies, multinational private sector corporations, and international banks.

In recent times, new categories of Eurobond issuers have emerged. The most significant of these are Japanese companies with no international profile who issued U.S. dollar and Swiss franc Eurobonds with equity warrants to achieve, via swaps, low-cost funding in yen. These issues have, in the main, been placed with Japanese institutional investors who were comfortable with the credit and were simultaneously backing the Japanese stock market. The second new category of issuer is the one-off special-purpose borrowing vehicle (SPV) with no profile whatever, which issued Eurobonds to refinance mortgages, bank loans, credit receivables, or leveraged acquisition finance. These issues, which are secured on the income stream from the assets, are termed *securitized* and are in many cases guaranteed by financial insurance. The latter financings have a complex structure and the issue, which is analyzed by the rating agencies, relies upon the award of a rating to be launched.

Currently, the pressure on international banks to meet and maintain capital adequacy ratios has forced a shrinking of their balance sheets and a reallocation of loan portfolios in favor of higher-quality (and lesser-weighted) risk. In effect, this has led many banks to contain or curtail their lending to private sector corporations which are obliged to turn increasingly to the bond markets for medium- and long-term finance. International issues by borrowers with a lesser credit rating or international profile will clearly require a rating to ease their distribution. The role of the independent rating agencies such as Moody's and Standard & Poor's, who are experienced in rating corporate issues in the United States, will be vital to the development of a new class of corporate issuer. As a general rule, the higher the profile and quality of credit of the borrower, the more readily acceptable will be the name and, other things being equal, the easier the distribution of their issues. Traditional issuers meeting these criteria can be categorized as follows. (See Table 5-1 for top 50 borrowers.)

Supranational Institutions. These comprise the development agencies (e.g., the World Bank, the Inter-American Development Bank, the Asian Development Bank, the African Development Bank, and Nordic Investment Bank) which borrow to fund regional development and typically seek long-term, low-coupon debt (Swiss franc, Deutsche mark, and yen) which is on-lent to the end user. The European Community institutions (the European Community, the European Coal and Steel Community, and the European Atomic Energy Authority) are also regular issuers, as well as the European supranational agencies (e.g., the Council of Europe, Eurofima and the European Investment Bank). These institutions borrow in a variety of strong and weak currencies but typically swap the proceeds for ECU or the currency of the end user.

Sovereign Governments. Most European sovereign governments have launched Eurobond issues (the Republics of Austria, Italy, Finland, Portugal, Iceland, Ireland, and Turkey, and the Kingdoms of Belgium, Denmark, Norway, Spain, Sweden, and the United Kingdom). Commonwealth countries (Australia, Canada, New Zealand) are regular borrowers. Latin American issuers include the Argentine, Mexican, and Venezuelan Republics. In the Far East there have been issues by Malaysia, Thailand and, more recently, the Republic of China. The motivation is invariably to raise foreign exchange to boost international reserves. Issues in minor currencies are generally swapped for U.S. dollars or Deutsche marks and, for large amounts, issuers resort directly to the larger U.S. dollar, Deutsche mark, and ECU Eurobond markets where many sovereign borrowers have an established presence.

Government Agencies, Regional and Municipal Authorities. These borrowers have a long record of issuance, are more numerous than their sovereign counterparts, and can offer risk of the highest quality. Issues are launched generally for twin purposes of (1) funding the working capital requirement of the agency, usually in local currency, and (2) raising foreign currency at the behest of the central monetary authority to boost interna-

Table 5-1. Top 50 Borrowers Ranked by Nominal Issue Amount

Rank	Name	Issues	Amount	%
1	EIB (European Investment Bank)	32	10970.21	4.74
2	Italy Republic of Italy	2	5438.79	2.35
3	Crédit Local de France—CAECL S.A	20	5122.86	2.21
4	Ontario Province	9	4182.77	1.81
5	Republic of Finland	11	3891.17	1.68
6	United Kingdom	1	3873.24	1.67
7	World Bank	11	3592.16	1.55
8	Belgium Kingdom of Belgium	5	3482.36	1.50
9	British Gas plc	7	3125.34	1.35
10	Compagnie Bancaire	20	2987.94	1.29
11	Crédit National	17	2674.67	1.15
12	EEC (European Economic Community)	5	2562.20	1.11
13	Crédit Lyonnais	10	2262.05	0.98
14	General Electric Co.	17	2227.82	0.96
15	Kreditanstalt fuer wiederaufbau	11	2171.39	0.94
16	Uorway Kingdom of Norway	2	2140.25	0.92
17	IADB (Inter-American Devt. Bank)	9	2084.70	0.90
18	Toyota Motors Corp.	13	2042.33	0.88
19	National Home Loans Corp. plc	12	2033.79	0.88
20	Deutsche Bank AG	12	1966.92	0.85
21	Nissan Motor Co. Ltd.	14	1954.53	0.84
22	Société Générale	12	1931.63	0.83
23	Swedish Export Credit Corp. (SEK)	11	1920.74	0.83
24	Quebec Province of Ouebec	6	1883.66	0.81
25	Oesterreichische Kontrollbank	10	1842.71	0.80
26	Council of Europe	9	1830.50	0.79
27	Eurofima	12	1701.80	0.73
28	Ford Motor Company	12	1594.71	0.69
29	Tokyo Electric Power Co. Inc.	4	1471.34	0.64
30	Alberta Province of Alberta	2	1429.55	0.62
31	Daimler-Benz AG	7	1415.65	0.61
32	Japan Development Bank	2	1374.32	0.59
33	Landeskreditbank Baden-Wuerttemberg	9	1366.41	0.59
34	Export-Import Bank of Japan	5	1338.70	0.58
35	CREDIOP (Cons. Cred. Opere Pubbliche)	7	1311.88	0.57
36	British Columbia, Province of	3	1304.82	0.56
37	ECSC (European Coal & Steel Community)	5	1267.15	0.55
38	IBM	10	1229.31	0.53
39	Nordic Investment Bank	10	1211.17	0.52
40	Finnish Export Credit Ltd.	6	1201.22	0.52
41	UEC Corporation	6	1177.69	0.51
42	Asahi Breweries Ltd.	4	1172.52	0.51
43	Gefco Guaranteed Export Fin. Corp. plc	2	1171.25	0.51
44	ABN (Amro Bank NV)	4	1119.17	0.48
45	Kobe Steel Co. Ltd.	5	1115.58	0.48
46	Spain Kingdom of Spain	1	1096.89	0.47
47	Hydro-Quebec	4	1092.49	0.47
48	Swiss Bank Corporation	6	1029.62	0.44
49	Banque Nationale de Paris	10	1028.81	0.44
50	Roche Holding AG (previously Hoffman-La Roche)	1	1000.00	0.43

tional reserves. Borrowers such as Ontario Hydro, Caisse Nationale des Télécommunications (France), and Swedish Export Credit, though having little cause to be known outside their domestic financial markets, have successfully created a strong perception of themselves in the Eurobond market by virtue of (1) a policy of regular issuance, (2) professional management of issues, and (3) the high quality of risk.

Some sovereign governments such as France issue Eurobonds only exceptionally in their own name, and instead raise foreign currency through the vehicle of public agencies, which borrow under the guarantee of the Republic. Similarly, Hungary and the former USSR eschewed the public bond markets and borrowed with success through government-owned banks and public agencies.

Multinational Companies. Traditional borrowers in this category are the foreign subsidiaries of U.S. companies who launched issues to fund their overseas operations following the embargo on capital exports from the United States under the Mandatory Restraint Program (1967). Most offerings are standard fixed-rate Eurodollar bonds and were rated by Standard & Poor's or Moody's. European names in the Eurodollar sector are few in number and include multinationals such as Unilever, Roche, or Volkswagen which have substantial U.S. investments and/or trading operations. Many names are reluctant to apply for a rating—a lengthy and expensive process—or their size of operation does not warrant a regular program of medium-term issuance and is better served by a Euro-commercial paper program. The focus of operations is in Europe itself and corporate borrowers occasionally launch Euro-issues to fund their European subsidiaries, e.g., Trusthouse Forte (French francs), Peugeot (Italian lira). Corporate borrowers with Europe-wide commercial operations have launched issues in ECU (Olivetti, Michelin, Pirelli, and Nestlé). More common are corporate issues denominated in their home currency, including Philips (guilder), Alliance and Leicester Building Society (sterling), Peugeot (French francs), Olivetti (lira), BMW (Deutsche mark). The motivation here is the speed and relatively lower cost of a Eurobond in relation to a domestic issue, or a denial of access to the domestic market which is reserved for government borrowing, as in Italy.

The most significant development in corporate Eurobond issuance was the explosive growth in the second half of the 1980s of equity-warrant-linked bonds. A sine qua non of these issues is a buoyant stock market. Issuance activity is in direct function of the strength of stock market expectations which sustain the speculative attraction of the equity warrant or "kicker." The most frequent names are from countries with more developed stock markets, i.e., the United States, the United Kingdom and, above all, Japan. The sustained buoyancy of the Tokyo stock market in the late 1980s and the availability of attractive US$/yen swaps provided the conditions for an unprecedented volume of Swiss franc and U.S. dollar-denominated Eurobond issues by Japanese corporations. In this instance, criteria of international perception no longer apply since the vast majority of issues are from little-known names and were placed almost entirely with Japanese investors.

Financial Institutions. These resort to the Eurobond market for the medium-term funding of international treasury operations and portfolios of international loans and securities. The requirement is generally for U.S. dollar LIBOR-based floating-rate funds which can be met in two ways: (1) by direct recourse to the FRN market or (2) by medium-term arbitrage through fixed-rate issuance in a third currency (for example, Canadian dollars, Australian dollars, New Zealand dollars, Danish krone, Italian lira) with a currency and interest rate swap into U.S. dollar floating-rate funds at below LIBOR.

A small number of financial institutions have resorted to the Eurobond market to meet capital adequacy requirements by raising junior subordinated debt in the form of perpetual FRN issues. Financial institutions also launch Euro-issues in foreign currency to fund their overseas operations and in their home currency for domestic operations. These issues are typically structured as fixed-rate issues with an interest rate swap to produce floating-rate funding.

The motivations of Eurobond issuers are principally cost, speed of issuance, and prestige. In terms of cost of debt, the variety of debt instruments and currency sectors offer contemporary issuers unparalleled choice of structure, and the use of derivatives (swaps, options, and futures) has brought an edge to financial engineering techniques which offer opportunities for substantial savings over domestic bond markets. Most issuers are familiar with swaps and have accepted the incremental risks of the product. None have exploited the concept better than issuers of Japanese equity-warrant-linked issues, which, in some instances, achieved a negative cost of funds.

Borrowers also issue in the Eurobond market for the speed and ease of issuance. The option of a foreign bond issue, placed in the U.S., Japanese, or U.K. domestic markets, is also available. These are subject, however, in the United States and Japan, to lengthy registration procedures (albeit shortened by the facility of shelf registration), and extensive disclosure of information on the issuer's business and financial condition is also stipulated at a heavy cost in time. By contrast, Eurobond issues are not subject to prior registration and the information disclosure requirements of a London or Luxembourg listing are much less onerous. This leaves only capital controls (e.g., Italy and Spain) as a source of procedural delay. The principal sectors, including the U.S. dollar, Deutsche mark, Australian dollar, Canadian dollar, sterling, ECU and Euro-yen markets, have no procedural requirements at all.

The Eurobond market also offers a worldwide investor base, which is expanding to include access to investors in many domestic markets. The domestic investor base afforded by the U.S. and Japanese domestic bond markets is larger, but reliance on one market is an added risk of the issue. In this respect, the variety of currency sectors in the Eurobond market offers issuers a much more broadly based capital market. It also provides a unique advantage of being able to offer issue structures in several alternative currencies for the same financing.

Finally, the Eurobond market has played host to leading borrowers worldwide and, by association, has acquired their prestige. Thus a Eurobond issue conveys an indication of the international standing of the borrower. In 1989, the Republic of Turkey seized an opportunity to confirm before the international capital markets the perceived improvement in economic performance and successfully launched its first fixed-rate Eurodollar issue. The prestige of the financing is not negligible, and a professionally managed issue for a first-time issuer will pave the way, other things being equal, for further issues on better terms.

The principal motivations for potential issuers in the Eurobond market may be summarized as follows:

- no restriction on frequency of issue
- no restriction on issue size
- ease and speed of issuance: a standard debt issue can be closed within two weeks
- no registration procedure and no queues
- less onerous information disclosure to secure listing
- lesser volume of documentation
- less restrictive covenants
- a variety of instruments not available in any foreign bond market
- financial engineering techniques to produce low-cost funding
- arbitrage opportunities against the issuer's domestic market
- worldwide investor market active in 15 currencies

The Intermediaries

The intermediaries are the securities trading houses, universal banks, and investment banks who are active (1) as brokers and market makers in the secondary trading of existing Eurobond issues and (2) as issuing houses in the design and primary distribution of new issues. The activities of broker, market maker, and issuing house are distinct, and intermediaries have often emphasized one or another activity reflecting natural advantages in the market. Not all market makers become issuing houses; however, houses active in the new issues market all have substantial market-making operations. Brokering and market making generates market information and wins investor clients. An issuing house looking to solicit mandates for new issues has to demonstrate both knowledge of the market and the ability to bring added placement of bonds with investors. There is therefore no legitimate claim by an issuing house to a capability in the new issues or primary market unless this is supported by a substantial Eurobond market-making and sales operation.

The Market Makers and Brokers

Brokers and market makers are intermediaries between investors, and their main source of revenue is from buying and selling bonds. Brokers deal as agents on behalf of buyers and sellers and act in their own name. They normally match each trade with an equal and opposite transaction and do not run positions in bonds, thereby assuming risk. Market makers use their capital resources to buy and sell as principals and generate holdings or positions in a variety of issues. By their respective activities, both brokers and market makers serve as counterparties of investors wishing to deal, and thus provide liquidity to the market.

Market Makers. Market making is a self-contained business, independent of that of an issuing house. While issuing houses invariably undertake market making, historically not all market makers were issuing houses. Although market makers are dependent on issuers for the supply of new paper, they are under no statutory or contractual obligation and are free to make markets in issues of their choice. The selection is motivated by a view on the opportunity of strong trading activity in a variety of securities. Where this view coincides with the intentions of the investors or other market makers, trading takes place. In fulfilling their functions, market makers normally quote the following:

- a two-way price in each security: (1) the buy or *bid* price and (2) the sell or *offered* price, the offered price being the higher; the difference between the bid and the offered is termed the *spread*
- prices in a range of sizes of trades, say, US$50,000 to US$5 million
- prices in a wide spectrum of securities, from AAA to A, and sometimes BBB equivalent rated risk

These functions impose risks on the market maker who at any one moment is unaware of whether his or her counterpart will deal on the quote and, if so, in what size, or whether he or she is a buyer or a seller. In this respect, the market maker's willingness to accumulate unwanted positions or reduce holdings as a result of the dealings is the key to the liquidity of an issue. Active dealing makes for a liquid market and provides the market's assessment of the value, or price, of the stock. Conversely, without market makers, dealings are ad hoc and investors do not know what value to put on their holdings.

Market makers generate trading revenue in several ways. The first element is the spread between the bid and offered price. The market maker

134

buys at the bid (or lower) price and sells at the offer (or higher) price. Spreads vary between ⅛ percent on very liquid issues (and less on FRNs) to as much as ½ percent and more on small-size issues with little secondary trading. The second and more important source of revenue is the capital gain realized on sales of Eurobond positions as yields fall. (Conversely, in anticipation of a rise in yields, market makers may also sell bonds they do not own—an activity known as *going short*—with a view to buying stock to close their position at a later date when prices have fallen.) A third source of revenue is the coupon interest on the bonds for as long as they are held, but against the income has to be offset the cost of funding the position. Given a positive (or rising) yield curve, the market maker expects to fund a holding of medium-term bonds with short-term deposits at a rate below the coupon rate on the bond. The difference between the funding cost and the coupon is termed the *carry* which, if positive, generates a profit for the market maker. Conversely, when short-term rates are suddenly raised—as was frequently the case in the United States in the 1980s—the yield curve can invert, the carry is negative, and market makers fund their bond holdings at a loss.

Historically, an important source of revenue for market makers was the knowledge of price discrepancies in the same stock in different markets. By buying in the "cheap" market and selling in the "dear," market makers engaged in arbitrage dealing. With the advent of screen-based information technology, prices are diffused instantly to all market makers worldwide (among other participants) and, coupled with trade reporting requirements to regulatory bodies, the opportunities for arbitraging individual bonds in different markets have virtually disappeared. The only way of generating off-market revenue is by being the first house to call an investor with an offer of stock or by performing a particular service, either of which may be reflected in an adjusted price which is agreed upon on the trade.

The pressure of competition among market makers and the level playing field promoted by information technology and regulatory controls have led market makers to divert their efforts away from customers to dealing for their own account. This is known as *proprietary trading* and, as market makers become investors themselves, a subtle change of behavior can be observed. In times of interest rate volatility, providing liquidity to customers tends to become secondary to the market maker's concern to protect his or her positions. Sudden adverse yield movements can lead to funding losses. The risks of carrying positions increases sharply and a forced liquidation can be costly. In these circumstances, market makers become risk-averse and reduce the list of securities in which they are prepared to make markets. Spreads are widened to discourage buyers or sellers, or the quote is limited to a bid or offer price only. In poor market conditions, traders will make a basis market; that is, they will deal only if they find a counterparty. At worst, market makers withdraw altogether and liquidity ceases, as was the case in the FRN market in December 1986.

Even as proprietary traders, however, market makers are interdependent with both investors and issuers and, far from trading in isolation, this interdependence serves as a reminder of their primary role, which is to provide liquidity—a function which in practice need not be at odds with the imperative of making money. Occasionally, where a market maker works within an issuing house, his or her dealing policy may be at variance with the interests of the new-issues department which manages relationships with issuers. While the syndicate desk has a duty to support a new issue, sudden adverse market conditions might lead the market maker to sell positions. This conflict arises because there is a clear separation between primary and secondary trading books which can only be resolved by a decision by senior management.

Brokers. Brokers intermediate between buyers and sellers of bonds, serving both market makers and investors. Brokers dealing between market makers are known as *interdealer brokers,* while brokers dealing with end investors offer a service which is complementary to that of market makers. In either case, their function typically includes:

- sourcing the best quotes (that is, the highest bid for sellers and the lowest offered price for buyers). In the case of poorly traded securities, investors often rely on brokers, in the absence of market makers, to find counterparty and a quote.

- enhancing client access to other market makers and investors worldwide. Large orders will typically be broken down among several market makers and brokers to avoid undue price movements.

- saving on clients' time and costs in finding counterparties.

- providing anonymity where required.

Interdealer brokers have also long provided a major service to the aftermarket of new issues (or "gray" market) by helping to even out surpluses and shortages of paper experienced by members of the management group and underwriters to new issues. The brokers' actions here help to stabilize the issue which thus "finds its (price) level" in the secondary market. This service, however—and in particular the anonymity it afforded—has been exploited by co-managers who join management groups of new issues for prestige reasons. These put in applications for allotments of paper to justify their position of managers but have no actual investor demand. In due course their holdings are sold in small lots or, worse, in a single trade, which depresses the price of the issue. Some lead managers have viewed the facility as being able to fall back on brokers to dispose of unwanted paper as the prime cause of price volatility and of the resultant (paper) losses inflicted on genuine investors. As a result, new syndication practices such as take-and-pay and fixed-price reofferings based on U.S. practice are being applied in new issues. These are intended, respectively, to (1) oblige managers to request allotments only for the amount of paper for which they have demand or (2) oblige the co-managers to resell bonds at a fixed price to their customers for a period of 2–5 days. In either case, these new issue practices preclude dealings in the gray market and make the role of inter-dealer brokers redundant.

The advent of screen-based price information services has also threatened the livelihood of brokers who, like market markers, generate little if any revenue from arbitraging individual bonds. Some brokers have then sought new brokering lines in derivatives such as swaps and currency options. Others introduce in-house financial engineering skills to devise and broker products which combine derivatives with bond instruments. These brokers develop a corporate finance niche and even embark upon limited market-making activity, thereby competing directly with the broader-based issuing houses.

The Issuing Houses

The activity of an issuing house is the third and ultimate degree of commitment of a financial intermediary to the capital markets. Issuing houses build on their experience of a wide variety of bond sectors and instruments to add a separate capability in the design and launching—or origination—of new issues. New issues typically rely for their prompt distribution to investors on not one but a dozen issuing houses to participate in the launch. New issues are also routinely underwritten—to provide the borrower with the guarantee of receiving the full nominal amount of the issue on the signing date—and the underwriting is syndicated with other issuing houses which together make up the management group of the new issue. Should adverse market conditions arise in the course of the launch, the underwriters may be left with unsold bonds which have to be retained and financed until such time as they can be sold. If poor conditions persist, the bonds may have to be realized and a loss taken.

An issuing house, in order to meet this function, has to commit substantial additional capital to assume underwriting commitments, to provide the technical expertise to structure new issues, to install a sales desk and develop a credible investor base, and to demonstrate an aptitude for risk selection and management on a scale which exceeds by far the parameters of market making or brokering bonds. The size alone of a new issue—rarely less than US$100 million equivalent—is likely to exceed all but the very largest secondary market trades. A new issue is often only one of several components in a complex and tailor-made transaction, which may also include a currency and interest-rate swap or other derivative products in its structure. Not least, a new issue is a much more visible transaction, as every aspect of its structure, pricing, and timing is rigourously scrutinized by other market players. The reputation of the issuing house is therefore also at stake on the occasion of each new offering.

The skills, expertise, and entry costs of becoming an issuing house have limited the number of candidates in many domestic bond markets to a half

Table 5-2. Bookrunners League Table, 1991
(Top 30, Ranked by Amount in US$ Equivalent*)

Rank	Name	Issues	Amount	%
1	Nomura International Group	121	21327.83	9.37
2	Daiwa Securities	99	16093.38	7.07
3	Crédit Suisse/CSFB Group	60	14708.59	6.46
4	Deutsche Bank AG	79	14323.90	6.29
5	Paribas	28	10994.46	4.83
6	Yamaichi	74	10168.05	4.46
7	Nikko Securities	73	9756.94	4.28
8	Goldman Sachs	50	9674.25	4.25
9	Morgan Stanley Co. Inc.	17	9272.88	4.07
10	Bank Corporation	35	7915.12	3.48
11	Union Bank of Switzerland	33	6954.84	3.05
12	Merrill Lynch	32	6690.93	2.94
13	Morgan Guaranty Trust Co. of New York	35	6553.22	2.88
14	S. G. Warburg Group	27	6454.93	2.83
15	Crédit Lyonnais	24	6083.44	2.67
16	Crédit Commercial de France	21	5373.84	2.36
17	Industrial Bank of Japan	23	5167.44	2.27
18	Dresdner Bank AG	31	5050.90	2.22
19	Hambros Bank Limited	51	4123.64	1.81
20	Canadian Imperial Bank of Commerce	22	2840.89	1.25
21	Salomon Brothers Inc.	14	2675.68	1.17
22	Baring Brothers Co. Ltd.	16	2588.90	1.14
23	Société Générale	18	2495.15	1.10
24	ABN (Amro Bank NV)	14	2433.00	1.07
25	Barclays Bank	15	2371.27	1.04
26	Bankers Trust	18	2145.87	0.94
27	Banque Nationale de Paris	10	2132.55	0.94
28	Banca Commerciale Italiana	10	2042.53	0.90
29	Ist. Bancario San Paolo di Torino S.p.A	9	1745.47	0.77
30	Westdeutsche Landesbank Girozentrale	9	1731.77	0.76

* Issue amounts partially adjusted.
SOURCE: IFR Bondbase.

dozen houses at most. For Eurobond issuing houses, which may be called upon to launch an issue in any one of 22 Euro-currencies, the scale of effective operations and concomitant entry costs are larger still. Since the time when the market served mainly offshore investors, the ranks of Eurobond investors have swelled to include large segments of domestic retail and institutional investors. Moreover, as these have begun to invest outside their home securities market, their interest has focused not only on Eurobonds but on the domestic securities issued in foreign countries. This has posed a challenge to Eurobond houses—anxious to provide a comprehensive coverage of bond markets for their issuer and investor clients—to extend their operations beyond the Eurobond market and to establish a trading and issuing capability in other domestic bond markets. The cost of such further establishment, coming at a time of compliance with capital adequacy rules and securities industry regulation, has lain within the reach of no more than some 20 international financial intermediaries. Had the benefit of an international trading and issuance capability been confined to bond products, the number would have been smaller but for the opportunity of adapting their establishment in other countries to both bond and equity products. Few houses, however, are genuinely competent in both areas and the population of Eurobond issuing houses has endured as much for reasons of mere prestige as for reasons of product coverage, and the resultant excess capacity has been signally detrimental to the health of the industry as a whole.

In the face of such immense demands on their resources, intermediaries seek to exploit every market advantage. There is a strong tendency, for example, for issuers in the Eurobond market to choose issuing houses of their country of origin. This rule holds good with borrowers in Europe and the United States, but especially with Japanese borrowers whose equity-warrant-linked issues are almost entirely in the grasp of the four leading Japanese securities houses. (The latter have in addition been successful in securing a significant portion of public Eurobond mandates and most, if not all, of the private placement business of many leading European borrowers.)

The same practice applies in currency sectors. In countries such as the Benelux, France, Germany, and the United Kingdom, the indigenous banks tend to be favored for the lead management of Euro-issues in their currency. This tendency is abetted by procedural requirements in certain countries (such as France, the United Kingdom, or Germany) that Euro-issues in their currencies have to be launched from the country of issue of the currency; and their dominance of domestic markets makes difficult the penetration by outsiders, such as Japanese and U.S. intermediaries. In currency sectors such as the U.S. dollar, the ECU, or the Australian dollar, where Eurobond issues are not required to be launched in the country of issue of the currency, banks have no natural advantage, and develop niches in particular currency sectors. As regards these currencies, issues are generally launched in London where most international issuing houses have their principal Eurobond issuance establishment.

Eurobond issuing houses have also developed niche capabilities in swaps and derivatives markets, which give an edge to their representations to participate in issues. These claims are readily heeded where issuing houses find themselves unable to provide both the issue and the swap on terms meeting the borrower's cost-of-funds target, and it is common to find the issue and the swap are provided by different institutions, each with special competence in their respective areas.

Such pockets of advantage, however, do little to offset the intense competition among intermediaries. The very scale of operations, the prestige attached to international issues, and the potential for generating large fees and commissions have exercised an enduring fascination on international and domestic financial institutions, most of which had no vocation whatever to be active in Eurobonds. Between the late 1970s and the mid 1980s, some 50 international commercial and investment banks aspired to the role of full Eurobond market intermediary. For want of investors, capital resources, or experience of bond markets acquired in home markets, many of these fell prey to adverse trading conditions—in particular, volatile U.S. dollar interest rates—and, after enduring several years of continuous trading losses, withdrew from the market. During the second half of the 1980s many of the remaining houses expanded into new currency sectors and in domestic markets and all competed to secure market share by pricing new Eurobond issues on break-even or even loss-making terms. These practices led to heavy layoffs and further closures in the late 1980s when the population of issuing houses shrank further and eventually stabilized into the current oligopoly of some 25 banks.

Competition and overcapacity are recurring phenomena in unprotected securities industries and, notwithstanding the process of attrition in the Eurobond market, there are still too many houses in relation to the volume of new issues. The competition encourages over-fine pricing and jeopardizes the underwriting fees of syndicate members. Operating returns become inadequate to meet the high "sunk" costs of information technology, professional staff, compliance, and capital adequacy. After a very poor year in 1990, profitability was restored in 1991 through the acceptance of fixed-price reoffering practices and an exceptional volume of new issues. Recently, some houses have broken ranks again, in a renewed bid to pre-empt competition. The battle is likely to be of long duration. The top 25 Eurobond issuing houses are all major financial institutions with sufficient resources to see out many years of poor trading—and with the commitment to do so if a more dominant position is perceived to be the prize.

The Clearing Systems

On agreeing to a trade in bonds, the intermediary and the investor exchange confirmation of details of the transaction and specify terms of *settlement* and *delivery*. The purchaser sends instructions for payment and the seller advises the receiving bank. The seller sends further instructions to the *depositary* who holds the securities in safe custody to either (1) deliver physically the bonds against receipt of payment to the buyer or his or her agent or (2) transfer the bonds to the buyer's own depositary.

In the early years of its activity, secondary trading volumes in the Eurobond market grew rapidly and the multiple instructions on settlement and delivery for each transaction led to major administrative risks, particularly where buyers and sellers were located on different continents. In response to this problem, a clearing system, Euroclear, was founded by Morgan Guaranty in 1968 and established as a cooperative to offer book-entry clearing to its members. A second clearing system, Cedel, was created as a limited liability company in 1970, offering similar services. Both clearing systems are dedicated primarily to the Eurobond market, but trades in other securities, including Euro-commercial paper, Euro-equities and internationally traded domestic government bonds (such as ECU U.K. Treasury bills, Canadian Treasury bills and ECU OATs issued by the Republic of France), are also cleared through these systems. Member institutions thus settle transactions by means of one instruction (by telex, SWIFT, or electronic link) to transfer securities from one member account to another against payment. Physical delivery of the bonds has become rare. The securities themselves are held with depositaries to the order of the clearing systems. The depositaries are usually banks which also act as paying agents to the issue. The ease of settlement has been further facilitated by the introduction of the ACE system, a joint project between the two clearing systems, to match and confirm several times each day trades involving members of both systems. The system, which was called the *bridge,* was amended in 1992 and abolishes a long-standing discrepancy in the delay between processing and the book entry of the stock which benefited Euroclear.

Both clearing systems offer customers both securities and cash accounts in the various currencies, albeit remunerated at low rates of interest. This enables them to finance bond inventories and to lend bonds to intermediaries that are short. Both activities have developed significantly in response to the needs of professional investors who maintain short positions beyond settlement date. However, their bond-lending rates are high and members have turned instead to the sale and repurchase (or *repo*) market in bonds, which is more economical and liquid. Normal practice on settlement of Eurobond transactions is delivery against payment within seven calendar days of the trade. The gradual harmonization of settlement and delivery practice in different markets will lead to common standards to all markets. In this regard, the practices of Euroclear and Cedel have anticipated the proposals put forward by representatives of different markets so as to minimize disruption in the Eurobond market. A shorter settlement delay is anticipated by 1994.

The Rating Agencies

The rating agencies provide an evaluation of the creditworthiness of Eurobonds for the benefit of investors and, indirectly, the issuers.

A rating is assigned to an individual issue, not the issuer, and provides twofold information: (1) an indication of the issuer's overall credit quality and (2) the ability of the issuer to service the particular security as defined by its provisions on status (senior or subordinate), security (unsecured or collateralized), guarantees, or covenants. The rating is thus an assessment of the borrower's creditworthiness, in function of the legal protection afforded to the investor by the particular provisions of the issue.

Ratings help investors to assess an issue in relation to other Eurobonds (and other outstanding securities) according to a single yardstick, regardless of industry, currency sector, or country of origin. The reliability of these credit ratings has led to their widespread acceptance:

1. The range of ratings begin with *AAA* or *Aaa* which is associated with the highest-quality credit and the smallest investment risk. This rating is usually granted to issues by supranational bodies and strong sovereign borrowers.

    AA or *Aa* also denotes a high-grade credit but with a lesser margin of protection than on AAA-rated bonds.

    A-rated bonds are considered good-quality investment-grade debt but vulnerable to some deterioration in the future.

    BBB or *Baa* are considered as medium-grade obligations; certain protections may be absent and the bonds may even have some speculative element. This rating is the lowest grade generally accepted by Euro-investors.

2. Subordinated or convertible debt is usually rated one grade lower than a standard unsubordinated issue.

3. Ratings may be assigned to private placements. This is usually done to comply with the investment criteria of the providers of funds, such as insurance companies and pension funds.

Most borrowers, whether frequent or first-time issuers, want a rating to facilitate the distribution of their issues and to maintain their credit image in the securities markets. Improvements in ratings ultimately lead to lower pricing in subsequent issues. The actual proportion of Eurobonds which are rated has fallen from two-thirds to just over half, partly as a result of the large number of equity-warrant-linked issues from Japanese corporations. These are placed mainly with Japanese institutions and are not considered to warrant a rating.

The rating agencies are for the most part independent of financial institutions and are remunerated by (1) the issuers who pay a fee when applying for a rating and (2) investors and financial institutions who subscribe to the ratings information services published by the agencies.

The international agencies providing ratings on Eurobonds are from the United States and include Moody's Investors Services and Standard & Poor's Corporation. Both perform a significant rating service in the U.S. domestic bond and commercial paper markets; another U.S. agency, Fitch Investors Service, launched a European subsidiary, Euroratings, whose ratings for a while were used on Euro-commercial paper. There is presently no indigenous Europe-wide rating agency for debt of European origin, for want of a structure appropriate for a commercial venture to allay concerns of national or shareholder bias. Presently, plans for European agencies include (1) a merger between a U.K. rating agency, IBCA, and Euronotation from France, and (2) the formation of a German-led consortium to establish a Europe-wide rating agency. Meanwhile, the U.S. agencies fulfill the need for ratings very adequately and are unlikely to face serious challenge until the installation of a single European capital market.

The one other international agency, Mikuni, is Japanese in origin but two-thirds of its customers are from outside Japan. The domestic Japanese rating agencies are backed by financial institutions and include Nippon Investors Services (backed by the securities houses), Japan Credit Rating Agency (the Trust banks), and Japanese Bond Research Institute (a publishing group).

The Stock Exchanges

Public Eurobond issues are listed on one or more stock exchanges. The principal exchanges for issues in U.S. dollars, ECUs, Canadian dollars, and Australian dollars are the Luxembourg Stock Exchange in Luxembourg city and the London Stock Exchange in London.* Issues denominated in European currencies tend to be listed on the home exchange: issues in French francs on the Paris Bourse, Eurosterling in London, Deutsche marks in Frankfurt and Duesseldorf, and Dutch guilder on the Amsterdam exchange.

An Exchange as a Marketplace. Stock exchanges are the traditional forum of securities markets. An exchange was a place where securities dealings were conducted and, by gathering under one roof a significant number of professional dealers, this location became a marketplace. The proximity of dealers ensured that price movements, size of trade, and other stock information was rapidly disseminated throughout the market. Where several dealers were dealing in the same security at the same time, this meant that such dealings were likely to be struck at the same "market-related" price. The dealers collectively brought depth and variety of clientele, and investors dealing through the exchange had indirect access to the widest possible range of counterparties for the execution of their orders. In these latter respects, the exchange provided, in some measure, transparency of price and liquidity. Even today, when most trading in securities is conducted off the floor of the exchange, institutional investors such as pension funds and insurance companies still look to a listing to provide a framework of last resort for trading.

The Eurobond market, unlike domestic securities markets, has no indigenous trading floor or exchange. Although Eurobond issues are mostly listed, there is no statutory or even contractual obligation on dealers to deal on the exchanges. From early on, dealers in Eurobonds dealt direct or over-the-counter (OTC). In this they adopted the practice of the money

---

* The London Stock Exchange, so designated in 1992, was formerly known as the International Stock Exchange of the United Kingdom and the Republic of Ireland.

and foreign exchange markets where the willingness of professional houses to deal relies on (1) a market comprising a large number of active and sophisticated investors, and (2) the widespread use of screen-based price information, in this instance from services such as Reuters and Telerate. These arrangements, however, provided no price transparency, and end investors relied on quotations from several houses to ensure that their dealings were struck at a fair price; but the poor liquidity of many early Eurobond issues meant that quotations might be offered by only one or two houses. The use by market makers of screen-based price information services also varied widely in extent, and could lead to sizable differentials in quotation in the same stock. In either instance the investors' interests were ill-served.

After having defeated voluntary measures at reform for many years, London-based Eurobond houses—which account for over three-quarters of secondary market trading in Eurobonds—were obliged to accept radical changes in their dealing practices in the wake of the U.K. Financial Services Act of 1986.* The absence of price transparency was addressed by the introduction of a check on the terms of each trade shortly after the event. Eurobond market makers and brokers are members of a trade association, the International Securities Market Association (ISMA),† which requires its London-based members to report the terms of their bargains through a trade-matching and confirmation system, TRAX. The ISMA in effect serves as an alternative stock exchange, and is designated a Recognized Investment Exchange under the terms of the FSA 1986. The ISMA, however, is unregulated by any higher authority and instead regulates itself, as it has always done. It has no trading floor, nor does it specify formal listing or issuer reporting requirements, which would merely duplicate the requirement of the official exchanges.

With no practical value for trading purposes, the main benefits of a listing lie in the requirements for admission to the exchange list. European stock exchanges stipulate disclosure of information on the issuer at the time of the issue, and the supply of financial accounts on an annual basis until the final maturity date. Evidence is also required of a system for disbursement of payments of interest and principal, undertaken by the paying agent. For the issuer, there is an element of publicity and prestige in the daily quotation of the price of its outstanding bonds. Issuers with a prior listing of, say, an equity stock, benefit from having to submit fewer listing particulars.

The London Stock Exchange. Listing requirements for Eurobond issues on the London Stock Exchange are set out in an official Stock Exchange publication, the *Yellow Book* (sections 3 and 7) and summarized in a further

---

* London-based intermediaries have to comply with the Financial Services Act 1986, which requires, among other things, systems which ensure price transparency.

† Formerly known as the Association of International Bond Dealers.

publication, the *Blue Book*. The requirements are referred to as *listing particulars* and comprise details of the terms of issue, the issuer's business and markets, a review of the economy of the country of operation, financial statements, and audit certificates, all of which are set out in the Offering Circular (see Chapter 11). The listing particulars are supported by documents relating to the issuer's incorporation, audited accounts, board resolutions, legal opinions, and, where necessary, consents to borrow in foreign currency.*

The issuer applies for a listing through a sponsor who is a member firm of the exchange that prepares the particulars in collaboration with the lawyers to the issue. The contents of the Offering Circular are also sent to an information service, Extel Statistical Services, which prepares a reference card. This reproduces the contents of the Offering Circular and is circulated to subscribers, including all the London-based intermediaries. Where an issuer already has a listing, the Offering Circular is dispensed with, leaving only the requirement for an Extel card. Extel cards are, however, no longer compulsory for London-listed Eurobond issues.

The Luxembourg Stock Exchange.   Listing requirements for a Luxembourg listing are set out in the *Requirements Concerning the Listing of Debt Securities on the Luxembourg Stock Exchange*. The principal requirement is an Offering Circular whose contents are virtually identical to those of a London listing. A shortened Offering Circular is accepted in the case of frequent borrowers. There is no requirement similar to that of an Extel card but, since Extel is regarded as a universal reference system, some issuers send details of the issue to Extel for inclusion in their service.

The Trustee, the Paying Agents, and the Fiscal Agent

The Trustee.   In issues governed by English law, a trustee may be appointed under a trust deed for the specific purpose of representing and protecting the interests of the investors in the issue. The relationship between the issuer and the trustee is contained in the trust deed which sets out:

- the terms and conditions of the issue—in particular, the issuer's covenants and the circumstances in which events of default are declared

- the trustee's duties and powers to act on behalf of investors and in the defense of their interests

* See Chapter 10, "Documentation," for a detailed account of listing particulars.

The trustee is usually empowered to use its discretion to waive technical defaults and agree to minor amendments to the terms of the issue which do not materially prejudice bondholders' interests. This discretion saves time for the investors and the issuer, who negotiates with only one party representing the investors. In case of serious defaults, such as nonpayment, the trustee has the discretion to call for repayment and, if so instructed by more than a certain percentage of bondholders by amount, is obliged to do so. Bondholders' meetings may also be called in the case of passive events of default, such as a change of ownership which materially affects the creditworthiness of the issuer.

The appointment of a trustee is not a legal requirement but is an added comfort to investors. It is more commonly found in issues by corporate and financial institutions than in sovereign or supranational borrowers who tend not to recognize the need for investor protection.

The Paying Agents. The paying agents are banks appointed by the borrower to undertake the receipt and distribution to investors of the interest and principal payments, as well as certain administrative procedures relating to the bonds, including:

- authentication of the temporary single global bond covering the full nominal amount of the issue and delivered on closing date in exchange for the net proceeds

- exchange of the global bond for definitive bonds and authentication of the definitive bonds

- issue of replacement bonds in the case of theft, loss, or destruction

- maintaining records of the issue, including payment against presentation of interest coupons, cancellation of coupons paid, and bond certificates repaid

The issuer usually appoints a principal paying agent and sub-paying agents in the major international banking centers in Europe, e.g., London, Brussels, Luxembourg, Zurich, Geneva, Basle, Frankfurt, and Paris, as appropriate.

The Fiscal Agent. The majority of Eurobond issues dispense with a trustee and, in such instances, a fiscal agent is appointed by the issuer with functions which are synonymous with those of the principal paying agent (that is, undertaking the mechanics of interest and payments to investors and the administration of the bonds on closing and repayment). As in the case of a principal paying agent, the fiscal agent acts only on behalf of the issuer. The bondholders remain unrepresented and, in the case of default, have only a direct and individual—and hence impractical—recourse to the borrower. These arrangements, however, are less costly and therefore more popular with issuers.

The Trade Associations

The International Securities Market Association (ISMA)*

The rapid growth of the Eurobond market gave rise to a need for participants to agree on industry codes of practice and standards. The AIBD (currently known as the ISMA) was launched in 1969 by some 150 banks active in the market to determine market conventions for the trading and settlement of Eurobonds. The organization was established in Zurich as a voluntary trade association and in the course of twenty-five years acquired a membership of 900 institutions from 40 countries, including market makers, brokers, and institutional investors such as central banks and some stock exchanges.

The initial objects of the AIBD were to provide rules of trading, a forum for discussion of market problems, and promotion of standards of market practice and behavior. There followed education courses for dealers and settlement personnel and an information service of current prices published daily and in a weekly booklet also containing basic terms of outstanding issues. From the early 1970s to the late 1980s, the AIBD developed considerably its functions and, from being a trade association, became a fully fledged self-regulatory organization with an exchange mechanism and a mission to promote the development of the market—in particular, automation by computer systems. In 1972, members were invited to adopt electronic market making systems as a means of more efficient and transparent trading. These were seen in many quarters to pose a threat to perceived niches of trading advantage and the proposal was dropped. The introduction of yet another electronic trading system, the AIBD Quotation system, or AIBDQ, was defeated in 1987, but part of the system included a trade matching and confirmation system, TRAX, which was installed in 1989 by London- and Hong Kong-based members to comply with reporting requirements under the United Kingdom Financial Services Act of 1986 (FSA) (see following) and which currently includes 260 members.

Currently, approximately 75 percent of all Eurobond trades in the secondary market are initiated in London and, until the enactment of FSA, the AIBD performed an informal regulatory role of the secondary market. The regulators appointed under the FSA recognized that this was an international market and invited the AIBD—rather than the Stock Exchange—to become a self-regulatory organization for the purposes of the formal regulation of the London-based market players under the terms of the act. Initially, such a status was considered by the AIBD not to be compatible with its position as an international organization. Under threat of national regulation, the AIBD, in order to preserve the professional self-regulatory character of the London-based Eurobond market, became a Designated

---

* Formerly known as the Association of International Bond Dealers (AIBD).

Investment Exchange under the Act. The implication of this status, as far as AIBD London-based members were concerned, was to make compulsory the installation of the TRAX system to introduce some price transparency in their trading, albeit after the event, and, more importantly, to leave the AIBD free to adjudicate on its own authority on trading practices. In these respects, the Association has established standards which are well in advance of many domestic systems.

Following proposals to regulate international trading in equity stocks, which would help members amortize the costs of installing TRAX, the AIBD changed its name in 1992 to the International Securities Market Association (ISMA) to reflect this broader role. Currently, ISMA encompasses four roles: (1) a regulatory body, (2) a trade association, (3) an investment exchange, and (4) a supplier of electronic trading systems. These activities are essentially designed to serve the international securities markets in a relatively regulation-free environment. This has well served the London marketplace which is perceived in some quarters to have developed at the expense of other smaller and less efficient continental European exchanges. The clawing back home, in particular of international equity trading business, is the motivation behind negotiations on the future roles of ISMA within the more restrictive terms of the proposed Investment Services Directive of the EC single market.

The International Primary Market Association (IPMA)

The IPMA was established in 1984 as a voluntary organization of some 50 issuing houses to promote standards in the primary market in Eurobonds in documentation, communication, information disclosure, and syndication practice. Ninety percent of issues now conform to the standards of the association which are set out in a list of "Recommendations."

Recently, IPMA members have been under pressure to make changes which would support efforts to restore profitability to the market. One key area is the stabilization of new issues in the gray market where, under IPMA rules, losses incurred by the lead manager in stabilization were deductible from the underwriting fees due to the co-managers. In cases where market makers have viewed a new issue as tightly priced, short selling has ensued and depressed the price. The lead manager with a duty to stabilize the price of the issue in the immediate after-market has often spent large sums in buying back paper to support the issue. Co-managers who successfully placed their allotments then found their underwriting fees eroded and even disappearing altogether. In the light of these circumstances, the rule on the deduction of stabilization costs has been suspended.

This move was part and parcel of members' attempts to restore sanity in their pricing and to price their new issues "in line" with market yield levels. To support this, new syndication techniques have been introduced from the United States, including take-and-pay allotment practices which are designed to weed out frivolous co-managers without final investor demand and to inhibit gray market dealings in the initial period of primary market distribution. Another technique, also adopted from practice in the U.S. domestic market is the fixed-priced reoffering which requires that new issues may not be sold at prices lower than the issue price for a specified period, thus dispensing with stabilization and eliminating short selling for the period in question. Their implementation, however, is voluntary and their effectiveness depends on (1) the correct or "on-market" pricing of the issue and (2) a voluntary consensus among the issuing houses to accept the price restriction on sales. After a poor trading year in 1990, the intermediaries, under pressure to restore profitability to their underwriting business, concerted themselves in 1991 to use fixed-price reofferings and with some success. Recently, some leading issuing houses, while adhering to a fixed price reoffer launch, have reduced the commissions on new issues or priced them on over-fine terms in a bid to preempt competition. In some instances, the banks have been abetted by the actual issuer who clearly stood to gain from a lower all-in cost of funds. The long-term effectiveness of these practices has therefore yet to be proven, both in terms of (1) a fair reward to issuing houses for their underwriting risk and (2) the interests of investors whose holdings of underpriced issues tend to be less liquid in the secondary market. Ultimately, the very intermediation of issuing houses will come under scrutiny as automated systems for primary distribution relieve intermediaries altogether of their role in what has become an unprofitable activity through continuing excess capacity and ferocious competition.

6
Preparing a New Issue

Questions Confronting an Issuer

The Nature of the Finance Requirement

The theoretical justification for a corporate borrower to raise marginal finance in foreign currency is to finance investment in further capacity which produces returns in foreign currency adequate to service and redeem the issue. However, the cash flow of bond issues rarely matches the cash flow of their projects. The cash flows of new ventures have typically a gradual drawdown of funds and an irregular payback, while the cash flow of a typical plain vanilla fixed-rate issue starts with a single drawdown, followed by level annual or semiannual interest payments and a bullet repayment. The initial capital requirement is more likely to be raised from bank facilities or by issuing paper under a commercial paper program. A bond issue is then launched at a later date to refinance short-term borrowings (or an existing medium-term liability) with the purpose of deferring repayment to a date which may or may not coincide with the time by which the project will have generated substantial positive cash flows. The selection of maturity date of the issue will depend primarily on the yield curve and investor demand for different maturities rather than a specific date in the commercial exploitation of the project. Indeed, rather than be linked to a specific project, the financing is more likely to constitute a component of a pool of debt whose size is dictated by prudent debt:equity ratios and the relative costs of an issue of debt rather than equity.

The rationale of a Eurobond issue by these different categories of borrower is very similar. Although it is commonplace for an issuer to refinance a specific project, as far as the borrower's presentation of its requirement to the market is concerned, the proceeds are normally declared to be applied for "general finance purposes." This statement is at its most accurate in the case of supranational, sovereign, and government-owned borrowers. Similar considerations apply to a bank issuer which is unlikely to apply the proceeds of a bond issue to fund-specific financial assets. Its motivation is more likely to augment a managed pool of below-LIBOR medium-term finance which serves to fund a portfolio of LIBOR-based assets. Sovereign borrowers, too, may undertake many projects, but typically consolidate the finance requirement to present a single general borrowing requirement to the market.

Currency Requirement

A Eurobond issue, however, is often raised in a currency which is foreign to the issuer, yet the end currency requirement is generally for funds denominated in its domestic currency. A Eurobond issue in foreign currency must therefore present a cost or other advantage in relation to (1) a domestic financing or (2) a Eurobond issue denominated in the domestic currency. A foreign currency Eurobond issue creates a foreign currency risk unless the issuer is able to service the debt out of revenues in the same currency. In order to assess this risk, the borrower compares the cost of a domestic issue with that of a Eurobond issue in foreign currency. This requires (1) an assumption of the likely appreciation or depreciation of the currency of denomination against the borrower's domestic currency, and (2) a calculation of the break-even exchange rate before a domestic issue becomes more attractive. Even if the calculation seems to justify an issue in foreign currency, the issuer cannot know in advance of adverse currency movements which may occur later and which would increase the cost of servicing the issue. Many issuers who require an exposure in domestic currency then add a medium-term currency swap to neutralize or alter their currency exposure. Where the end currency of exposure is the borrower's home currency, the all-in cost of financing (including the swap) is compared to that of a domestic issue or a Eurobond issue in the borrower's home currency.

The advantage of a Eurobond issue in foreign currency, however, may not always be one of cost. An issue may be justified in terms of longer maturities, early call options, or issue sizes which are not available in the issuer's domestic bond market. In some cases, access may be restricted, as for example in the case of Italian borrowers, whose domestic bond market is reserved almost exclusively for the State's own debt-financing operations.

Borrowing Strategy

A borrower's borrowing strategy—given an overall amount of debt—seeks to reconcile the borrower's optimum combination of short-, medium-, and long-term debt with the different sources available—such as a commercial program, bond issues, and bank facilities. While the prime concern is one of cost, most borrowers also have an eye to relationships with their fund providers, be it a bank or an investor. Where bond investors are concerned, this is reflected ideally by a program of continual issuance in issue sizes sufficient to develop a broad investor base, to promote liquidity, and generally to establish the name. Few borrowers, however, in European domestic bond markets,* aside from the sovereign, have substantial ongoing borrowing requirements and most issuers, whether from the public or private sector, issue only occasionally and in a size which makes for poor liquidity and hence an indifferent image. This applies also to issuers of Eurobonds, the majority of whom have launched only a single issue motivated as much by prestige as by financial reasons. These issues are poorly traded and add nothing to the image of the borrower or of the market.

Indeed, the weight and depth of the Eurobond market relies mainly on the continual issuance activity of some fifty frequent and sophisticated borrowers. These have issued extensively in a variety of instruments in a wide range of currencies and maturities, and the investors they tap in different Eurobond markets are often complementary or overlap only slightly. The prime example is the World Bank which, in accordance with a policy of borrowing in low-coupon currencies, has issued extensively in the Euro-yen, Euro-Deutsche mark, and Swiss franc bond markets. The concern for such frequent issuers is to achieve an orderly program of issuance to achieve the best cost, to promote liquidity (with a view to achieving even better terms), and to avoid saturating any one market. Thus, the World Bank has ongoing demand for Swiss francs—but to avoid saturating the market and the risk of paying a premium, has launched Eurodollar bond issues linked to cross-currency swaps into Swiss francs to achieve Swiss franc exposure at a cost approximately equal to that of a direct issue. Following a series of issues in a particular market, such a borrower may leave the public bond markets and raise any additional finance requirement through private placements.

Due Diligence

The target investor audience of a new issue is potentially large, and few investors have the time or the facilities to inform themselves independently on the issuer and the proposed bond issue. An important function of the issuing house, therefore, is to inform itself and the investors in the issue and, more importantly, to verify what that information represents about the issuer and the issue. This verification is a process known as *due diligence* and denotes the practical—but not legal—responsibility of the issuing house to the financial community for the standing of the issuer and the

---

* This is not the case in the U.S. domestic bond market, which has a mature corporate bond market offering a regular selection of new issues in a wide range of credit quality.

merits of the issue, and normally entails a visit by representatives of the issuing house, accompanied by lawyers to the issue and independent accountants to the issuer's business premises and an inspection of business operatons and assets.

At its most detailed, the verification is exhaustive and comprises first a complete audit of the borrower's financial condition; comparative financial statements are drawn up including a balance sheet as of a date close to the date of issue. Extensive discussions are held with senior management of the issuer on the constitution, the business, the markets, prospects, and financial standing of the issuer, together with a statement on the use of the proceeds of the issue. The substance of these discussions, together with a description of senior management, statements of the capitalization, financial statements of the previous five years, and present financial condition of the issuer are set out in a prospectus (or "Information Memorandum" or "Offering Circular"). To situate the borrower in its context, the prospectus includes an analysis of the industry in which the issuer is operating and a political and economic report of the country in which it is incorporated and, where applicable, those countries in which its main markets are situated. The prospectus also includes the terms and conditions of the issue (as printed on the actual bonds) and details of the subscription, underwriting, and sale. The sum total of the process of due diligence is not to perform a credit analysis of the issuer or the issue but to provide the fullest and most factual account of the issuer (and, where applicable, the guarantor on whose credit the issue relies). The prospectus is a catalogue on the basis of which investors make their own credit analyses and serves by the same token as one of the main listing particulars of the issue for listing purposes.

The process of due diligence is routine for all issues but in the case of first time issuers, or borrowers which may be recently privatized or amalgamated, or a bank which has written provisions against nonperforming loans, the scrutiny is long and painstaking. Because of the time and expense of the exercise, the work is generally undertaken by one issuing house which is appointed de facto lead manager. For experienced issuers in the Eurobond markct, such as supranational, sovereign, or government agency names, the preparation of a new issue can be abridged and the duration of the entire operation limited to two weeks. The process is accelerated by a fluent relationship between the issuer and the issuing houses which, by maintaining regular contact, are fully conversant with the borrower's requirements, funding strategy, and investor markets. In such instances, the prospectus for a new issue is largely a matter of updating a recent past prospectus.

Proposals

Issuers need to keep informed of market developments, and regular borrowers maintain relationships with half a dozen or so of the leading issuing houses. Their attention is shown by the regular receipt of unsolicited proposals which keep them abreast of market opportunities and pricing and, when the issuer asks for new issue proposals, help to ensure competitive bidding. Each house offers some niche of expertise in placement or in derivative products which together bring the issuer a broad understanding of the marketplace. Borrowers look to issuing houses which demonstrate commitment and competence in the analysis of their borrowing requirement in the submission of timely, cost attractive, and marketable proposals.

The varieties of currency sector and instruments are a unique source of continual arbitrage opportunities. With a choice of some ten major currency sectors, an issuer looks to an issuing house to advise on the choice of market and selection of instrument, and on the pricing and construction of the swap, where appropriate. Given these parameters, the proposal also includes a detailed analysis of:

- bond market conditions in the designated currency sector
- the yield curve, to determine acceptable maturities in the particular sector
- the attraction of the selected currency to investors
- the likely sources and volume of investor demand for the proposed issue

A proposal also includes recommendations for (1) a syndicate of underwriters who enhance the placement and (2) the timing of the launch.

Selecting a Lead Manager

Pressures of market share and poor profitability have contributed to highly variable degrees of professionalism in the preparation of new issues and maintenance of a secondary market. While proposals demonstrate considerable thought and originality, actual issues commonly suffer from incorrect pricing, wrong timing, and inadequate aftermarket support. The selection of a professional issuing house to lead-manage the issue is therefore a critical decision with direct implications (other things being equal) for the primary placement of the issue, secondary market making, the image of the issuer in the market and, ultimately, the cost of subsequent issues.

For many issuers, the selection of a lead manager follows naturally from a scrutiny of proposals. For major borrowers, the choice is simplified by the prior selection of intermediaries with whom they maintain relationships. Other borrowers make clear their willingness to work with any house, and include even frequent issuers with heavy borrowing requirements for whom the criteria of selection is the cheapest cost of funds. However, mandates are not normally awarded on cost alone and potential issuers look for assurances with regard to other criteria, including:

- cohesion of the syndicate: arguments put forward by the lead manager for the coordinated placing of the issue on the terms proposed

- capital commitment of the lead manager: the ability to submit a fully underwritten offer and assurances to support the issue in the primary market by buying in and holding paper in the event of adverse yield movements

- effective market making: the commitment of the lead manager and other banks in the syndicate to making a market, which is essential to promote liquidity and thus support the image of the issuer in the secondary market

- the ability to deliver a wide range of derivative products which may enter into the structure of the issue

- market standing: the ability of an issuing house to demonstrate good relationships with other market participants on which it depends to fulfill the above tasks

Commercial considerations may also enter into the decision. Universal banks solicit both lending business and bond issues, and a cost-effective loan transaction may be acknowledged by the award of a mandate for a new issue.

Questions Confronting an Issuing House

The issuing house is the counterpart of the issuer in the preparation of an issue and its concerns mirror the questions confronting the issuer. The issuing house is continually conveying to the issuer information on interest rates and the bond, swaps, and currency markets. In return, it hopes to obtain an accurate picture of the issuer's general borrowing strategy and the specific finance requirement, for which it will then submit proposals. This is only the beginning of the issuing house's task. Its major contribution lies in bringing to bear its expertise with respect to the presentation of a first-time issuer; the selection of a syndicate with strategic placement; the decision on a timely launch; the deployment of capital in its underwriting function and in support of the issue in the aftermarket; and, ultimately, the maintenance of an effective secondary market. In assessing a borrower's eligibility to issue Eurobonds, the issuing house has to apply further criteria which are peculiar to an international market and which also serve as a guide to the contents of the prospectus.

Country of Origin

The country of incorporation, or home market, of the borrower is a key element of international investors' perception of the borrower. The health of the national economy, fiscal, monetary, budget, exchange control, and industrial policies indicate the quality of the environment in which the issuer operates, its potential performance, and its ability to service a debt in foreign currency. In this regard, the image and performance in the secondary market of issues by the sovereign borrower will have direct impact on investor attitudes to issues by the government agencies or corporate borrowers of that country.

Industry Sector

For private sector corporations, investors—in assessing issuers—will tend to prefer:

- a sector of activity or industry on an international scale.
- an industry with steady growth in world markets (say, computers and telecommunications, which are more prized than oil or automobiles); no sectors with negative connotations, such as armaments.
- the prominence of the borrower within its industry nationally and internationally.
- the quality of profile: a middle-ranking company which has gained prominence through technical innovation and demonstrates high quality of future earnings may achieve pricing terms no worse than those which would apply to a market leader with lackluster performance. Similarly, an issue by a company with a high profile in retail markets may find a better reception than a poorly known government agency of larger size with a better rating.

Financial Standing

The financial strength of sovereign borrowers is assessed according to an economic analysis of country risk. This covers three areas: (1) the domestic economy, including demographic factors; natural resources; industrial structure; central fiscal, monetary, and budgetary policy; and economic indicators of growth, employment, and inflation, (2) the external economy is assessed in terms of visible, invisible, and capital account items on the balance of payments, foreign currency reserves, public and private sector external debt, exchange controls, and exchange rate policy (several ratios are included, in particular that of foreign currency debt-service payments to export earnings, which should not exceed 20 percent), and (3) an account of the domestic political environment and memberships of international political and financial organizations (e.g., UN, IMF, OECD, BIS, and the World Bank). Strength of government and quality of economic management count for as much as the size of the country.*

---

* There is a widely held belief that sovereign borrowers cannot go bankrupt, which rests on the notion that governments have a unique right to raise revenue by levying taxes. This is true as far as domestic obligations are concerned. (There are of course limits to theamount of revenue that can be efficiently raised in this way, at which point governments resort to printing money.) Clearly, however, governments do not have such powers to meet their external debt, where there are many examples of payment defaults by sovereign borrowers.

Borrowers within the public sector other than the sovereign are assessed first in terms of the quality of country risk (see previous). This is followed by a detailed examination of the constitution and status of the borrower—for instance, as a government province, department, wholly owned public utility, or semiprivatized undertaking. The economic assessment covers the scale of activity and source of revenue; the source of repayment of the issue (whether out of the state budget or revenues from commercial undertakings); the ability to purchase foreign exchange to service the debt and the need for consents to do so, if any; and the existence, if any, of a state guarantee and whether this is explicit or implicit in its statutes.

The analysis of the financial standing of an international bank comprises a review of the balance sheet, lending, money market and foreign exchange operations; fee-generating businesses; currency and interest rate exposure; the maturity spread of assets and liabilities and mismatch, lending provisions, loan loss record, contingent risks, and off-balance sheet commitments; and capital adequacy.* The financial standing is expressed in terms of ratios, including shareholders' funds to total balance sheet size, to short- and medium-term debt, and to risk assets. Profitability is expressed in terms of the return on assets and return on equity. Gearing ratios of 20:1 and a net worth of US$100 million are considered acceptable.

Private corporations outside the financial sector are analyzed similarly to banks but with due regard to the industry sector. An analysis will typically review shareholders' funds; short-, medium-, and long-term debt; the maturity profile of outstanding debt; currency exposure; liquidity; investments; capital expenditure; and contingent liabilities. The financial standing is expressed in terms of ratios, including shareholders' funds to debt and current assets to current liabilities. Gearing ratios are much lower than for banks and do not usually exceed 1× capital funds.† The ability to service debt is measured by a debt coverage ratio of net profits to financial charges where a multiple of 2× is generally accepted.

Financial Information

Issuers are required in the course of the due diligence process to provide financial and commercial information which is published in the prospectus

---

* Banks incorporated in OECD member states which sit on the Basle Committee on bank supervision have implemented capital adequacy rules which calculate the capital allocation for each of their risk assets. For many institutions, raising capital in the form of equity has been precluded by poor profitability, and raising long-term subordinated debt, which qualifies as capital, has been expensive and difficult. Thus, many banks have diminished the size of their operations in order to comply with capital adequacy rules.

† Higher ratios, however, would be acceptable for corporates with heavy current assets (e.g., real estate or auto sales companies which operate on higher levels of debt).

to the issue. Eurobond issues have adopted the standards of foreign bond markets which require financial statements to be prepared according to "generally accepted accounting principles" (known as GAAP) and audited by a firm of international standing.

How Is the Issuer Perceived?

In a name-conscious market, the importance of adequate perception of the issuer on the part of issuing houses, market makers, and investors cannot be overestimated. Frequent issuers in the Eurobond market hold regular discussions with issuing houses and investors to acquaint them with their business development and financial requirements. The issuing house then acts as a channel of information which is disseminated to the market as a whole. The investment in management time for the issuer is small in relation to the benefits of sustained or enhanced investor perception. Ideally, these discussions generally support a program of regular issues in a particular currency sector, with a view to attracting the widest range of investors and thus optimizing the placement and cost of subsequent issues.

In the case of first-time issuers, the issuer is introduced to investors through a series of presentations to investors and the financial press (or "roadshow") in major financial centers arranged by the lead manager. A roadshow can span several months of preparation and the presentations should be timed to conclude just before the launch of the issue when their impact is still fresh. The presentations include an account of the borrower's constitution; an analysis of business strategy; a report and comment on the financial condition; the purpose of the borrowing; and, where appropriate, an outline of future approaches to the Eurobond and other capital markets. Where the issuer is a corporate name active in the retail market or luxury consumer goods (such as Benetton or Moët Hennessy), the task of familiarizing the investor with the name is already done; and, while the content of the presentation remains the same, the focus is on the financial condition of the issuer. Subject to correct pricing, such issues tend to sell easily. Conversely, issues by triple-A-rated government agencies have fallen to deep discounts after launch for lack of prior introduction to investor markets.

Underwriting and the Syndicate

Issues of debt and equity securities to a wide investor audience have traditionally been partly or wholly underwritten to protect the issuer from the risks of sudden changes in market conditions, interest rates, or currency expectations which could prejudice investor demand.* A fully underwritten issue guarantees the issuer that all the issue will be bought and that the issuer will receive the full proceeds of the issue at the specified date and on the agreed terms and conditions (as opposed to a nonunderwritten issue which is placed on a "best-efforts" basis—that is, with no commitment from the issuing house as to the amount of bonds sold). Underwriting risks are shared or syndicated among issuing houses acting as underwriters and remunerated by underwriting fees. Eurobond issues are commonly underwritten by a syndicate of issuing houses comprising the issuing house which has won the mandate or "lead manager" and other banks with the designation of "co-manager." Together these constitute the "management group" of the issue.

The lead-manager in selecting banks to make up a management group is concerned with two priorities: (1) sharing the underwriting risk and (2) supplementing its placement. The two roles are connected: the underwriters are expected not to solicit a share of the underwriting risk unless they also bring with them some incremental placement capability through their own distribution systems. Throughout the history of the Eurobond market, there have been abuses of syndication practice, which have resulted in a significant erosion of the value of co-management groups in favor of the lead-manager.† The value added of co-managers has also been reduced by the change in the composition of investor markets from predominantly retail to predominantly institutional. Institutional investors are counted not in millions but in thousands and are known to, and solicited by, all the major issuing houses. As their participation in new issues has become gradually more important, lead managers have tended to preplace issues with institutional investors on a conditional basis prior

---

* Underwriting risks assumed by issuing houses cover mainly financial events within or closely related to the capital markets during the launch of the issue. Events of a political nature or major economic upheavals are not included but are covered in subscription agreements under the heading of a force majeure clause which, if invoked, triggers the cancellation of the issue. The subscription agreement (see Chapter 11) also itemizes representations and warranties on the part of the issuer as well as a "no material adverse change" clause, all of which are deemed to be continuing until the payment date of the issue.

† Traditional co-managers included banks from the Benelux, Switzerland, and the Federal Republic of Germany. Institutions from other countries with little or no investor demand also secured invitations into management groups of Eurobond issues, but their motivation was not to place bonds so much as to demonstrate to the market and to their customers a commitment to the Eurobond market with a view to soliciting mandates to lead-manage issues. These banks then justified their commitment to the lead manager by requests for bonds. Allotments of bonds, for want of investors, were sold back via brokers to other members of the management group. These sales tended to depress the price of the issue, especially when the issue was perceived to be underpriced, and encouraged short-selling by trading houses outside the management group. The downwards pressure on the price then obliged the lead manager to support or stabilize the issue through purchases in the market, and losses incurred on stabilization were deducted from underwriting fees. The participation of derelict co-managers without placement (or a lead manager underpricing an issue) thus penalized other co-managers with genuine placement. These houses then declined to participate and supplied paper to their investor clientele by simply purchasing bonds in the secondary market after the issue price had fallen to a discount.

Chapter Six

to the actual launch. This clearly diminishes the contribution and reward of co-managers who, in the case of a successful launch, find their investor clients to be already satisfied.

The contribution of co-managers is also diminished in retail placement. Genuine retail placement is still brought by the new issues departments of universal banks with substantial retail branch networks. Issues (for example in Australian dollars) were tailored directly to specific retail investor markets (such as Germany). However, these issues tend to be placed entirely by the lead manager within its own network and with only minor support from co-managers whose added value is negligible.

The underwriting function of co-managers has likewise been eroded. Nowadays, proposals for issues commonly include cross currency and interest rate swaps or options whose pricing is sensitive to market changes. To take advantage of the coincidence of market-sensitive opportunities in the bond and swap markets, issuing houses are obliged to submit fully underwritten offers with firm pricing on both the bond issue and the derivative for acceptance within a short time. This often means that issuing houses have to make fully underwritten offers in their sole name. This is the technique of the bought deal, introduced in 1979 at a time of volatile U.S. dollar interest rates when a "window" of favorable bond market conditions had to be seized quickly.* In theory, the lead manager's underwriting risk is syndicated only after acceptance of the terms by the issuer. In practice, the lead manager routinely consults the potential co-managers on pricing prior to submission of such offers and, in so doing, will gauge their interest in the issue. However, the co-managers give no commitment and in the event of adverse yield movements may decline the invitation. If the underwriting risk is poorly syndicated and a large portion unsold, the lead manager must rely on its own financial strength to hold such a portion until such time as the market improves.

The bought deal rapidly became popular with borrowers because it removed the risk of price changes and speeded up the process of launch. Today it is the norm rather than the exception. The assumption of the full underwriting risk by one institution, albeit a short period until the risk is subsequently syndicated among co-managers, implies a heavy initial commitment on the part of the lead manager. The very magnitude of the risk and the relative capital commitment are within the grasp of no more than some 25 major international issuing houses which now have come to dominate the management groups of most Eurobond issues. The task of the issuing house in selecting members of a syndicate is therefore simplified and will be decided on nuances of relationship with the issuer and perhaps returns of earlier favors.

---

* The original motivation behind bought deals was to counter premarket—or gray market—dealing introduced some time before by a leading broker, Ross & Partners, and which effectively dictated the pricing on hitherto "open priced" issues.

Placement

The anonymity of Eurobond investors makes for little detailed discussion between issuers and issuing houses on the placement of their issues. Issuing houses are inclined to be defensive and issuers tend to defer to pretexts of customer confidentiality, so discussions are conducted largely in general terms. Issuers, in any event, are rightly more concerned with a fully underwritten issue and many assume that the lead manager who has submitted a fully underwritten offer must by implication be confident of the effective distribution of the issue.

More experienced issuers do not take such statements at face value and will seek an analysis by the lead manager of the intended placement of the issue. Regular issuers such as the World Bank with an AAA rating are concerned not to saturate their investor markets and insist on careful segmentation, with a view to conserving investor demand for later issues. Thus, carefully orchestrated placement will normally lead to a rapid distribution (and create a somewhat misleading impression that the issue sells itself).

Placement strategy is also valuable in the case of lesser-known or lesser-rated issuers without the World Bank's advantages. Here the professionalism of the lead manager is demonstrated by:

- an initiative to inform and sell to its own investor base (investor presentations, though time-consuming, greatly assist this process).
- the skill in selecting co-managers who bring incremental demand for paper.
- the willingness to buy and hold paper where necessary to ensure orderly and firm primary placement. Dramatic yield movements have on occasion led a conscientious lead manager to repurchase 50 percent or more of an issue and thus carry substantial positions for periods of six or even twelve months. These positions, however, may be hedged through forward purchases of similar instruments or futures contracts, but at some cost.
- the willingness and ability to put together a group of houses, including itself, which will each make a secondary market in the issue and thereby provide liquidity.

Placement strategy must also take account of selling restrictions which regulate the placement of international issues in many jurisdictions. (See Appendix B.) Historically, access to domestic markets was restricted out of concern for:

- the protection of nonprofessional investors from investment in international securities issued on less onerous terms and/or less disclosure of particulars on the issuer
- the control of capital outflows

- reserving access to the domestic markets to domestic, in particular sovereign, issuers
- preventing the holding by residents of any security which could facilitate the avoidance or evasion of revenue taxes

The most notorious sales restrictions are in the U.S. securities markets. These derive from the provisions of U.S. Securities Act, 1933, which impose a registration with the U.S. Securities and Exchange Commission (SEC) of an Offering Circular containing extensive information on the issuer. Issues launched outside the United States are not specifically excluded from the ambit of the act, and sales of nonregistered securities into the United States are a criminal offense entailing sanctions against both issuer and investor. Eurobond issues are exempted from registration provided the placement is "under circumstances reasonably designed to preclude distribution . . . to nationals of the United States." The meaning of this wording has in time been translated into a number of criteria which have been accepted by the U.S. authorities and which are set out in statements contained in the invitation telexes, selling-group agreements, and the Offering Circular relating to the issue. They are as follows:

1. The Bonds are not and will not be registered under the U.S. Securities Act of 1933.
2. Each manager, underwriter, and selling group member undertakes:

- not to purchase bonds for the account of or sell to a U.S. person (exceptions include (1) purchases by U.S. banks acting as underwriters only or (2) an offer through a private placement to a limited number of sophisticated investors who buy for their own account only and agree to abide by the restrictions on resale into the United States).
- not to sell to a U.S. person within 90 days of closing; this is the seasoning period or lapse of time accepted by the SEC to be sufficient for U.S. investors to inform themselves on the issuer and for the issue to "settle."
- to notify any purchaser that the securities are not registered.

Countries such as Canada, Japan, and Australia also regulate the placement of international securities. Placement in the U.K. domestic market is governed by the Financial Services Act 1986 and the Companies Act 1985 which treat Eurobond issues in effect as securities issues intended for professional investors. This implies less stringent disclosure requirements in the listing particulars (the Offering Circular) than for a domestic issue. On the other hand, issues may be distributed only to professional houses. In the case of issues listed abroad, sales to the United Kingdom fall within Part V of Financial Services Act which requires managers and underwriters to undertake:

1. to sell only to persons whose business it is to sell securities

2. to distribute offer documents (the Offering Circular) only to those persons who are professional persons under Article 9(3) of FSA

Eurobond issues listed on the London Stock Exchange still fall within the scope of Part III of the Companies Act 1985 and, in due course, within Part IV of FSA whose import is equivalent to the provisions on non-London-listed issues.

Issuance Procedure

Issuance procedure begins with the award of a mandate for a new issue and concludes with the closing or payment of the proceeds. In the run-up to launch, the management of a new issue draws on the skills of different departments within the issuing house.

Premandate

The corporate finance department, which manages relationships with borrowers, is responsible for ascertaining the finance requirement and designing the issue. The department coordinates with (1) the syndicate department (responsible for syndicating the underwriting risk and launching the issue), the bond traders and salespeople on pricing, and (2) the transaction or financial engineering group on the structure and terms and conditions. Issues are almost invariably underwritten and the syndicate department draws up a draft syndicate of managers. Proposals are submitted to the borrower, including outline terms and conditions, a draft timetable, and syndicate. Internal discussions are held continuously by syndicate department with the bond traders and salespeople to update pricing and to determine their strategy for distributing the securities in the primary market and to amend, where necessary, the composition of the management group. Updated market reports, terms for the issue, and any amendments to the structure are conveyed to the borrower by the corporate finance department who, in the course of their conversations with the borrower, may detect the existence of competitive bids and the degree of their preferment. This guides the extent of the preparatory work prior to the award of the mandate, in particular the drafting by the legal department of the Offering Circular and legal documentation of the issue. In the case of frequent issuers, the preparatory work can be minimal. The syndicate group is drawn up from a list of issuing houses that typically feature in most of the borrower's issues, and work on the Offering Circular and legal documentation generally consist of adapting precedents. In the case of less frequent borrowers, the winner of the mandate will expect to be notified (if only informally) well before launch.

Borrowers generally defer taking a decision to award a mandate until they have several proposals which indicate some convergence of market views. After obtaining internal and/or external approvals, the borrower is ready to proceed and invites banks to update their proposals at daily or shorter intervals. If market conditions are volatile, if the proposed structure includes several products whose price is market-sensitive, or if there is simply competition for the mandate, the issuing houses at this point submit fully underwritten offers (to purchase the issue) on firm pricing terms for acceptance within a short period of 4–12 hours. In such cases the syndicate department approaches the proposed members of the syndicate beforehand to indicate likely terms and conditions, pricing and timing, and to request their interest in joining the syndicate. Firm offers are then submitted in the knowledge of likely, if uncommitted, interest on the part of the managers' group.

The Mandate

On acceptance of terms, the issuing house receives from the borrower a mandate, often only verbal, which appoints the bank formally to put together the proposed syndicate of issuing houses who will jointly commit to subscribe for or underwrite the issue on the specified terms and conditions. The mandate is confirmed by a short telex instructing the lead manager to proceed along the lines proposed. This implies careful drafting by the issuing house of its offer to cover the key terms and conditions and organization of the issue, which typically include the following:

- the issuing vehicle (or issuer) and, where applicable, the guarantor
- the issue amount, currency, maturity, amortization, coupon, or (in the case of an FRN issue) the margin, status, negative pledge, default provisions, denominations, etc.
- pricing of the bonds
- the choice of Stock Exchange
- appointments of the issuing house as lead manager (or "syndicate manager" or "bookrunner"); subsidiary appointments of trustee or fiscal agent and paying agents are also mentioned
- a force majeure clause
- commissions and reimburseable expenses

Postmandate

Following the award of the mandate, the preparation of the issue is split among four different departments working simultaneously within the issuing house.

1. *Syndicate.* Once the composition of the proposed management group has been agreed with the issuer, the syndicate department telephones the issuing houses concerned and invites them to become co-managers subject to accepting (1) the outline terms and conditions of the issue and (2) their level of underwriting commitment. The issue is actually "launched" when telexes are sent to the managers, confirming the terms and conditions and the invitation to underwrite (see Appendix B for draft invitation telex). A response is requested within hours and, on acceptance, the terms of the invitation and its acceptance are confirmed by the co-managers by telex.

Further invitations may be sent to banks acting as underwriters with lesser underwriting commitments than the co-managers; these subsidiary commitments, when received, are then applied in pro rata reduction of the underwriting commitments of the management group.

Co-managers and underwriters are also requested to indicate their final demand for bonds in the new issue. The management group and other issuing houses and intermediaries approached by the lead manager who express demand for bonds are members of the selling group.* The response time in this instance is longer to enable selling group invitees and investors unfamiliar with the issuer to analyze the credit risk and the terms of the issue. Once it has received all indications of demand, the lead manager then confirms individual allotments of bonds to selling group members by telex, which are subject to the signing of the underlying subscription or purchase agreement entered into by the management group and the issuer (see Appendix C).

2. *Documentation.* The most time-consuming task of the documentation group is the drafting, printing, and proofreading of the Offering Circular. Wherever possible, precedents are drawn upon and updated. In the case of infrequent or first-time issuers, the preparation of the Offering Circular will have begun several weeks prior to launch.

The documentation group also drafts the legal agreements relating to the primary distribution of the issue, including the subscription or purchase agreement, agreement among managers, underwriting agreement, and selling group agreement, all of which are standard and vary little from issue to issue. The drafting of the terms and conditions of the bonds is more time-consuming. The terms of plain vanilla bond issues are fairly standard and vary in few respects such as status (subordination), representations (constitution and ownership), and covenants (financial ratios). Bond issues with warrants attached, index-linked issues, convertibles, deferred payment bonds, and asset-backed securities

---

* The selling group historically comprised not merely the management and the underwriting group but also a more numerous group of securities houses having end investors with demand for the issue. The change in the composition of the investor market and the practice of bought deals and preplacing of issues have all but made the selling group redundant.

necessitate extensive additional documentation. Application is made for the listing of the issue (and, where applicable, of any securitized options such as equity warrants attached to the bonds). Supporting documentation is finalized and sent to the exchange, including the preliminary and final Offering Circular, the legal agreements, borrower resolutions, official consents, and specimen bonds. Agreements are also drafted relating to the appointment of (1) a trustee or fiscal agent and (2) the paying agents.

3. *Signing and Closing.* Signing refers to the signing of the purchase or subscription agreement which may take place as early as 10 working days following launch. Traditionally, this was a formal occasion; however, the volume of new issues is such that most signings are now conducted at the offices of the issuing house using powers of attorney from the co-managers. The signing commits the management group to subscribe to the totality of the issue and provides, in particular, for the payment of the proceeds of the issue on the closing date. The managers' commitments are protected until the closing date by a force majeure clause which relieves them of their obligations in the event of a major economic, political, or financial crisis which would have a material adverse effect on the primary distribution of the issue.

The closing, or payment of the proceeds, follows later, usually within another fortnight and is set as a function of the period required to complete the placement of the issues with end investors. During this delay, the documentation group gathers documents to be produced immediately prior to the transfer of the proceeds of the issue to the borrower. Key documents include the trust deed or fiscal agency agreement, paying agency agreements, confirmation of admission of the bonds to a listing, legal opinions, exchange control consents where required, and a certificate of no material adverse change.

4. *The Settlements Office.* This department opens clearing accounts with the selected clearing system(s) and appoints depositaries—usually the principal paying agent—to hold the securities in safe custody. Instructions are sent to all subscribers to the issue to pay the lead manager acting as collecting agent. The closing of the issue is evidenced by a telex from the lead manager instructing the payment of the proceeds to the issuer, against receipt by the clearing system of a temporary global bond, for the full nominal amount of the issue. Further instructions are sent to credit individual clearing accounts of other issuing houses and investors that have bought bonds against receipt of subscription monies by the lead manager. Further payment instructions may be required in the event of an interest rate or currency exchange being attached to the issue.

Gray Market. At the time of launch—or even beforehand—premarket, or gray market, dealings in the issue may commence among trading houses unconnected with the issue. Gray market dealings take place in the period between the launch and closing dates, and trades are termed on an "if and when issued" basis, allowing for the possibility of the issue being canceled, under the force majeure clause of the subscription agreement. If necessary, the lead manager intervenes to buy or sell bonds to intermediaries dealing in the gray market with a view to stabilizing the price. The issue is said to be in the secondary market following the closing date.

7
Introduction to Pricing a New Issue

Elements of Pricing

Pricing a fixed-income public issue is one of the critical functions of an issuing house—and the one which is also the most criticized. Leading intermediaries with long experience of Eurobond and derivative markets bring into play their skills to (1) read a market, (2) structure and price an issue, (3) anticipate market changes and interpret their impact on pricing. Yet pricing is commonly flawed because competition induces lead managers to underprice in the dubious interest of market share and rarely in the interests of their issuer or investor clientele. However, the problem of mispricing through pressure of competition is not the remit of this chapter. Issues are also vulnerable to an incorrect reading of the market; their structure is often too complex and makes for poor distribution; and market developments may not be anticipated or may be ignored. This results in underpriced or even overpriced issues—with similar damaging consequences for the issue in the secondary market.

The pricing of a bond issue is its most visible aspect and is therefore a matter for particular care. The process of pricing involves not merely the collection of information, but also an evaluation of those facts and the exercise of an instinct for the behavior of the market which is neither taught nor acquired. Clearly, the issuer and the investors have a vital interest in correct pricing, but it falls primarily on the issuing house to form a view which it then has to back up by committing substantial amounts to underwriting the issue.

Factual Information

Outline Borrowing Requirements. The borrower's funding requirement determines the amount to be raised over a certain period and it is left to the issuing house to submit, from time to time, proposals for issues whose structure may vary according to market circumstances. The borrower will normally indicate to the issuing house for each issue details such as the currency of exposure, amount, maturity range, call option, and target cost of funds. The issuing house then determines the most cost-effective route, including market opportunities for issuing in other currencies, the availability of currency and interest rate swaps and, in the case of corporate borrowers, the merits of a convertible issue or an issue with equity warrants attached.

Outstanding Issues and Spread Analyses. Before attempting to price the structure, the issuing house examines the market's assessment of the borrower's outstanding issues. This is the most reliable, though not necessarily sufficient, guide to pricing a new issue. An analysis will also routinely cover trading history, quality of market makers, liquidity, the perceptions of professional and end investors, and yields on outstanding issues. Benchmark issues are now widespread in most Euro-currency sectors, so the analysis of yields deals essentially in terms of the "spread" over the yield of the benchmark issue. Where there is no Euro-issue outstanding with a maturity similar to that of the proposed offering, an analysis is prepared of:

- the spreads of other Euro-issues by the borrower in the same currency but in different maturities
- the spreads of issues by equivalently rated borrowers in the same currency and in the same selection of maturities
- the spreads of other Euro-issues by the borrower in different Euro-currencies against the appropriate benchmark
- the spreads of domestic issues by the borrower against the sovereign borrower of its domestic market
- where the sovereign also has Euro-issues outstanding in the proposed currency, the spreads of any such issues against the benchmark issues in that currency

Not all the spreads information will be available for any one borrower, and some yield information may also be distorted by the operation of prepayment (or call) options and sinking funds built into existing issues. Generally, however, it is possible to ascertain from the analysis the spread and hence the yield at which the new issue should be offered.

Market Conditions. A review of market conditions is essential as it situates the pricing of the issue in relation to what is going on in other markets. This review takes account not only of Eurobond markets but government bond markets (where, for example, a heavy schedule of new issues could depress the market) and foreign exchange markets (where forthcoming economic announcements could have an impact on the currency and hence the appetite of foreign Eurobond investors). The review may also cover derivative markets such as swaps and even expectations in stock markets (where the redemption structure of the issue may be linked to the performance of a stock index). Other relevant information may include credit ratings of Euro-issues by the borrower and by the sovereign of its country of origin; economic information such as inflation, growth, balance of payments, and foreign exchange reserves of the country in whose currency the issue is to be denominated. The issuing house also takes account of general market activity which can influence investor demand including:

- current Euro-issuance volume in the currency of exposure and in other currency sectors
- reflows of capital to investors (through payments of interest and principal on outstanding bond issues) in the currency of exposure and other currency sectors

Perception of the Issuer. By their continuous trading activity in the market, issuing houses gather factual and subjective information which may— or may not—corroborate their research on a borrower's existing issues. The input of the bond traders and the bond sales force is vital. Traders have continuous contact with professional investors and the sales force with institutional and retail end investors and will canvass both overtly and discreetly their interest in structure and pricing of particular new issues. This may reveal areas where some education is required and will help to refine the structure, for example to meet demand for a particular maturity or coupon. * In the case of a first-time issuer, an enquiry into the market's perception of the issuer may cover:

- perception of the borrower by its competitors within its own industry, nationally and internationally.
- the perception of the issuer within its domestic financial markets in relation to other borrowers.
- the perception of the borrower, if any, in the Euromarkets. Prior activity by way of a syndicated loan is a useful indicator. In the absence of a track record, the lead manager may arrange a series of investor presentations to inform investors and professional houses

In the case of an existing issuer, the perception of the borrower is already molded and reflected in the performance of outstanding issues. An issue that trades poorly may be the result of lack of support at launch, too small an issue

* Japanese institutional investors, keen to boost their current income, bought new issues with higher coupons—even at the cost of a higher issue price—to produce the same redemption yield as a conventionally priced issue with an issue price of par.

size, wrong timing, or the withdrawal of the market makers. The resulting lack-luster perception of the issuer is not irreversible, and a change of perception may be achieved at the cost of a more expensive issue and a determined effort on the part of issuer and issuing house and market markers to restore the image of outstanding issues by buying back paper and promoting liquidity.

Evaluation

The next step is to evaluate the factual information and subjective percep-tions of the issuer. In the past, pricing occasionally took on the character of informed guesswork, as in the case of the early ECU issues. In mature mar-kets, however, proposals and offers for new issues are noted more for their convergence than differences on pricing. This is only natural, since issuing houses exchange market views, and market makers by definition concur on price when they transact a bond trade.

The evaluation process does not fall on the issuing house alone. Experi-enced issuers are able to gather a perception of themselves and their out-standing issues from other intermediaries and challenge the proposals they receive. Ideally, a relationship of trust develops between issuing house and issuer so that market information is exchanged freely and the final decision emerges by common agreement. The remainder of this chapter attempts to cover the thought processes used and steps which may be encountered in this calculation.

Case Study: Dashitall Carpet Baggers Ltd.

Dashitall Carpet Baggers Ltd. (DCB) ranks 14th among the top 20 U.K. industrial companies. It is a leader in its field in the United Kingdom, has strong commercial relationships worldwide, and has several major subsidiaries in continental Europe. It is a regular issuer in the Swiss franc bond market where it commands best terms for corporate borrowers. It has not issued in sterling in either the domestic or Euro-markets and none of its outstanding issues are rated.

The company has recently completed a series of acquisitions in the United States. These were financed by bank lines for a total of US$165 million, which DCB now proposes to refinance with medium-term debt. A flow of U.S. dollar-denominated receivables and a low U.S. dollar interest rate structure point to a Eurodollar issue. The borrower would prefer a bullet repayment (i.e., without amortization) and no early repayment option is sought.

The Eurodollar bond markets are presently buoyed by U.S. economic data above expectations; these have helped the U.S. dollar, which has been trading strongly for some time in the foreign exchange markets, on a trend of improving balance of trade figures—but there is some question as to whether or not this performance can be sustained.

The primary market has quickly absorbed a recent ten-year Euro-U.S. dollar issue by Electricité de France (under the guarantee of the French Republic and carrying an AAA rating). A spate of five-year Eurodollar issues was also quickly placed, notwithstanding tight terms dictated by the accompanying swaps. There has been no issuance for some time in a seven-year maturity.

Bond markets conditions are generally favorable. Cost-attractive swaps are available from the Australian dollar, but in maturities up to five years only. The Canadian dollar bond market is also buoyant, but is expecting several issues by Canadian Crown agencies.

DCB has a creditable track record in the international bond markets but no Eurodollar issues to its name. For guidance on the magnitude of spread the market may require, we turn to issues by similar borrowers from both the United Kingdom and overseas, as follows:

- DCB's major international competitor is a U.S. company, Kellogue Kravitz (KK), a conglomerate that has launched several Eurodollar issues, one of which has approximately seven years remaining life. The issue has a call two years from now and is currently trading at a yield equivalent to a spread of 58 basis points over seven-year U.S. Treasury stock. The company is well regarded but results are unexciting and DCB is perceived to be encroaching on KK's traditional markets.

- In the United Kingdom, DCB has no peer in its range of activity, but related businesses are undertaken by Consolidated Industrial (CI). The group has grown rapidly through acquisitions and owns several luxury brand names. It presently ranks 29th in the top 50 leading U.K. companies. The company successfully launched its first Eurodollar issue earlier in the year; the issue has six and three-quarter years remaining life, no call, and presently yields 50 basis points over U.S. Treasury stock.

- Some larger U.K. companies have also issued Eurodollar bonds, and those outstanding with a seven-year maturity trade within a range of 48 to 58 basis points over U.S. Treasury stock.

Evaluation. The KK issue is trading at a relatively high spread. This may be accounted for by numerous factors at the time of the launch of the issue, or subsequently in the secondary market. Some such factors are as follows:

1. At the time of launch
   - a poor lead-manager and/or weak syndicate
   - pricing which was too fine
   - an issue size not large enough to sustain liquidity
   - the nature of credit: KK is a conglomerate and therefore more difficult to assess
   - poor timing

2. In the secondary market
   - a poor trading history, leading some market makers to withdraw
   - deterioration of the credit or image of the business
   - the likelihood of exercise of the call option discouraging investors from buying as interest rates fall

   Consolidated Industrial enjoys a better perception which may result from the following:

- the high profile of its luxury brand names
- strong trading expectations following its acquisitions
- correct pricing at launch; a strong syndicate and firm placing
- large issue size
- committed market-making by several houses
- the bond's status as a good "switch" instrument

The trading performance of the KK and CI issues may be accounted for in part by questions of syndicate, the borrower's constitution, the timing of the issue, its size, or the market's perception of the issuers. The more certain factors behind the poor trading spread of the KK issue are (1) the borrower's call option—a feature which tends to inhibit investor demand, (2) its conglomerate status which makes it less easy to analyze, and (3) the perception that the company is losing market share. The CI issue, on the other hand, has fared better in spite of being a smaller group. The issuer's brand names are highly visible to potential retail investors. In credit terms, the company is highly regarded and enjoys a market perception normally given to companies of larger size.

DCB's track record in the international bond markets is limited but very positive. The fact that its issues in the Swiss franc bond market have been well received indicates that DCB enjoys a good perception in at least one major bond market. Swiss financial institutions manage large U.S. dollar-denominated portfolios and, given favorable bond market conditions, there is likely to be good demand for a Eurodollar issue by DLB from these houses, which are already familiar with the name. This points firmly to the inclusion of Swiss issuing houses in the management group.

These observations on the perception and track record of DCB and related issuers enables the lead manager to attempt an outline of the structure of a Eurodollar issue for DCB as follows:

Amount: For a first issue in the Eurodollar sector, the issue size should be sufficient to promote liquidity, but not so much as to strain a smooth placement process. This suggests an issue size of US$100 million with a possibility of an increase to US$150 million if the initial placement is well received.

Maturity: The clear choice of maturity is seven years. Market conditions would permit a longer maturity to be chosen; however, for a first-time issue a shorter maturity is preferable.

Yield Spread: An aggressive spread would be 50 basis points over U.S. Treasury stock. This could be justified by:

- the strong perception of DCB's business
- the size and ranking of the company
- the identification of substantial demand from at least one major investor market
- good bond market conditions

Although DCB is larger than CI, it does not enjoy the same high profile, and a yield level of 50 basis points would be more appropriate for subsequent issues. For a first-time issue, a small premium is suitable to attract investor interest. This points to a spread of, say, 52 basis points.

These decisions enable the lead manager to formulate detailed pricing as follows:

U.S. Treasury yield (assumption):	8.765% semiannual
DCB spread:	0.52% semiannual
DCB yield:	9.285% semiannual or, using the conversion formula on p. 72, 9.50% annual

The investor will therefore be offered a seven-year DCB Eurodollar bond at a price to yield 9.50 percent annual. The pricing is expressed in terms of the issue price—normally 100 percent or par—and a coupon in this instance of 9½ percent per annum (annual).

With the issue price fixed at par, the issuing house structures its proposal to the issuer in the form of an offer to "buy" the issue from the issuer at a lower price with a view to "selling" bonds in turn to investors at the issue price of 100 percent and thereby generating a profit on the distribution of the issue to investors. In this instance, the issuing house buys in at 98¾ percent. The difference between the buy-in price and the issue price of 100 percent is the selling concession, which in this instance is 1¼ percent flat. In addition to the *selling concession*, the issuing house charges fees for managing the issue and for making an underwriting commitment. In the case of a seven-year Eurodollar issue, these are as follows:

Management fee:	¼% flat
Underwriters' commission:	⅜% flat

The selling concession, management fee, and underwriting commission are all expressed as percentages of the issue amount and are paid by deduction from the proceeds of the issue. In percentage terms, the total commissions amount to 1⅞ percent and, assuming an issue price of 100 percent, the issuer will receive net proceeds of 100 percent less 1⅞ percent or 98⅛ percent of the issue amount.

In competitive bidding, issuing houses may forgo some—or even all—of the fees so as to lower the all-in cost of the issue. In the present example, if the borrower forgoes the selling concession of 1¼ percent, bonds would then be bought and sold without profit at 98¾ percent. However, at a price of 98¾ percent, the coupon required to yield 9.50 percent is lower. Using the HP-12C we key in:

$n = 7$
$PV = 98.75$
$i = 9.50$
$FV = -100.00$

and, solving for *PMT*, we derive –9.2475 percent for the coupon. Thus a redemption yield of 9.50 percent is derived from bonds with a coupon of 9.2475 percent and a price of 98¾ percent. If the coupon is rounded up to 9¼ percent, we key in 9.5 CHS PMT and solving for *i*, we obtain a redemption yield of 9.5026 percent, or slightly above the desired level of yield.

In the case of DCB, the lead manager decides, under pressure of competition, to forgo the selling concession and to lower the coupon from 9½ to 9¼ percent. The issue is said to be priced "at the selling concession." By joining the syndicate, other members of the management group then rely solely on the management fee and underwriting commission for their remuneration on the issue.

The issue's commission structure will still include a selling concession of 1¼ percent but the management group forgoes the benefit of the concession and sells the bonds at 98¾ percent so as to give the investor the same yield of 9.50 percent at the lower coupon of 9¼ percent. The management group is thus out-of-pocket and the investor is no better or worse off. The only party to benefit is the issuer, who benefits from the lower coupon.

Expenses.   Expenses on the issue include the following items (and reflect typical current market costs):

1. *Paying Agency.*   Assume US$50 million in US$1000 denominations, and US$50 million in US$10,000 denominations.

Total number of bonds:	55,000
Coupon charge p.a.:	US$0.07 per coupon payment or US$3850 (p.a.) payable in arrears
Redemption charge:	US$0.70 per bond or US$38,500 flat on redemption
Authentication:	US$2000 flat on delivery of bonds
Administration:	US$1000 (p.a.) payable in arrears

2. *Listing.*   US$10,000 flat payable in advance

3. *Trustee.*   US$4000 (p.a.) payable in advance

4. *Printing, fees of lawyers to the managers, traveling, and managers' out-of-pocket expenses.*   These are reimbursed up to a negotiated maximum amount, say US$60,000 flat

Detailed pro forma terms of the issue may then be set out, as follows:

Borrower:	DCB Ltd.
Guarantor:	None
Amount:	US$100 million

Maturity:	7 years
Coupon:	9¼% p.a. annual
Issue price:	100%
Amortization:	Bullet repayment on final maturity date
Issuer's call option:	None
Listing:	London
Denominations:	US$1000 and US$10,000
Form:	Bearer securities
Status:	Direct, unconditional, and unsecured obligations ranking equally with all senior unsecured debt of the issuer.
Negative pledge:	Undertaking not to enhance the status or security of any outstanding senior unsecured debt of the issuer without granting the benefit of such enhancement to the bonds under the issue.
Events of default:	Standard including cross-default
Rating:	Applied for and expected to be AA
Tax status:	All payments of interest and principal to be made free of deduction or any withholding. In the event that such withholding or deduction is required under the laws of the jurisdiction of the issuer, the issuer will pay additional amounts which, after further withholding or deduction, will fully compensate the holders as if no such deduction or withholding has been levied. In the event that such a requirement is imposed on the issuer, the issuer shall have the option to redeem the issue on 30 days notice.
Event-related investors early repayment options (event risk):	In the event that: (1) DCB is taken over by a predator, *or* (2) DCB takes over another company, *or* (3) DCB makes shareholders a substantial distribution out of earnings retained profits or reserves, *or* (4) DCB implements a repurchase program of its own shares, *or* (5) DCB distributes assets for an amount equivalent to half the net worth of DCB; *and* the effect of any one or several of such events is (1) to reduce the rating of the issue from AA to BBB or (2) in the opinion of the managers to reduce substantially the ability of DCB to service its obligations under the issue; *then* the holders shall have the right to request immediate redemption of their bonds under the issue at 100 percent.
Commissions:	1⅞% flat
Yield:	9.25% (at issue price) 9.50% (at 98¾% or after deduction of full selling concession)

Table 7-1. Cash Flow of Dashitall Carpet Baggers Ltd. (%)

	End of year							
	0	1	2	3	4	5	6	7
Principal	+100,000,000*	—	—	—	—	—	—	-100,000,000†
Interest	0	-9,250,000	-9,250,000	-9,250,000	-9,250,000	-9,250,000	-9,250,000	-9,250,000
Commissions (Mgmt. fee, Underwtg. comm. + selling con.)	-1,875,000							
Paying agency	—	-3,850	-3,850	-3,850	-3,850	-3,850	-3,850	-42,350
Paying agency authentication and administration	-2,000	-1,000	-1,000	-1,000	-1,000	-1,000	-1,000	-1,000
Listing	-10,000	—	—	—	—	—	—	—
Trustee	-4,000	-4,000	-4,000	-4,000	-4,000	-4,000	-4,000	—
Reimbursable expenses	-60,000	—	—	—	—	—	—	—
Cash flow	+98,049,000	-9,258,850	-9,258,850	-9,258,850	-9,258,850	-9,258,850	-9,258,850	-109,293,350

* Plus sign denotes incoming payment.
† Minus sign denotes outgoing payment.

Cost of Funds

Cost of Funds Inclusive of Commissions and Reimbursable Expenses

This figure is commonly used to express the all-in cost of the issue and takes account of the coupon, the commissions of 1⅞ percent flat on the issue amount, and the reimbursable managers' expenses. On the DCB issue, the commissions amount to US$1.875 million and the reimbursable expenses to US$60,000, or a total of US$1.935 million. The issuer then receives notional net proceeds of: US$100,000,000 − US$1,935,000 = US$98,065,000, or 98.065 percent of the issue amount.

Using the HP-12C, we key in:

$PV = 98.065$
$n = 7$
$PMT = -9.25$
$FV = -100.00$

and solve for i to obtain a redemption yield equivalent to the all-in cost of 9.6428 percent per annum annual.

Cost of Funds Inclusive of Commissions, Expenses Listing, Trustee, and Paying Agency

The various additional costs impact at different times and it is advisable to draw up a cash flow (see table) and calculate the total cost of funds using the HP-12C through an IRR calculation. Using the HP-12C, key in as follows:

98,049,000, g, CFo
9,258,850, CHS, g , CFj

The payment of 9,258,850 occurs six times and the in-putting of the figure for the IRR calculation may be abridged by keying in:

6, g , Nj

The last payment is keyed in as follows:

109,289,350, CHS, g, CFo

and solving for IRR, we key in:

f, IRR

to obtain 9.658348 percent per annum annual.

In the course of preparing the issue, DCB has taken a view of the likely favorable course of interest rates and decided to convert the interest base of the funding from U.S. dollar fixed to U.S. dollar floating rate using a 6-month LIBOR base.

The lead manager of the issue obtains a swap quotation from a counterpart C. In the U.S. dollar "rate swap" market, this quotation is typically expressed as:

6-month LIBOR v. U.S. Treasuries plus 92/102 in 7 years

This means that C will enter into a 7-year exchange of interest rate obligations and either make fixed-rate payments at a rate equal to 92 basis points or receive payment at 102 basis points over the redemption yield on 7-year U.S. Treasury stock. In either case the countervailing payment would be 6-month U.S. dollar LIBOR flat.

In the case of DCB, the issuer wishes to neutralize the fixed-rate obligations under the bond issue and so, under the swap, it receives fixed-rate payments (that is, at a rate of 7-year U.S. Treasury stock yield plus a margin of 92 basis points). (*Note:* U.S. Treasury yields and the swap margins are expressed in semiannual bond terms.) The swap can then be structured so that the fixed-rate payments to DCB coincide with the bond coupon payments (that is, annually on the anniversary of the issue in arrears). In exchange for receiving fixed-rate payments, DCB is required under the swap to make payments to the counterpart at a floating rate equal to the 6-month London Interbank Offered Rate for U.S. dollar deposits ("6-month US\$ LIBOR"). The first such payment is made six months after the date of the start of the swap, which is generally fixed to coincide with the payment, or closing, date on the issue.

Accordingly, the fixed-rate payment made to DCB by C may be expressed as follows:

U.S. Treasury yield (assumption):	8.765% p.a. semiannual
Margin:	0.92% p.a. semiannual
Total:	9.685% p.a. semiannual

or, converting into annual using the formula on p. 72, 9.9195% per annum annual.

The effect of the swap is to add two further and separate cash flows. (The issuer is by no means relieved of its debt service obligations to the investors under the issue.) Leaving aside expenses related to the issue, the issuer's cash flows take the following form:

End of year	Bond		Swap	
0	+98,125,000	—	—	
1	−9,250,000	+9,919,500	−6 month US\$ LIBOR	
2	−9,250,000	+9,919,500	−6 month US\$ LIBOR	
3	−9,250,000	+9,919,500	−6 month US\$ LIBOR	
4	−9,250,000	+9,919,500	−6 month US\$ LIBOR	
5	−9,250,000	+9,919,500	−6 month US\$ LIBOR	
6	−9,250,000	+9,919,500	−6 month US\$ LIBOR	
7	−109,250,000	+9,919,500	−6 month US\$ LIBOR	

IRR (bond issue alone): 9.630462%

Clearly, the fixed-rate receipts under the swap exceed the payments under the bond issue:

Receipts: 9.9195% annual

Payments: 9.6305% annual

Surplus: 0.2890% annual, or 28.9 basis points per annum (annual bond basis)

The floating-rate cash flow obligation of 6-month LIBOR is effectively reduced by this annual surplus. Unlike a fixed-rate issue, LIBOR interest payments are calculated on a money market basis (see section on FRNs on p. 34). To derive the end cost of funds to DCB, we convert the swap surplus (expressed in annual bond terms) into money market terms, as follows:

9.9195 annual = 9.6850 semiannual

9.6305 annual = 9.4092 semiannual

Surplus = 0.2758 or 27.58 basis points semi annual

The surplus expressed in semiannual terms is converted to money-market as follows:

$$27.58 \times \frac{360}{365} = 27.20$$

Thus DCB's cost of floating-rate funding is expressed as:

6-month US$ LIBOR − 27.20 basis points

The actual cash flows can be managed in one of several ways. DCB may choose to retain all three cash flows as set out here. Alternatively, were DCB to require the fixed-rate receipts under the swap to match exactly the fixed-rate obligations under the issue, then the fixed-rate receipts under the swap would be reduced to the level of the coupon payments on the issue and, similarly, DCB's obligation under the swap to pay floating-rate interest at 6-month U.S. dollar LIBOR would be diminished by 27.20 basis points.

A third possibility permits DCB to match its debt-service obligations under the bond issue to pay LIBOR flat under the swap and to commute the annual surplus into a single payment by C to DCB on the start date of the swap, which normally coincides with the payment date of the bond issue. To calculate the amount, we create a fictional cash flow (with the same IRR of 9.630462) as the bond issue but with the first payment unknown, as follows:

End of year	
0	X?
1	9,919,500
2	9,919,500
3	9,919,500

End of year	
4	9,919,500
5	9,919,500
6	9,919,500
7	109,919,500

IRR: 9.630462%

Using the HP-12C, we derive the first payment, by keying in:

$FV = -100$
$n = 7$
$i = 9.630462$
$PMT = -9.9195$

and solving for PV, we derive 101,424,444.

Thus, on a bond with interest payments at 9.9195 percent and an IRR of 9.63 percent (as in DCB's issue after commissions), the closing payment would have been US$101,424,444, or an excess of US$3,299,444 against the net proceeds of DCB's issue of US$98,125,000. The single payment by C to DCB is therefore US$3,299,444.

The same result can be obtained by a present value calculation of the interest payment surpluses of US$669,500 per annum (US$9,919,500 − US$9,250,000) discounted at 9.630462 percent. Using the HP-12C, we key in:

$PMT = 669,500$
$n = 7$
$i = 9.630462$
$FV = 0$

and solve for PV to obtain −3,299,444.

The motivation of commercial banks and corporate issuers such as DCB to launch fixed-rate issues arises in most cases only because of the attractive below-LIBOR funding derived from attaching a swap to the debt service of the issue. Swaps quotations are driven by demand and supply for fixed- or floating-rate funding and, in currency sectors where there is an active government bond market, these are generally priced in terms of a spread or margin over the redemption yield of government stock of equivalent maturity. This applies to U.S. dollar, sterling, French francs, Canadian and Australian dollar rate swaps. The swap may not always produce below-interbank rates, in which case the issuer may resort directly to issuance in the relevant market.

Exercise: The issues and the names of issuers used in this study are fictitious.

Crédit Vinicole (CV) has recently been set up by the French Government under statute to finance wine growers in France. It has an identical constitution to Crédit Communal whose senior Eurodollar bond debt carries an AAA rating. However, these issues trade at a higher spread over U.S. Treasury stock than other French AAA-rated

182

Euro-issues which carry the guarantee of the French Republic (e.g., Electricité de France and Crédit Foncier).

The launch of Crédit Vinicole was heralded in the press and by investor presentations held in Paris, London, Frankfurt, Geneva, and Zurich in anticipation of issuance in the Eurobond market.

Under a policy of complementing its core business, which is essentially cyclical, CV has created a portfolio of short-term U.S. dollar assets in excess of US$450 million. Until now these have been funded by six-month roll-over borrowings in the Eurodollar money markets. The business is now tried and tested, and CV proposes to refinance a substantial figure through a medium-term fixed-rate Eurodollar issue and a swap into floating-rate U.S. dollars. Discussions with the rating agencies have indicated that a AAA rating would be likely.

The Eurodollar market is buoyant but has seen a spate of issues in longer maturities which are showing signs of strain; interest rates are stable but several new issues are trading at or "outside" their fees. Among these was a 10-year Eurodollar issue by Société Régionale des Chemins de Fer Bretons (SRCB) guaranteed by the French Republic. This is a popular name, well established in the market, whose issues have an AAA rating. The issue was priced at 55 basis points over U.S. Treasury stock. The market considered the pricing tight, and the price in the aftermarket reflects a redemption yield of 59 over U.S. Treasury stock.

Crédit Communal's outstanding Eurodollar issues are trading at 62 over U.S. Treasuries (7-year maturity) and 69 over U.S. Treasuries (10-year maturity). Neither of the issues was for a large amount, and trading activity is not substantial. There is no 5-year issue outstanding. The spread differential between Crédit Communal and state-guaranteed names has been 9–10 basis points (annual). The present yield curve on French AAA risk indicates the market is looking for a 7-basis-point differential between 5-, 7-, and 10-year maturities. As a further pricing reference, there are two issues outstanding by Caisse Centrale de Communication Digitale (CCCD) with four and six years' maturity and trading at 45 and 51 basis points, respectively, over U.S. Treasuries. CCCD is a government agency which also issues under the guarantee of the French Republic, but issues infrequently and is not as strongly perceived as are other, more regular, issuers.

You are head of syndicate in a leading issuing house. The sales desk in your trading room reports demand from institutional investors and, where top credits are offered, in substantial amounts. Crédit Vinicole was appreciative of your contribution to the investor presentations and has asked you for a proposal. Your marketing team tells you there will be substantial competition for the deal.

What do market conditions tell you about the following?

- demand for paper
- choice of offering (open priced or bought deal)
- issue size and maturity

Where would you price Crédit Vinicole's issue in terms of spread over Treasuries? (*Suggestion:* Draw a grid of maturities against the various issuers mentioned and insert the spreads which are given in the market report.)

Suggested Solution

1. Given the recent spate of issues and the lackluster reception of the 10-year issue for SRCB, your inclination is toward a shorter maturity for Crédit Vinicole's issue. The sales desk is reporting substantial demand for top-quality credits from institutional investors which central banks invest principally in AAA-rated names with a 5-year

maturity. Clearly, a shorter maturity is indicated, which makes for a larger issue size and hence greater liquidity of the issue.

2. Your decision on the choice of offering is made in conjunction with the following:

- Signs of saturation are emerging. You are under pressure to launch the deal while market sentiment is still positive.

- The need for a swap into floating-rate U.S. dollars implies that terms of the bond issue and the swap (or swaps) should be contracted at the same time.

- There is competition for the mandate and you would not wish to lose the deal to a smaller house which offered firm terms.

You are therefore going to propose a bought deal.

3. Your advice to the borrower is to offer a US$250 million issue with a 5-year maturity. This is a large enough size to interest major institutional investors who are looking for liquidity, but not so much as to strain market appetite. Any paper left with the underwriters could easily be hedged in this maturity. The shorter 5-year maturity is ideal for a first-time issue and the expected AAA rating will ensure the widest possible reception.

4. Spreads grid

Years	4	5	6	7	10
Crédit Communal	—	(55)	—	62	69
SRCB/State gtee	—	(45)	—	(52)	59
CCCD/State gtee	45	—	51	—	—

Note: Spreads in brackets are estimates only.

How can one assess a spread for Crédit Vinicole in five years? Some of the spreads are given in the market report, but there is no market indication of the spread appropriate to state-guaranteed risk or Crédit Communal in this maturity. The spread therefore must be deduced. If there is a 7-basis-point differential between 5 and 7 years, then a 5-year issue for Crédit Communal would be expected to yield 55 basis points over U.S. Treasuries. SRCB, as state-guaranteed risk, would issue at a spread of 10 basis points less in this maturity, or 45 basis points, which tallies with the spread differential of 14 basis between a 5- and a 10-year maturity presently sought by the market in that risk. CCCD is also state-guaranteed risk, but the name perception costs CCCD 2–3 basis points more, and it would be priced at a spread of 47/48 basis points.

For Crédit Vinicole, an equivalent risk to Crédit Communal, there are arguments for tighter pricing:

- a good-size issue

- strong demand in five-year paper

- CV having been well introduced to the financial community

You are also under pressure to win the deal, which inclines you to a spread of "52 over," or a mere 7 basis points over, SRCB. Your sales desk then confronts you with the following arguments:

- Crédit Vinicole does not carry a government guarantee.

- This is their first issue ever and (you learn from marketing) the issuer is looking for a successful issue.

You therefore settle on a spread of 54 over U.S. Treasuries and decide to forgo your selling concession. This enables you to keep the coupon low and to maximize the benefit of the swap.

Questions

1. What is the coupon on the issue if the bond yields 54 basis points over 5-year U.S. Treasury stock. Assume an issue price of 100 percent and a 5-year U.S. Treasury yield of 8.335 per annum semiannual bond.

2. The commissions on a 5-year Eurodollar issue include a management fee of ¼ percent flat, an underwriting commission of ¼ percent flat and a selling concession of 1¼ percent flat. If the reimbursable expenses amount to US$70,000, what is the all-in cost of the issue, inclusive of commissions and reimbursable expenses only?

3. What denominations would you recommend for the issue?

4. What event risks would you envisage for an issue by an institution such as CV?

5. Write down the cash flow of the issue.

6. The swaps quote obtained by your swaps department is: 6-month LIBOR v. 87/92 basis points over U.S. Treasuries. What is the end cost of funds expressed in money market terms?

7. If the issuer were to receive the benefit of the swap as a single payment on the closing date of the issue, how much would CV receive?

8. CV likes the idea of an "up-front" payment, but its ideal cash flow on the financing would be to have the bond payments neutralized and to pay floating-rate interest at a rate of LIBOR less 15 basis points throughout the life of the issue. Does this leave anything to be paid up-front and, if so, how much?

Solutions

1. 5-year U.S. Treasury yield: 8.335 p.a. semiannual
   CV spread: 0.54 p.a. semiannual
   Issue yield to investor: 8.875 p.a. semiannual
   Or, using conversion
   formula on p. 72:   9.0719 p.a. annual

   CV's issue is priced at the selling concession—that is, the investor receives his or her required yield of 9.0719 at a price of 98¾ percent. Using the HP-12C, we key in:

   $i = 9.0719$
   $n = 5$
   $PV = 98.75$
   $FV = -100.00$

   and solve for *PMT* to obtain: –8.7499.
   The coupon on the issue is therefore 8¾ percent per annum annual.

2. Total commissions amount to 1¾ percent of the principal amount of the issue or US$4,375,000. Reimbursable expenses are US$70,000 to bring

the total of commissions and reimbursable expenses to US$4,445,000 and the net proceeds to US$245,555,000, or 98.222 percent of the principal amount. Using the HP-12C, we key in:

$PV = 98.222$

$PMT = -8.75$

n and FV remain unchanged, and we solve for i to obtain 9.209599 per annum annual, or using the conversion formula on p. 72, 9.006793 per annum semiannual.

3. The predominant institutional interest points to larger denominations, which helps to reduce paying agency costs. You recommend:

   US$50 million in denominations of US$10,000

   US$150 million in denominations of US$100,000

   US$50 million in denominations of US$1,000,000

4. Event risks associated with an issue for Crédit Vinicole would relate to a change of ownership through privatization. This would remove the underlying backing of the French State for the bank's business activities. However, this need not affect CV's ability to service the debt. Therefore, any event risks would be linked to the rating of the issue, which would have to be downgraded before investors' right to prepayment was triggered.

5. The cash flow of CV's issue after commissions and reimbursable expenses (totaling US$4,445,000)

End of year	
0	+245,555,000
1	−21,875,000
2	−21,875,000
3	−21,875,000
4	−21,875,000
5	−271,875,000

IRR: 9.209599%

6. Under the swap Crédit Vinicole receives fixed-rate payments at a rate of 5-year U.S. Treasury stock plus 85 basis points to offset its fixed-rate payment obligations under the bond issue.

5-year U.S. Treasury yield:	8.335 p.a. semiannual
Swap margin:	0.87 p.a. semiannual
Total:	9.205 p.a. semiannual
or, using the conversion formula on p. 72:	9.4168 p.a. annual

The swap pays 9.4168 per annum (annual) or 9.2050 per annum (semi-annual bond). The cost of the issue is 9.209599 per annum annual, or 9.006793 per annum semiannual. The surplus of the swap payments over the cost of the issue is therefore:

$$9.2050 - 9.006793 = 0.198207 \text{ or}$$
$$19.8207 \text{ basis points (semiannual)}$$

This surplus expressed in semiannual (bond) terms is then converted to money market terms as follows:

$$19.8207 \times \frac{360}{365} = 19.549 \text{ basis points (money market)}$$

The swap therefore produces a net cost of funds of 6-month U.S. dollar LIBOR less 19.55 basis points.

7. The swaps pays 9.4168 per annum (annual bond) or, on a principal amount of US$250 million, US$23,542,000 per annum. A fictional cash flow on the basis of the swap payments would be as follows:

End of year	
0	?
1	−23,542,000
2	−23,542,000
3	−23,542,000
4	−23,542,000
5	−273,542,000
IRR: 9.209599%	

Using the HP-12C, key in:

$n = 5$
$i = 9.209599$
$FV = -250,000,000$
$PMT = -23,542,000$

and solve for PV, which amounts to 252,003,939.

This represents a surplus over the net proceeds of the issue of:

$$252,003,939 - 245,555,000 = US\$6,448,939$$

Thus if CV requires its payment obligations under the issue to be exactly matched and to pay LIBOR flat under the swap, it should receive a payment of US$6,448,939 up front. This can be verified by the following calculation. The fixed-rate payments received under the swap (US$23,542,000) exceed those on the bond issue (US$21,875,000) by

US$1,667,000 per annum. This stream of surpluses may be discounted to calculate their present value as follows. Using the HP-12C, we key in:

$i = 9.209599$
$PMT = -1,667,000$
$FV = 0$
$n = 5$

and solving for PV, we derive 6,448,939.

8. In summary, if the fixed-rate payment obligations under the bond issue are exactly matched, CV floating-rate obligations under the swap equate to one of the following: (1) 6-month LIBOR less 19.55 basis points per annum (money market) throughout the life of the issue and no up-front payment, or (2) 6-month LIBOR flat, in which case it also receives a up-front payment of US$6,448,939.

If CV is looking to pay LIBOR less 15 basis points, (i.e., a higher rate of floating-rate interest), then under the terms of the swap the difference of 4.55 basis points may be commuted into a single up-front payment. This payment is the difference between the equivalent up-front payments on two swaps against the issue, one producing LIBOR less 19.55 basis points and the second producing LIBOR less 15 basis points.

The equivalent up-front payment on a swap-producing LIBOR less 19.55 basis points is US$6,448,939 (see solution 7). To ascertain the equivalent up-front payment on a swap-producing LIBOR less 15 basis points, the calculation in solution 7 is performed in reverse. Fifteen basis points (money market) is first expressed in semiannual (bond) terms as follows:

$$15 \times \frac{365}{360} = 15.208 \text{ basis points (s.a. bond)}$$

The cost of DCB's issue in semiannual (bond) terms is 9.006793 percent (semiannual bond), to which we add the swap benefit expressed previously in semiannual (bond) terms 0.15208 to obtain a notional swap rate of 9.158873 per annum (semiannual bond) or 9.3686 per annum (annual bond).

On a principal amount of US$250,000,000, the fixed-rate receipts at this notional rate of swap would amount to:

$$250,000,000 \times \frac{9.3686}{100} = \text{US\$23,421,500 per annum}$$

We then create a further fictional cash flow as follows:

End of year	
0	?
1	−23,421,500
2	−23,421,500

End of year	
3	−23,421,500
4	−23,421,500
5	−273,421,500

with an IRR of 9.209599%

Then, using the HP-12C we key in:

$n = 5$
$PMT = -23,421,500$
$FV = -250,000,000$
$i = 9.209599$

and solve for PV to derive a payment of US\$251,537,774. This represents an excess of US\$5,982,774 over the net proceeds of the actual issue of US\$245,555,000.

The excess of US\$5,982,774 is, however, smaller than the up-front payment under the original swap of US\$6,448,939 (see solution 7). The difference between them (6,448,939 − 5,982,774 = US\$466,165) represents the new up-front payment due to CV if the swap is structured so that the bond obligations are matched and CV pays LIBOR less 15 basis points under the swap.

This can be verified by converting the difference between the two floating-rate payments into a rate expressed in annual bond terms. The difference between the two floating-rate cost of funds is:

6-month US\$ LIBOR less 19.5492 basis points
−6-month US\$ LIBOR less 15 basis points
4.5492 basis points (money market)

To convert this into annual bond terms, we convert the differential into semiannual (bond) terms:

$$4.5492 \times \frac{365}{360} = 4.61238 \text{ basis points (semiannual bond)}$$

The direct conversion of this figure into a yield expressed in annual bond terms is distorted by the scale of the calculation. We therefore assume a level of interest rate to add to the differential, and, for this purpose, take the cost of the issue of 9.006793 (semiannual bond) and add the differential of 4.61238 basis points (semiannual bond) as follows:

$$9.006793 + 0.0461238 = 9.052917 \text{ semiannual (bond)}$$

which in annual terms converts to 9.257805 (annual bond).

The base figure of 9.006793 semiannual equates to 9.209599 annual (bond). The difference between the two rates expressed in annual terms is:

$$9.257805 − 9.209599 = 0.048206 \text{ or } 4.8206 \text{ basis points (annual bond)}$$

Thus the differential of 4.549 basis points (money market) converts into 4.8206 basis points (annual bond). In cash terms this represents a payment of:

$$250,000,000 \times \frac{1}{100} \times \frac{4.8206}{100} = US\$120,515 \text{ p.a.}$$

Discounting a stream of payments of US$120,515 by a factor of 9.209599, we obtain a figure of roughly the same order, namely US$466,233.

8
Equity-related Eurobond Instruments

The practice of linking a Eurobond issue to the issuer's equity was borrowed from the U.S. and the U.K. domestic bond markets. Investor interest in early Euro-convertibles was, like that of their domestic counterparts, localized. Issues were launched against stocks traded mainly in their home stock markets, which attracted little investor interest from overseas. Liquidity was poor and the low coupons inherent to the structure aggravated their secondary market performance. These markets did not develop until the mid-1980s, when deregulation and new information systems promoted the emergence of worldwide debt and equity securities markets working continuously round the clock. At this juncture, rising stock markets in 1986–1987 provided the necessary catalyst for relaunching equity-linked debt instruments.

The initiative, in any event, surpassed all expectations and in 1988–1989, equity-linked Eurobonds accounted for well over a third of all new Euro-issues (see Table 8-1). The rapid development was due largely to the activity of investors and corporate issuers from Japan, where stock markets proved relatively impervious to events such as the crash of October 1987. The most popular instruments by far were equity warrant issues, placed chiefly with Japanese investors but also with international investors who familiarized themselves with the more prominent names. To issuers, the principal attractions were, first, the opportunity to issue equity at a premium; and, second, the low cost of the debt in local currency compared with a domestic financing. Thanks to a highly efficient swaps market, the proceeds of Eurodollar equity warrant issues were typically swapped into yen at negative interest

Table 8-1. Issues of Equity Warrant-linked Fixed and Floating Rate Eurobonds and Equity Convertible Eurobonds (in US$ millions)

	1984	1985	1986	1987	1988	1989	1990	1991
Total Eurobond issuance	79,290	132,875	180,182	135,023	175,913	211,819	175,857	247,773
Equity warrant-linked*	2,646	2,743	15,092	23,535	28,491	67,112	19,574	27,345
Convertible†	4,161	4,638	6,413	14,068	5,794	5,249	4,179	7,139
Equity-linked Eurobonds as % of total Eurobonds	8.6	5.6	11.9	27.9	19.5	34.2	13.5	13.9

* Includes issues of equity warrants linked to fixed- and floating-rate Eurobond issues.
† Includes issues of convertible preference shares.

SOURCE: Euromoney Bondware.

rates in 1987 and at rates between 0 and 2 percent in 1988.* As dollar/yen swaps became uneconomic (that is, producing a yen cost of funds over 2 percent per annum), Japanese corporate borrowers launched equity warrant issues denominated in Deutsche mark or Swiss franc.

The fortunes of this market changed dramatically in 1991 when tight monetary policies in Japan led indirectly to falling equity prices. The fall has been virtually continuous since, and has not only wiped out the value of most outstanding equity warrants on Japanese stocks but also has virtually closed the market for any new issues using this structure. New convertibles and equity warrant issues rely essentially on the expectation of a rising and buoyant stock market to be successfully placed. Leaving aside the particular circumstances of the Japanese economy, most Western economies with potential issuers of such instruments are only just emerging from the generalized recession of 1991–1992, and it will require considerably more business confidence for the market in equity-related Eurobonds to reopen.

Convertibles

A convertible bond (or *convertible*) is a standard fixed-rate bond issued by a private sector corporation that is convertible, at the investor's option, into an equal amount in cash terms of the equity stock or shares of the issuer. Investors have the right to convert at any time, normally until the final maturity date of the issue, on terms which are fixed at launch. These include the following:

- the price of the shares or conversion price at which conversion takes place and which is set at a premium over the share price at the time of launch. The number of shares derived from converting one bond is calculated by dividing the denomination of the bond by the conversion share price; this is called the *conversion ratio*.

- an exchange rate that applies throughout the life of the issue to all conversions. This is necessary where the bond and shares are denominated in different currencies.

Clearly, investors will exercise their conversion right if and when the current share price exceeds the conversion price.[†] However, if the value of the

---

* If the end cost in yen were above 2 percent, the borrower would find it as cheap to launch a convertible issue in Japan.

[†] *Example:* A U.K. corporation launches an issue of convertible bonds in denominations of £1000. Investors may convert their bonds into shares at a price of £4 and therefore, on conversion, the investors receive 250 shares. If the share price rises to £5, the investor may convert (subject to whether the coupon rate on the issue is higher than the historic dividend yield) and certainly converts if the prevailing share price is above £4 as the bond approaches maturity; however, if the share price is £3.50, the value of the conversion is only £875, so he does not convert. (*Footnote continued on page 194.*)

shares never exceeds that of the bond, the investor has no incentive to convert and, on maturity, the convertible would normally be redeemed, as in the case of ordinary bonds, for cash.*

Convertibles are issued at par, or 100 percent, of the nominal value of the bond. This price includes the value of the investor's option to convert (or the conversion right), as well as the value of the bond as a straight debt instrument (which must therefore be less than par). It follows that to produce a redemption yield in line with current yields, the coupon level of the issue will be below-market. In practice, the coupon is set above the yield of the stock to encourage the investor to buy a convertible bond rather than the stock itself. The rule of thumb is to set the coupon at a level halfway between the yield of the stock and the coupon on a conventional straight bond.†

Having set a coupon level, we calculate the price of the bond alone and subtract this from 100 percent to derive the value of the conversion right per bond.‡ The value of the conversion right is thus calculated on the basis of an arbitrary assumption of the coupon level. Whether or not this is a fair market value is measured by the level of an index called the *global premium*,§ which is compared with the volatility of the underlying stock over the life of the convertible.[1]

Where the bond and the share are in different currencies, the investor will also take into account any change in exchange rates since the launch in relation to the fixed exchange rate specified in the terms of the issue.

Example: Substitute a Belgian company for the U.K. corporation. The bonds are still in denominations of £1000, but the conversion price is BF2400 per share. The exchange rate, fixed at launch, is BF60 = £1. The value of each share in sterling terms is BF2400/60 = £40 and, on conversion, the investor receives £1000/(2400/60) = 25 shares.

Assume the share price rises to BF3000 and the Belgian franc appreciates to BF50 = £1. The 25 shares arising from the conversion of each bond will be worth BF75,000 or, in sterling terms, £1500, so the investor converts. If the share price has fallen to BF2300 but the Belgian franc has appreciated to BF55 = £1, then the shares are worth BF57,500 or, in sterling terms, £1045.45, so he still converts.

* A variation of the convertible bond is the equity note. This is the same as a standard convertible except for redemption which is made in shares only.

† Stock yields are generally well below the yields on fixed-rate debt.

‡ *Example:* A corporation whose stock yield is 5 percent issues a 20-year U.S. dollar convertible. The current share price is US$75 and the conversion price US$100. The coupon on a straight dollar bond of equivalent maturity would be 9 percent and a redemption yield of 9.25 percent. If the coupon on the convertible is set halfway, at 7 percent, a calculation of the *PV* on the HP-12C produces a value of the bond of 79.821 percent. The conversion right is therefore worth 100 − 79.821 percent = 20.179 percent or US$201.79 per bond of US$1000. The bond is convertible into 10 shares, and the conversion right is worth US$20.18 per share.

§ The *global premium* is derived through the following formula:

$$\text{Global premium} = \frac{\text{Conversion right per share} + \text{Conversion price}}{\text{Current share price}}$$

From the previous footnote example, the global premium is:

$$\frac{20.18 + 100}{75} = 1.6024 \text{ or a premium of } 60.24\%$$

[1] See following section on equity warrants for volatility analysis.

The conversion right remains part of the convertible throughout its life and the performance of the convertible reflects both the price of the bond and its conversion value. Each of these, however, has a separate behavior and influence on the price. As the share price rises, the conversion value of the bond rises; assuming there is no change in the exchange rate or in bond yields, the price of the convertible rises in proportion to the profit realized on the sale of the shares arising from notional conversion in relation to the nominal value of each bond. But if bond yields rise while the share price and exchange rates remain constant, the price of the convertible falls (as in the case of a standard fixed-rate bond). Thus a rise in the share price and the rise in bond yields have an opposite effect on the price of the convertible. On the other hand, a rise in the share price and a fall in bond yields would have the same effect and, if occurring simultaneously, can reinforce each other.

The share price can also fall below the conversion price, at which point the conversion right may become worthless. But if bond yields meanwhile remain constant, the decline in the price of the convertible has a downside limit, which is the price of the bond as a bond alone. At this point the convertible ceases to trade like a share and reverts to trading like a deep-discount bond as a function of bond yield movements or variations in the credit risk of the issuer. However, even at this level of share price, the price of the convertible bond will contain a "time" value, reflecting the notion that the conversion may regain intrinsic value at a future date.

These two components, however, are only alternative ways of expressing the worth of the convertible and neither gives on its own a correct indication of value. To circumvent the problem, the market assumes that the price is determined by supply and demand and uses a measure of premium P calculated as follows:

$$P = \frac{\text{Conversion price}}{\text{Current share price}} \times \frac{\text{Bond price}}{100}$$

Examples: Calculate the premium on the following convertibles.

1. Issue: American Can US$175 million 5½% convertible due 22 April 2002.

Conversion price:	US$66¾
Current share price:	US$27¾
Current convertible price:	66–68%

$$\text{Premium} = \frac{66\frac{3}{4}}{27\frac{3}{4}} \times \frac{68}{100}$$

$$= 1.6357 \text{ or a premium of } 63.57\%$$

2. Issue: Elders US$75 million 5% convertible due 5 November 1997.

Conversion price:	A$4.4625
Conversion exchange rate:	US$1– = A$1.50534
Current share price:	A$3.00
Current exchange rate:	US$1.– = A$1.43328
Bond price:	88–90%

To calculate the premium, we convert (1) the conversion price at the conversion exchange rate, and (2) the current share price at the current exchange rate, which are then both expressed in U.S. dollar terms. Thus:

$$P = \frac{\text{Conversion price/conversion exchange rate}}{\text{Current share price/current exchange rate}} \times \frac{\text{Bond price}}{100}$$

$$= \frac{4.4625 / 1.505344}{3.00/ 1.43328} \times \frac{90}{100}$$

$$= 1.27466 \text{ or a premium of } 27.47\%$$

For the borrower, a convertible issue is in effect raising:

- until conversion, debt finance at rate below the cost of a standard bond issue (but above the level of stock yields)
- on conversion, equity capital at a premium to the share price on launch, instead of at a discount which would apply in a conventional equity stock issue*

Thus a convertible may be construed as a means of raising equity capital which, until conversion, costs more than the rate of dividends but which, on conversion, produces a larger amount of new equity capital. Clearly, issuers have an interest in early conversion by investors. The earlier the conversion, the earlier the fall in convertible debt service costs to the lower rate of stock yields. To precipitate conversion, convertible issues usually include an issuer's option to call the issue whose exercise is contingent upon the share price having remained at a 30–50% premium to the conversion price over a period of several weeks. The threat of redemption for cash triggers the conversion by investors who would otherwise forgo their capital gain in relation to the conversion price.

Maturities on convertibles are long, and 15- and 20-year maturities are commonplace, reflecting the equity character of the instrument. Issues sizes range from US$20–500 million but an issue of US$1 billion was launched by Texaco. The principal issuers are Japanese,[†] U.S. and British, reflecting their more developed stock markets. The principal currency of issue is the U.S. dollar, but convertibles have also been issued in sterling, Deutsche mark, yen, ECU, and French francs. The drawback of convertibles from the issuer's standpoint begins when conversion does not take place: the financing reverts to a debt issue which must be redeemed from sources other than an issue of capital. If denominated in a foreign currency, the issuer is also confronted with a currency risk whose exposure cannot be managed through a swap, since the amount outstanding at any future date cannot be known.

---

* This benefit can turn into an opportunity loss. In the event that the stock price appreciates sharply during the life of the convertible, the issuer in effect foregoes the opportunity of issuing the same equity at a higher premium still.

† Japanese convertibles are like standard convertibles except that they have lower coupons, which is acceptable because of the traditionally low yields on Japanese equities. In compensation, the conversion price is close to the share price at the time of launch, so the convertible effectively becomes straight equity but offers a slightly better yield. The strong yen is a further attraction for non-yen-based investors.

For investors, convertibles present significant attractions:

- Convertibles offer a higher income than stock yields.
- At best, investors participate in the appreciation of the stock.
- At worst, they enjoy the relative protection of capital of a bond.

They also present some drawbacks:

- Given their convertibility into equity, convertible bonds are generally subordinated in rank to senior nonconvertible debt and therefore present a greater credit risk.
- The convertible will not track the underlying stock directly and may appreciate more slowly.
- The poor performance of the stock price may be due to a deterioration of the credit of the issuer and, should the conversion become worthless, the investor is left with a bond of poor quality trading at a below-market price.
- Where the bond and the stock are in different currencies, the investor has a foreign exchange risk on conversion: the stock price may have risen but, if the currency of the stock has depreciated, conversion may not be attractive.

These risks acted as a deterrent to investors, especially as regards issuers of lesser quality. Convertibles issued in mid-1970s sought to remedy this problem by including a further investor option, exercisable, say, after five years, to redeem the bond at a large premium over par. When redeemed in this way, the investor achieved an overall yield which was equal to or better than the yield on sovereign risk of the currency of the bond. In return for yield protection, investors were offered, and accepted, a coupon lower than that on a standard convertible. Issuers consented to this additional risk in the expectation of fast-rising stock markets. The formula was successful for issuers in Japan, where the expectation was verified. Elsewhere, the record has been mixed in the wake of the stock market crash of October 1987. Next plc's issue of £100 million 5¾% due 2003 carried high conversion premiums, and the sharp fall in the stock price made the conversion strike price appear unrealistic. The investor option for early redemption, however, became increasingly attractive, and the issuer was obliged to set aside substantial reserves to meet the potential liability of the premium on early redemption by investors.*

---

* If the convertible is redeemed, the issuer has the further extra cost of refinancing the debt in the form of a conventional bond at market (that is, much higher) rates. Other convertible issues, such as Burton plc's £110 million 4¾ percent due 2001, whose stock also fell sharply, have offered incentives to investors to defer exercise of their early redemption option for a further five years in the hope of a recovery of the stock price.

Eurobond Issues with Equity Warrants Attached

Eurobond issues with equity warrants attached (*equity warrant issues*) became, in the 5 years to the end of 1989, the second largest category of instrument in the Eurobond market. Japanese borrowers issued 95 percent of all equity warrant issues, denominated principally in U.S. dollars and Swiss francs and, to a lesser extent, in Deutsche marks. Issuance by non-Japanese corporate borrowers remains low, reflecting in part smaller and less buoyant stock markets. Unlike convertible bonds, equity warrant issues comprise two separate components: a standard fixed-rate Eurobond issue, and a detachable equity warrant.

The bond is priced as normal in line with current market yields and the warrant is priced separately as a function of the desired warrant premium and equity content (see following). The two components are issued as a package with a combined price of either (1) 100 percent, in which case the bond price will be at a discount to par (as in a convertible bond) and the coupon at a below-market level (*discount bond*); or (2) in excess of 100 percent where the bond is issued at a normal market price, that is, close to 100 percent (*full coupon bond*).

Following launch, the equity warrant is typically detached from the package, leading to a secondary market in three distinct securities (each of which may be listed separately). These are *the bond and the warrant* (cum-warrant); *the bond alone* (ex-warrant); and *the warrant alone*.

Since the warrant and the bond are separate, the principal amount of the debt remains constant in nominal amount and has a set maturity. It can be swapped, and cost-effective swaps out of U.S. dollars into yen largely account for the fivefold greater popularity of equity warrant issues over Euro-convertibles.

Equity Warrants. An *equity warrant* is a medium-term option (a right but not an obligation) to purchase the stock of a company over a period of time (the exercise period) and at a fixed price (the strike price or exercise price). Equity warrants pay no interest and, if not exercised beforehand, the exercise rights lapse on the expiry date of the warrant. In losing these rights, the holder of the warrant then forfeits his or her initial investment.* During its life, the warrant value is made up of the intrinsic value (the amount by which the current share price exceeds the strike price) and a time value (the value of having an option for the period of the life of the warrant).

Equity warrants, like convertibles, are an instrument for raising equity capital at a premium to the share price ruling at the time of launch.† Unlike

---

* A variation on equity warrants is the redeemable warrant which pays a fixed redemption amount on expiry, in addition to the standard warrant rights.

† Equity warrants may be structured to entitle the holder to purchase new or existing stock, in particular (1) the stock of the corporation which issued the bond; (2) in the case of an issue

convertibles, however, the amount of equity raised through the exercise of the warrants is not tied to the nominal amount of the bond issue. The ratio of equity raised to the issue size is called the *equity content,* or warrantability, and can range from 100–150 percent or even 200 percent of the nominal amount of the bond issue. On the other hand, it is not possible to force the exercise of the warrants, and experience shows that these will often not be exercised until close to expiry. This pattern, however, mitigates another drawback—which is the duplication of funding which would result from an earlier exercise.

On launch, equity warrants attached to Eurobond issues are priced out-of-the-money, which means that the strike price is above the then ruling share price. The intrinsic value of the warrant at launch is thus nil and the warrant has time value alone. In pricing the warrant several factors are taken into consideration:

- *The exercise period of the warrant.* The longer the exercise period, the higher the time value. On U.S. dollar bond issues which offer maturities of up to 10 years, the exercise periods generally range between 4 and 7 years. Bond issues in Swiss francs, Deutsche marks, or sterling, which offer longer maturities, permit longer warrant exercise periods.

- *Volatility.* Shares fluctuate in price, and the degree and frequency of fluctuation is indicated by a measure of the stock's volatility. The greater the volatility, the earlier the likelihood of the share price reaching and exceeding the strike price and hence the greater the attraction of the warrant. When the warrant has no intrinsic value, as at launch, the price of the warrant is a direct function of the value put by the market on the future volatility of the stock. Various statistical models are used to calculate the future volatility, which serves as a guide to the level of global premium on the warrant (see p. 204).*

launched out of a special purpose issuing vehicle, stock of the (quoted) parent or holding company; (3) a separate corporation altogether—in which case the warrants are termed *covered warrants.* (*Note:* Company legislation in many jurisdictions makes the issue of warrants to purchase equity subject to a waiver of shareholders' preferential subscription rights, which protects them from earnings dilution).

* The most widely accepted models are those of Black and Scholes and Cox & Rubinstein. These, however, rely on an assumption being made of the future volatility of the stock that is sought. Clearly, this is unknowable a priori and instead the calculation uses an extrapolation of historic volatility data.

Another method is to assume the level of future volatility and to calculate a warrant price, which is then compared with the issuer's outstanding warrant prices, if any. If comparable, the assumed future volatility is said to be the implied volatility of the stock.

Interested readers are invited to read (1) Cox & Rubinstein's article in *The Journal of Financial Economics,* vol. 7, September 1979, p. 229, entitled "Option Pricing: A Simplified Approach," and (2) Black & Scholes "The Pricing of Options and Corporate Liabilities," *The Journal of Political Economy,* vol. 81, May 1973, p. 687.

Aside from its theoretical value, the price of the warrant is also assessed on the basis of practical standards and the "feel" of the market:

- The accepted range of value of global premiums is 2–25 percent (the lower premiums being for Japanese warrants) and equity warrants are usually priced within these parameters.

- The warrant traders make a judgment of what a warrant is worth by reference to (1) the prices of other warrants in the market, (2) market perception of the company, and (3) expectations of the performance of the stock market over the life of the warrant—none of which may be factored into the theoretical model.

The absence of intrinsic value when issued ensures that the price of the warrant is small in relation to the stock price at launch. Following launch, the price of the warrant will fluctuate in accordance with demand and supply for (1) the underlying stock and (2) the warrant itself. As the stock price approaches and exceeds the strike price, the warrant's value becomes closely related to the profit which could be realized on exercising the warrant and selling the stock. Warrant holders have a much smaller outlay than stockholders buying at the strike price to achieve the same profit. The ratio of the outlay to potential gains is termed *leverage;* in the case of warrants and other options, leverage is high because of the potentially higher return for a given investment. Conversely, as the share price falls, the warrant loses intrinsic value very quickly and the investment of warrant holders becomes worthless but for the time value which, unlike the share, has a limited life.

Case Study

Le Pétrole Parisien S.A. (LPP) is one of the leading private sector industrial companies in France and is engaged principally in the exploration and exploitation of oil deposits in the Parisian basin. The shares, widely held in France and overseas, are listed in several European financial centers. Recently, the oil price has been edging upwards. The French economy is in good shape: inflation is 3 percent, growth is sustained, and the stock market is buoyant. The balance of trade is improving sharply and the French franc is well supported on the foreign exchange markets. LPP's share price has been boosted by its recent announcement of the discovery of substantial new oil deposits of commercial value under La Défense. Some medium-term bank loans of the company, amounting to US$200 million, have come up for refinancing and you have been asked to submit proposals.

Your inclination is to suggest an equity-linked financing for the following reasons:

- The French stock market is strong.
- Uncertainty in the oil industry is focusing the attention of investors on those companies with demonstrable oil reserves.

- The share is held by international investors; the strong perception of the franc is a good climate into which to launch an equity-linked issue.
- LPP's growth and development will require further issues of equity capital to preserve safe gearing ratios.
- An AGM of shareholders is due shortly when resolutions may be tabled for an increase in capital and, if necessary, a waiver of shareholders' preferential subscription rights.

Your choices include:

- an issue of equity capital by way of rights; the shares would be issued at 7 percent discount to the current share price and the fees and expenses would be in excess of 3 percent.
- a convertible bond issue with a 15–20 year maturity.
- a straight bond issue with equity warrants attached.

LPP tells you that it is in no hurry for the extra capital and that before issuing equity direct they have to renegotiate the terms of some outstanding preference capital. It is also averse to the high cost of issuing ordinary equity. You therefore submit proposals for a convertible bond issue and a straight bond issue with equity warrants attached. Many of LPP's international shareholders are institutions with substantial U.S. dollar portfolios, so your proposals are denominated in U.S. dollars. Market sources report the following additional data:

U.S. Treasury yields:	5 years	7 years	15 years (interpolated)
	7.31 s.a.	7.55 s.a.	7.93 s.a.
LPP Euro-U.S. dollar bond yield:	U.S. Treasuries + 120 basis points (all maturities)		
Current share price:	FF270		
Historic share yield:	4.47%		

Historic Share Price Volatility

Previous 12 months:	19.89%
Previous 3 years:	22.50%
Previous 10 years:	28.60%
Previous 15 years:	36.16%

Outstanding Warrants

Remaining Life:	4¾ years
Current price:	US$5–5.50
Current exchange rate:	US$6.20 = US$1

With this information you are now in a position to prepare proposals for a convertible and an equity-warrant-linked Eurobond issue for Le Pétrole Parisien. A convertible issue offers the advantage of a longer maturity and your selection is for a 15-year issue. A 15-year U.S. dollar bond issued by LPP should yield:

$$7.93 \text{ s.a.} + 1.20 = 9.13 \text{ s.a.}$$

Dividends are paid semiannually and the yield is expressed in semiannual terms. Adding the bond and dividend yields and dividing by 2, we derive a rough estimate of the coupon of the convertible:

$$\frac{9.13 + 4.47}{2} = 6.80$$

or, rounding to the nearest ⅛ percent, 6¾ percent.

Using the HP-12C, we calculate the *PV* of a bond with a 15-year maturity, a yield of 9.13 percent semiannual and a coupon of 6¾ percent semiannual. Keying in:

n = 30 (30 six-month periods)
FV = −100
i = 4.565 (9.13 divided by 2)
PMT = −3¾ (the annual coupon divided by 2)

and solving for *PV*, we derive 80.76 percent as the value of the bond. Deducting this from 100 percent, we derive the value of the conversion right, or 100 − 80.764 = 19.236% of each bond.

Let us assume denominations of US$1000, a conversion price of Fr310, and a conversion exchange rate based on the current exchange rate of US$1 = Fr6.20. Then the number of shares derived by converting a bond is:

$$\frac{US\$1000}{310} \times 6.20 = 20 \text{ shares}$$

The conversion right is then worth:

$$\frac{19.236}{100} \times US\$1000 \times \frac{1}{20} \times 6.20 = Fr59.63 \text{ per share}$$

The global premium is then calculated as follows:

$$\frac{310 + 59.63}{270} = 1.369$$

or a premium of 36.9 percent, which is acceptable in the light of the historical 15-year volatility of 36.16 percent.

Typical pro forma terms of the issue may now be set down as follows:

Borrower:	Le Pétrole Parisien
Amount:	US$200 million
Issue price:	100%
Denominations:	US$1000
Number of bonds:	200,000
Final maturity date:	2 January 2005
Conversion exchange rate:	Fr6.20 = US$1.00
Amount of equity raised through conversion:	Fr1,240,000,000
Conversion price:	Fr310
Number of shares arising through conversion:	4,000,000

Number of shares arising from the conversion of one bond:	20
Issue price of the bond:	80.764%
Value of conversion rights:	19.236%
Value of conversion right per share:	Fr59.63
Conversion premium:	14.81% (see formula on p. 195)
Global premium:	36.90%
Coupon:	6¾% per annum
Fees:	2½%
Cost of funds:	7.02 semiannual bond
Interest payment dates:	2 January and 2 July. The January date is chosen to coincide with LPP's accounting year end date on 31 December and to allow for the fact that conversion is made without accrued interest. Investors converting on 2 January therefore lose little interest and are entitled to both dividends paid in the year of conversion.
Conversion period:	At any time after the first interest payment date.
Early redemption at the option of LPP:	LPP may redeem on 60 days' notice outstanding bonds on the third, fourth, or fifth anniversary of the issue, provided that the average share price shall have exceeded 145 percent of the conversion price over a continuous period of 45 days. On the tenth and subsequent anniversaries of the issue, LPP may redeem on 60 days' notice outstanding bonds at an initial premium of 1¼ percent and declining by ¼ percent in each successive year.
Redemption at the option of the investor:	Investors are entitled to be redeemed on the fifth, sixth, seventh, and eighth anniversaries of the issue at a price such that the redemption yield on the bonds shall equal the redemption yield of U.S. Treasury stock of equivalent maturity at the time of launch plus a margin of 150 basis points. (*Example:* 5-year U.S. Treasury yield is 7.31 semiannual. The redemption yield in the event of early redemption is 8.81. The redemption price of a bond with a 6¾ percent semiannual coupon, a five-year life, a present value of 97½ percent, and a yield

of 8.81 percent semiannual, using the HP-12C, is 108.75 percent.)

Note: The level of the premium acceptable to LPP would depend on expectations for the appreciation of its own share price and market conditions at the time of launch which, if poor, could necessitate a higher premium.

In the case of an equity warrants issue, the amount of equity raised is not tied to the issue amount. However, normal market practice requires the relationship between the two, or the equity content, to range from 100–150 percent of the issue amount. This is the first assumption of the proposal and is determined by the borrower's requirement and market conditions. LPP needs new equity in due course and present market conditions are good. This suggests that an equity content of 150 percent would be acceptable; however, for the sake of comparison, the proposal provides for a 100 percent equity content.

In order to put a value on the warrants, we examine the various elements with a bearing on the price. The in-house economist has calculated that the historic volatility of the stock price over the last three years was 22.50 percent. By extrapolation, he has calculated a theoretical price of a five-year warrant of Fr28.

LPP has equity warrants outstanding with 4¾ years' remaining life and currently quoted US$5–5.50 or Fr31–35.75 at today's exchange rate of US$1 = Fr6.20. The exercise price is Fr300, which produces a global premium of 24.35 percent.*

This suggests that the warrants could have a five-year life and the global premium could be set at 25 percent. You assume a slightly higher strike price of Fr310 and write the equation of the global premium as follows:

$$1.25 = \frac{310 + \text{warrant price}}{270}$$

and thus derive a notional warrant price of Fr27.5, which is low in relation to the market price of the outstanding warrants (with a shorter life). Given the low equity content you are proposing, you opt for a price of Fr30. This produces a global premium of

$$GP = \frac{310 + 30}{270}$$
$$= 1.259 \text{ or } 25.9\%$$

In order to check whether this is fair value, you arrange for a theoretical calculation of the warrant price. This shows that the implied volatility of a warrant price of Fr30 at the strike price of Fr310 is 26.75 percent. Given the historical volatility of the stock, the level of global premium is acceptable.

Further assumptions are now required on the terms of the issue. Market conditions indicate a 7-year maturity, an issue amount of US$200

---

* Global premium = $\dfrac{\text{Strike price} + \text{warrant price}}{\text{Current share price}}$

million and denominations of US$1000. Given an equity content of 100 percent of the issue, we derive the following terms:

Amount of equity raised:	US$200M × 1.0 = US$200M = Fr1.24 billion.

Number of shares created on exercise:	$\dfrac{Fr1,240,000,000}{310} = 4$ million
Number of bonds:	200,000
Exercise ratio:	1 warrant entitles the holder to purchase 1 share
Number of warrants:	4 million
Number of warrants per bond:	20
Value of the warrants attached to each bond of US$1000:	20 × 30 = Fr600 = US$96.77 (9.677% of the nominal amount of each bond)

The seven-year U.S. Treasury yield is 7.55 semiannual and we add the spread of 120 basis points (applicable to LPP) to derive the desired yield to the investor of 8.75 percent semiannual or 8.94 percent annual. The deal is competitive so you decide to forego part of your selling concession of 1½ percent and offer bonds at 99.04 percent to allow you to reduce the coupon to 8¾ percent annual (to offer the same yield of 8.94). You also opt for a full-coupon bond which trades better in the secondary market than a discount bond.

The pro forma terms of the issue may then be put down as follows:

1. The bond

Amount:	US$200 million
Maturity:	7 years
Denominations:	US$1000
Number of bonds:	200,000
Repayment:	In one amount at maturity
Coupon:	8¾% annual
Issue price:	100%
Commissions (as % of issue price):	2¼%

2. The warrants

Price of the warrant:	Fr30
Exercise price:	Fr310
Period of exercise:	5 years
Exercise premium:	9%
Global premium:	25.92%
Implied volatility:	26.72%

Issue price	
(bonds and warrants):	109.68%
Cost of funds (based on total issue price less commissions of 2¼%):	7.354% annual or 7.22% semiannual

The cost in semiannual terms is 33 basis points below the yield on 7-year U.S. Treasury stock. If LPP then accepted a swap into floating-rate funds at, say, 90 basis points over U.S. Treasuries, the benefit would be worth 123 basis points in semiannual bond terms or, in money market terms, 121.31 basis points (below LIBOR). In any event, LPP declines the proposal for an equity-warrant issue because of the slightly higher cost and the absence of control over the exercise of the warrants, which could lead to a potential duplication of debt and equity funding.

Exercise: Another oil major, Oberoesterreichische Oel und Mineral Forschung (OOMF) was privatized three years ago and is planning to finance oil exploration under the Tirolean Alps. The company has an excellent reputation in exploration, and geological surveys suggest substantial reserves which could place Austria among the leading oil-producing countries. The company's balance sheet is strong but the current exploration program, which will reach its peak in five years' time, could begin to stretch gearing ratios. World demand for oil is steady but stocks are high, production and refining plants have been working at well below capacity for some years, and there is little prospect of a hike in oil prices. OOMF's principal customers are located in its domestic market: Switzerland, Germany, and Czechoslovakia.

The Austrian stock market is buoyed on strong foreign demand in the Deutsche mark zone. Economic indicators are good and the currency is stable. The first and second part of the exploration have been financed through a domestic bond issue and an international bank loan. You are asked for proposals for the third stage financing of $250 million (equivalent) with an equity "kicker." Other data:

OOMF's current stock price:	S480
Historical volatility of the stock (3 years):	18.76%
Gross stock yield:	3.5%
Current exchange rate:	US$1 = S14

The tone of the bond markets is generally positive. The U.S. dollar market has seen a large volume of issuance activity on the strength of the solid performance of the U.S. dollar in the foreign exchange markets; however, swaps out of U.S. dollars are uneconomic. The Swiss franc market is showing strong institutional demand in medium-term maturities. The Deutsche mark market is less receptive following a DM5 billion issue for Deutsche Aussenhandelsbank, which had a lukewarm reception.

In formulating a proposal, consider first the arguments for and against a convertible and equity-warrant-linked issue in function of the borrower's requirement and equity content. Then establish which currency you would advocate. Is the currency of exposure acceptable to the borrower or will your choice dictate a swap?

Suggested Solution*

1. *Choice of equity instrument.* OOMF's equity requirement will need to be in place in five year's time, so the equity should be raised beforehand. A convertible

---

* This solution is one of several possibilities. Others are feasible but should be argued.

is an attractive option because of the possibility of a longer maturity, but this is of no benefit in this instance and the issuer would want to force conversion at an early stage. An early call provision in the structure of the issue would deter investors, unless the share price were expected to appreciate very quickly. On present market readings this is unlikely—given, for example, that no major oil price rise is in prospect. A convertible also limits the amount of equity OOMF can raise.

An equity-warrants issue enables OOMF to raise more equity, and the exercise of the warrants can be encouraged by a short exercise period and a low strike price. The price of the warrant itself would then be determined principally in function of the equity content. OOMF's ongoing exploration activity makes a possible duplication of resources quite manageable but, in order to strengthen the balance sheet further, the package might also include a second, cheaper warrant with a higher strike price. The income from the sale of both warrants would serve as an injection of shareholders' funds right away. An equity-warrants linked issue also allows the issuer to manage if necessary its interest and currency exposure and provides the issuer a broader choice of investors to target. On balance, you opt for an equity-warrants issue.

2. *Choice of currency.* OOMF's customers are in fact predominantly in the Deutsche mark zone and therefore the currency of exposure should be Deutsche marks or Swiss francs. A U.S. dollar financing would target a large range of international investors; however, as far as the issuer is concerned, swaps out of U.S. dollars into Deutsche mark or Austrian schilling are currently uneconomic. An issue in Deutsche marks is not an attractive alternative since the Deutsche mark bond market is presently overblown. On the other hand, the market report indicates there is strong institutional demand in Switzerland. This is the one area close to the borrower which is showing positive appetite and your choice therefore inclines away from a Eurobond issue in favor of a Swiss franc issue with longish maturity, say, 10 years.

You are now required to price the financing, which begins by making assumptions on the levels of:

- the strike price
- the equity content
- exchange rates (use current exchange rates)
- the bond denominations
- the exercise ratio

Hints: Consider the level of global premium. Can the historic volatility of the stock serve as a guide in any way?

For the purposes of pricing the bond in Swiss francs, assume you are pricing a full-coupon bond with a coupon of 5¼ percent and total issue commissions and taxes of 3⅜ percent.

Solution: The following data are provided by the market:

- a Swiss franc/U.S. dollar exchange rate of US$1 = SFr1.60;
- a Swiss franc/Austrian schilling exchange rate of SFr1 = S7.80

and the following are assumptions (which may be altered in the light of the overall shape of the financing):

- an equity content of 140 percent
- denominations of SFr5000
- an exercise ratio of one warrant per share

Given the borrower requirement for US$250 million (equivalent), we now formulate the following parameters of an issue:

Issue amount:	SFr400 million
Equity raised on exercise of the warrants:	SFr400 × 140% = SFr560 million or S4.368 million

The high equity content is alleviated by introducing two separate warrants, A and B, with different exercise periods. Warrant A will serve the equity requirement 5 years hence and account for ten-fourteenths of the total equity content. The exercise period will be four years and the strike price will be low so as to optimize exercise of the warrants. Other things being equal, these terms will ensure the warrant acquires intrinsic value soon, which would allow a medium to high price to be placed on the warrant. However, the package has a high overall equity content and you decide to price the warrant within conservative parameters as follows:

Amount of equity raised through warrant A:	1 × SFr400 million or S3.120 million
Strike price (assumption):	S520
Number of shares issued at the strike price of S520:	6 million
Number of bonds:	80,000
Number of A warrants per bond:	75
Warrant price (assumption):	S60
Current share price:	S480
Exercise premium (warrant price divided by current share price):	12.50%
Global premium:	20.83%

Your economist works out for you the level of implied volatility of certain warrant prices at the strike price of S520 as follows:

	Exercise period (years)			
Price	3	4	5	7
S35	16.21	18.34	20.41	23.59
S60	18.47	21.41	22.23	25.04
S90	20.71	23.08	24.60	28.60

The implied volatility of a four-year warrant priced at S60 is 21.41 percent. The theoretical global premium is a direct function of the implied volatility, which serves as a guide to the degree of accuracy of the warrant price and size of global premium. The actual global premium of 20.83 percent is therefore acceptable. At S60 warrant price, the implied volatility of the warrant for a three-year exercise period is also within the historical volatility of the actual underlying stock over the past three years (18.76 percent) and provides additional comfort on the suggested levels of warrant price and global premium.

Value of the A Warrants Per Bond

$$\frac{\text{Number of A warrants per bond} \times \text{(assumed) schilling warrant price}}{\text{Swiss franc/Austrian schilling exchange rate}}$$

$$= \frac{75 \times 60}{7.8} = \text{SFr576.92 (11.54\% of each SFr5000 bond)}$$

B warrants will account for the four-fourteenths remainder of the equity content. Their purpose is to offer investors a more speculative instrument, while giving the issuer the reasonable prospect of raising still more equity at a higher premium at a later date. The exercise period should therefore be longer and the strike price higher. On the other hand, the price of the warrant should be moderate because of the greater delay in acquiring intrinsic value.

Amount of equity raised through warrant B:	4/14 × SFr560 million = SFr160 million or S1.248 million
Exercise period:	7 years
Strike price (assumption):	S600
Number of shares issued at the strike price of S624:	2.080 million
Number of bonds:	80,000
Number of B warrants per bond:	26
Warrant price (assumption):	S24
Current share price:	S480
Exercise premium:	5.00%
Global premium:	30.00%

Your economist tells you that at a strike price of S600, the implied volatility of a warrant priced at S24 is 28.74 percent. The global premium of 30 percent on the B warrants is greater, but is still acceptable given the intentionally speculative character of the warrant and its cheap price.

Value of the B warrants per bond:	$\dfrac{24 \times 26}{7.8}$ = SFr80.00 (1.60% per SFr5000 bond)
Value of A and B warrants per SF5000 bond:	1.60 + 11.54 = 13.14%
Issue price of package:	113.14%
Cost of funds: Using the HP-12C, key in:	PV = 109.765 (113.14% less commissions and taxes of 3.375%) PMT = −5.25 FV = −100 n = 10

and, solving for i, you obtain 4.0435 percent per annum bond.

OOMF is delighted with this proposal and awards you the mandate.

Bull and Bear Bonds

A bull and bear issue is a standard fixed-rate Eurobond issue whose principal redemption payments are linked to the performance of a stock market index. On maturity, the index may be higher or lower than its level at the time of launch, and the structure accommodates both expectations by offering two tranches.

The Bull Tranche. The principal amount on redemption varies in a direct ratio to the performance of the selected stock market index. Investors receive a current yield and, if their expectation of a stock index rise is realized, the bonds are redeemed above par, at a price calculated by reference to the rise in the index on redemption date. If the stock market index has fallen in relation to its initial level at the time of launch, the redemption price is below par, and is calculated according to the fall of the index. In effect, the bull bond equates to a straight bond and the simultaneous purchase of a share index composite stock. It is designed to appeal to investors who buy fixed-interest securities but who also wish to benefit from an anticipated share market rise, hence the name *bull.*

The Bear Bond. The bear bond rewards the investor for (justified) pessimism by gradually increasing the redemption price as the stock index falls. The formula is similar to that used on the bull tranche with the difference that the redemption price varies in inverse ratio to the performance of the stock index. In effect, the bear tranche serves as a long-term hedging instrument for share portfolios against stock market falls by enabling the investor to offset the potential loss on the portfolio with the capital gain on the bond.

The price of the composite stock index is reflected in an identical below-market coupon on both tranches. The issuer is at no risk on the level of the index on redemption, since the *sum* of the redemption prices of the respective tranches is constant at any given index level. In early issues, the sum was set at a level in excess of 200 percent, but the below-market coupon ensured that the cost of funds of the package was still below that of a standard fixed-rate issue.* Clearly, the choice of index was directed to more volatile stock markets, including Nikkei Dow (Japan) and Standard and Poor's 500 (United States), but the FAZ index in the Federal Republic of Germany has also been used.

Example: Deutsche Bank Finance issued in July 1986 a DM200 million bull and bear bond in equal tranches of DM100 million, whose redemption price was linked to the performance of the FAZ stock index on the following terms and conditions:

Maturity:	5 years
Coupon:	3% p.a. (annual bond)
Issue price:	100% for each tranche
Redemption price:	The redemption price of each tranche is calculated on the basis of a redemption index. The redemption index is the percentage ratio of the level of the stock index on redemption date (the "final index") to the level at the time of launch (the "initial index"). Thus:

$$\text{Redemption index} = \frac{\text{Final index}}{\text{Initial index}}$$

and is expressed as a percentage

---

* This applied even where the index on the maturity date turned out unchanged in relation to the initial level, because the formula for calculating the redemption price was different in each tranche.

The redemption price of each tranche is calculated as follows:

1. Bull tranche: Redemption price = redemption index × 0.94
2. Bear tranche: Redemption price = 217% − (Redemption index × 0.94)

Initial index level:	610.79
Final index level:	Index prevailing as of close of business on August 15th, 1991
Other terms:	Standard

In this example, the sum of the redemption prices of both tranches was 217 percent regardless of the level of final index (or, in effect, 108.5 percent of the total principal amount). Assuming fees of 2½ percent, the all-in cost of funds of the DM200 million financing is 5.1140 percent. By contrast, a conventionally priced issue with a coupon of 5¼ percent would have had an all-in cost of 5.8409 percent. Within these parameters, a matrix of redemption prices was constructed as follows:

Percentage change of final index	55	70	85	100	115	130	145	160	175
Bull redemption price	51.7	65.8	79.9	94	108.1	122.20	136.30	150.40	164.50
Redemption yield	−8.43	−4.48	−1.11	1.84	4.48	6.87	9.06	11.08	19.0
Bear redemption price	165.3	151.2	137.1	123.00	108.90	94.8	80.7	66.6	52.5
Redemption yield	13.1	11.2	9.2	7.0	4.62	2.0	0.93	−4.28	−8.19

Calculation of the Redemption Price of the Bull Tranche

Let us assume:

Initial index:	610.79
Final index:	612.76
Redemption index:	$\dfrac{612.76}{610.79} = 1.0032$ or 100.32%
Redemption price:	$100.32 \times 0.94 = 94.30$

Given the coupon of 3 percent and a life of 5 years, the investor's redemption yield is 1.90 percent (assuming a purchase price of par).

Calculation of the Redemption Price of the Bear Tranche

Let us assume:

Initial index:	610.79
Final index:	540
Redemption index:	$\dfrac{540}{610.79} = 0.8841$ or 88.41%

Redemption price: $$[217 - (88.41 \times 0.94)] \times \frac{1}{100} = 133.89\%$$

Redemption yield: 8.697% (assuming a purchase price of par)

The linkage to a stock index caused bull and bear issues to perform erratically in the secondary market. Unlike an equity convertible whose price tracks the performance of a share, the price of a stock-index-linked bond was a function of something unknowable (i.e., the final index and standard calculations of the present value, or price, of the bond during the course of its life lacked credibility). Positive or negative sentiment in the stock market was reflected in exaggerated price swings as most investors sought to buy one tranche rather than the other, which then gave rise to liquidity problems. In an attempt to remedy these shortcomings, the redemption amount on later issues was fixed by reference to the level of the stock index after one year. Following the first anniversary, the issue then acquired a fixed redemption price and traded like a normal straight bond. This ensured that secondary market performance was smoother, somewhat more predictable, and therefore in closer relation to the actual performance of the stock index.

9

Introduction to Financial Engineering

Currency Option-linked Bonds

The performance of the U.S. dollar in the foreign exchange markets during the two decades 1970–1990 has similarities to that of sterling after the Second World War. The fundamental weakness of the U.S. dollar from growing budget and trade deficits, against the background of the currency's continuing role as the leading international reserve asset, compounded the potential for fluctuation or volatility in relation, say, to the Deutsche mark which, by contrast, is fundamentally strong and plays a lesser role in international transactions. The U.S. dollar has fluctuated against some major currencies by as much as 40 percent in the course of a year. This presents obvious risks to parties active in international trade and commerce and to international investor portfolios with diverse currency exposure and, for both, the management of currency risk became a major concern.

Traditional currency hedging instruments include the forward currency markets and the more recent foreign currency futures markets. However, both commit the customer to an exchange of currency at a set rate at a future date. In the mid-1980s, options were applied to currencies for the first time to provide a much more flexible and economical tool. A currency option, which shares most of the mechanics of an equity option (or warrant, as reviewed in Chap. 8), is a right (but not an obligation) to enter into a foreign exchange (FX) transaction over a period of time (the exercise period) and at a prespecified FX rate (the strike price). Currency options are presently offered against all major currencies and traded in active and liquid options markets. However, the maturities offered on traded currency options are short and contract sizes are large, with a minimum of US$/£12,500 or US$/DM62,500. The price of the option, or premium, is determined by

213

open competition between buyers and sellers on the exchange for foreign currency options and reflects intrinsic value and time value. Premiums are quoted in U.S. cents per unit of the underlying currency.

Currency option lexicon (reproduced from "Understanding Foreign Currency Options" published by the Philadelphia Stock Exchange) is as follows:

Exercise price. The exchange rate at which the holder may exercise the option. Exercise prices are expressed in terms of U.S. cents per unit of the underlying currency.

Call option. An option to purchase a stated amount of the underlying currency at the exercise price within the specified period.

Put option. An option to sell a stated amount of the underlying currency at the exercise price within the specified period.

Option premium. The price of the option expressed in terms of U.S. cents per unit of the underlying currency.

At-the-money. A currency option is at-the-money when the exercise price (or exchange rate) is the same as the current spot exchange rate.

In-the-money. A CALL option is in-the-money when its exercise price is *below* the current spot exchange rate; a PUT option is in-the-money when its exercise price is *above* the current spot rate.

Out-of-the-money. A CALL option whose exercise price is above the current spot rate; or a PUT option whose exercise price is below the current spot rate.

Intrinsic value. An option has intrinsic value if it is profitable to exercise it. Thus a CALL option has intrinsic value if the exercise price is below the current spot rate.

Time value. An option has time value if the exercise period is unexpired.

Example: British American Engineering (BAE) expects to receive US$5 million in three months and wishes to sell this in due course for pounds sterling. The US$/pound sterling rate today is US$1.75 = £1.00. BAE has three possible courses of action, as follows:

- It can buy sterling three months forward against U.S. dollars and thus hedge fully against a possible depreciation of the U.S. dollar. The hedge exchange rate will be a less favorable rate than today's exchange rate at, say, US$1.82 = £1.00 and produce £2,747,252.75.
- It can do nothing and run an "open" position. The dollar could depreciate to US$1.90 = £1.00, and BAE would realize no more than £2,631,578.94.
- It can buy a currency option to sell US$5 million dollars for sterling at US$1.75 = £1.00 within three months. The cost of the option is $0.05 per pound sterling and must be added to the cost of the transaction.

Assuming BAE takes the third course, on the expiry of the option, one of three scenarios could arise:

1. If the U.S. dollar is weaker, say, US$1.83 = £1.00, then BAE would exercise its option and sell U.S. dollars against sterling at a rate of US$1.75 = £1.00. The effective

exchange rate including the cost of the option is US\$1.80 = £1.00 and BAE realizes £2,777,777.78.

2. If the U.S. dollar appreciates to US\$1.50 = £1.00, the currency option serves no purpose and is allowed to lapse. BAE sells its dollars in the spot market. Again, BAE has to deduct the cost of the discarded option at \$0.05 per pound, which increases the effective rate to US\$1.55 = £1.00 and BAE realizes £3,225,806.45.

3. If the U.S. dollar appreciates, but only to US\$1.72 = £1.00, it would still discard the option. BAE does better to sell in the open market because the effective rate would be below US\$1.80 = £1.00.

Eurobond Issues with Currency Options Attached. Linked to a Eurobond issue, a currency option is securitized as a tailor-made listed warrant. This presents several advantages over standard currency options, including the following:

- It overcomes the prohibition in some countries that prevents retail and institutional investors from buying currency options per se.

- Currency options can be purchased (1) in smaller denominations or contract sizes and (2) with longer exercise periods.

For the issuer, adding a securitized option reduces the cost of the borrowing. The proceeds of the sale of the currency option warrants are applied (as in the case of an equity warrant) as a once-and-for-all income to reduce the IRR of the financing. However, in selling the warrants, the issuer is creating foreign currency exposure for itself. Let us assume that a U.S. issuer such as General Motors Acceptance Corporation issues a U.S. dollar Eurobond with a sterling call option attached at US\$1.75 = £1.00. If, on reaching expiry, the dollar has depreciated against sterling to US\$1.90 = £1.00, holders of the options will exercise their warrants and the issuer must deliver sterling against dollars at US\$1.75 = £1.00. If the issuer is unhedged and buys sterling in the spot market, it is liable for a loss of US\$0.15 per pound sterling. The issuer, however, may protect itself in turn by purchasing an offsetting currency option to hedge its currency exposure. The cost benefit of the issue is reduced but the issuer still benefits from the structure. The issuer hedges itself in the wholesale FX market but issues the warrants at a higher retail price.

Example: Aerospazio Italia S.A. decides to launch a DM bond issue with tradeable two-year warrants attached giving entitlement to an American DM put option. The terms of the bond issue are as follows:

Amount:	DM200 million
Maturity:	5 years
Interest:	6% p.a. payable annually in arrears and calculated on a 360/360 day year
Issue price:	100%
Early redemption:	None
Redemption price:	100%
Issuance commissions:	2%

Listing:	Frankfurt
Listing fee:	½%
Denominations:	DM1000

Terms of the Warrants

Exercise price:	US$1.00 = DM2.10
Exercise period:	At any time within a period commencing 2 weeks after settlement date and terminating on the second anniversary of the issue
Current spot rate:	US$1.00 = DM2.00
Structure:	Each bond of DM1000 has a detachable warrant giving the holder the right to receive the difference between (1) the DM equivalent of US$500 at a rate of US$1.00 = DM2.10 (the exercise price) and (2) the DM equivalent of US$500 at the then prevailing spot rate.
Warrant price:	$0.0375 per DM1. At the current exchange rate, this is equivalent to DM0.075 per DM1 or DM75 per DM1000 bond or 7.5%.
Issue price:	100% + 7.5% = 107.5%
Premium of exercise price in relation to current spot price:	2.10/2.00 = 1.05 or 5%
Global premium:	12.5%
Cost of funds (excluding paying agency, expenses, warrant listing, and exercise fees):	4.85% p.a.

The warrants are a two-year securitized American out-of-the-money put option which would be listed on the selected stock exchange separately from the bond. Pricing warrants relies, as in the case of equity warrants, on (1) option pricing models to provide a theoretical calculation and (2) a market view based on supply and demand, and currency expectations that are not factored into the theoretical assessment. Common sense also dictates that the time value of a 2-year option must be greater than that of a standard 3- or 6-month option, and this is reflected in the warrant price.*

In the secondary market, the warrant price should track the time value and intrinsic value, if any, of the warrant and, given adequate market making in the instrument, warrant holders are more likely to trade their warrants than exercise them, which would imply surrendering their time value. In the example just shown, provided the warrant is in-the-money, holders exercise their warrants as the expiry date approaches in exchange for a cash settlement. For example, if the spot rate remains at US$1.00 = DM2.00, the investor has no interest in exercising the warrant. If the spot rate deteriorates to US$1.00 = DM2.50, the investor exercises his warrant and receives:

$$\left(US\$500 \times \frac{DM2.50}{US\$1}\right) - \left(US\$500 \times \frac{DM2.10}{US\$1}\right) = US\$500 \times \frac{DM0.40}{US\$1}$$
$$= DM200$$

From this figure must be deducted the cost of the warrant of DM75 to derive a net profit of DM125.

---

* Standard options are also written with a one-, two-, nine-, and twelve-month life.

In this instance, the issuer's exposure arising from the currency options is unhedged. If we assume that all holders exercise on the expiry date and that on that date the dollar has appreciated to US$1 = DM2.50, then the issuer has a liability of DM200 × 200,000 = DM40 million in addition to the debt service costs. To hedge itself against such a liability, Aerospazio Italia purchases an identical currency option from, say, the lead manager of the issue at a cost of US$0.02875 per DM1 or DM0.0575 per DM1. This equates to DM57.50 per DM1000 or 5.75% of the nominal amount of each bond. The cost of the issue is much higher than if the currency option were unhedged, but still lower than a conventional straight DM bond issue as illustrated in the following cash flows. (All amounts in DM millions. Cash flows ignore paying agency fees and issuance expenses.)

End of year	Straight bond	Currency option bond (*unhedged* and warrant *not* exercised)
1	195.00	210.00
2	−12.00	−12.00
3	−12.00	−12.00
4	−12.00	−12.00
5	−212.00	−212.00
	IRR: 6.6033%	IRR: 4.8499%

End of year	Currency option bond (unhedged and warrant exercised by all holders on 2nd anniversary at $1 = DM2.50)	Currency option bond (hedged)
1	210.00	198.50
2	−12.00	−12.00
3	−52.00	−12.00
4	−12.00	−12.00
5	−212.00	−212.00
	IRR: 9.0423%	IRR: 6.1789%

Dual Currency Bonds

One of the early variations on currency option-linked Eurobonds was to issue bonds with warrants into currency options whose life extended to the maturity date of the bond. The warrants were securitized European options, that is, exercisable on expiry date only. An example of an issue structure might be a standard Eurodollar bond issue with a seven-year maturity and US1000 denominations with warrants attached. The warrants equated to a French franc call option (against the U.S. dollar) with an exercise price equal to the spot exchange rate at launch (that is, a nil exercise premium). The holder of the warrant—if exercising his or her right on maturity date—was entitled to receive, in U.S. dollars, the difference between (1) US$1000 and (2) the dollar equivalent at maturity of US$1000 worth of French francs at the time of launch. Thus, if the spot rate at launch was US$1.00 = Fr8.00, the French franc equivalent of each bond was Fr8000. At maturity, if the French franc had appreciated to US$1.00 = Fr6.00, then Fr8000 is worth US$1333.33. The warrant holder therefore receives the difference between US$1333.33 and US$1000, or US$333.33. The bond holder meanwhile received repayment of US$1000 in the normal way. In effect, the liability of the borrower at maturity under the combined bond and warrant was the French franc equivalent at launch of the dollar amount of the bond issue. Should the French franc depreciate to say US$1.00 = Fr8.50 the option would be worthless, since the dollar equivalent of Fr8000 was worth only US$941.18.

A notable variation of the currency option bond is the "heaven and hell" bond, which substitutes currency for the stock index linkage of bull and bear bonds. This structure comprises a standard Eurodollar bond issue with repayment linked to a below-market exchange rate, typically US$/yen. Thus, if the spot rate at launch was US$1.00 = yen 178, the peg rate on redemption might be, say, US$1.00 = yen 148. On redemption, if the then spot rate were equal to the peg rate, investors were repaid at par in U.S. dollars. If the U.S. dollar rate were stronger than the peg rate, say, US$1.00 = yen 158, then the U.S. dollar repayment goes up in consequence, and vice versa if the U.S. dollar is weaker. For non-US$-based investors, there is a leveraged or double FX risk hence the *heaven and hell* name of the instrument. In effect, the structure comprises a long-term currency contract at the expense of the investor who was compensated—in theory—by an above-market coupon on the bond.

Issue structures with medium-term currency derivatives present several drawbacks. Pricing is somewhat haphazard and, in case of currency warrants, although option pricing models provide a reasonable theoretical guideline, the contribution of a market view of the worth of the option has proved elusive. Similarly, in the case of heaven and hell issues, the theoretical value of the redemption feature embedded in the structure may bear little relation to its market worth. In the secondary market, it became apparent that long-term European currency options did not trade like plain vanilla bonds, and liquidity suffered. Subsequent medium-term structures have been tailored to specific requirements of a few large investors and were, in effect, private placements.

Public issues have then sought to overcome the uncertainty over pricing by offering currency option-linked structures with short exercise periods. Many structures offered options on one of the more volatile currencies—such as the Australian dollar against the U.S. dollar, itself relatively volatile. These currencies were deliberately selected because the time value of the option over a short period is minimal and, without some degree of volatility, the benefit to the issuer from selling it is very small. Again, fair pricing has been an issue. One of the more controversial structures was a one-year issue denominated in Australian dollars with a borrower (not an investor) currency option to repay in U.S. dollars. The benefit to the borrower of its option was acknowledged in the form of a higher coupon; however, the options were often in-the-money and held to be undervalued. Inevitably, the complexity of the debt and currency risk inherent in these structures points to the need to restrict their placement to sophisticated investors able to analyze and understand the different components.

Debt Warrants

Debt warrants were conceived in 1980 by Salomon Brothers and were first issued in the Eurobond market in conjunction with a Eurodollar bond issue by a French borrower, Crédit National. Debt warrants are not a debt obligation and pay no interest or principal. Instead, the instruments act as an interest rate call option, giving the right but not the obligation to purchase over a period of time (the exercise period) a separate standard fixed-rate Eurobond on prespecified terms. The option is securitized in the form of a tradeable warrant issued for cash by the issuer to the investor. The warrant usually comes attached to a host bond and both are issued at the same time; following launch, the warrant becomes detachable and is listed separately. The maturity and the coupon of the new bond do not bear any necessary relation to the host bond, but the redemption yield would normally be set lower than the yield on a bond of equal maturity at the time of issue of the warrants. Thus, debt warrant bonds, like FRN convertibles and partly paid bonds, are designed to be launched in an expectation of falling interest rates and an upward-sloping yield curve.

The attractions of debt warants for investors include:

- the leverage effect created by committing only a small amount of capital to the purchase of a right, the bulk of the investment being called into play only if the right is exercised. As and when yields fall below the redemption yield of the new bond, the option acquires intrinsic value and the price of the warrant rises in line with the rise in bond prices. The investor's gain is disproportionately large in relation to the small initial outlay on the warrant.

- a longer exercise period than for standard options.*

- a tool of investment strategy.†

---

* The Abbey National Building Society issued warrants exercisable into 10-year sterling bonds over the period May 1989–May 1990. The warrants in effect offered a 12-month interest rate option, or twice the maturity of the longest traded option in the sterling gilts market.

† In this example, a typical investor strategy might be to switch out of 10-year gilts into the option, place the proceeds of the sale of the gilts on 12-month deposit at the high level of rates prevailing then and, on maturity of the deposit and assuming a fall in rates a year later, exercise the option and purchase the bond from the proceeds of the deposit at a premium in yield. If money markets at the time of issue of the warrants are sufficiently high, the interest on the deposit will cover the income forgone by the sale of the gilts, plus the cost of the warrant.

The drawback for investors in debt warrants lies in the poor quality of the secondary market. Investors are largely professional and institutional and are inclined to hold the warrants until close to expiry date. Should the expectation of yields change for the worse, liquidity disappears.

Debt warrants also present merits for issuers.

- The warrants are issued for cash and the proceeds are applied in reduction of the cost of the host bond issue.

- The leverage of the warrant enables the issuer to price the host bond more aggressively than a conventional straight bond.

Against this, the issuer must take account of certain disadvantages.

- The warrants create a commitment to further future borrowing at a rate that, though lower than today's, could yet be higher than that prevailing for such a bond at the expiry date of the warrant. This opportunity cost disinclines borrowers to issue warrants for long exercise periods.

- The exercise of the warrants may lead to an excess or duplication of funding.

To overcome this last problem, several further structures were devised.

- A number of debt warrant issues were designed so that the exercise of the warrants was linked to the call date of the issuer's outstanding bonds and would in effect refinance the prepaid bonds at a lower cost.

- A further response was the invention of the "harmless" warrant, under which a conventionally priced Eurobond would include a call feature halfway to maturity and would be accompanied by warrants into a bond with identical terms and pricing, but without a call feature. The investor option was exercised, not with a further investment of cash, but by surrendering the old bond. Clearly, this was not an attractive proposition for the investor who would have to retain the host bond and warrant and pay the warrant premium to purchase the same bond again. On later issues using this structure, the warrants and the bonds were sold to separate investor groups, but this did not alter the fact that the structure was a device to reduce the cost of the financing, and it gave little away to the investor. Eventually the structure fell into disuse.

- A further solution to the duplication of funding was to bonds was to issue bond warrants alone or "naked" warrants. The Dutch utility, Gasunie, issued naked in-the-money debt warrants in 1986 exercisable until 1988 into an 11 percent bond at par, to refinance outstanding high coupon fixed-rate Eurodollar debt at 11⅞ percent due 1991 and callable in 1988. Because of the long exercise period, the warrants themselves were remunerated at 6 percent per annum of the issue price of 4.4 percent.

Debt Warrant Pricing.   Pricing debt warrants, as in the case of other options, follows two alternative procedures. A theoretical price level may be derived by using the Black & Scholes option-pricing model to calculate the implied volatility of the underlying bond on the basis of the exercise price, the exercise period, and an assumption of future volatility. However, few participants value the warrant premium with the help of models alone and construct alternative price scenarios where the break-even yield and the cash price are assessed in relation to the leverage of the warrant. The theoretical price is in practice viewed as a minimum value which is then augmented by a premium, reflecting the market's perception. The difficulty lies in the evaluation of this further premium: the market has only a small number of outstanding debt warrant issues to serve as a basis for comparison, and secondary market performance is poor.

Example: The National Mortgage Institution has issued a tap-bond financing of ECU200 million, of which ECU150 million is issued, leaving ECU50 million still to be launched. The issue carries a final maturity of seven years and a coupon of 7⅝ percent. The current price is 96¼ percent (offered) or a redemption yield of 8.42 percent. The borrower will not launch the remaining ECU50 million unless it can obtain a redemption yield of 8.34 percent, or a price in today's market of 96.43 percent.

You are an issuing house and propose to buy the remaining ECU50 million from the borrower at its price. Confident that ECU rates will fall over the next six months, you decide to offer naked warrants to the market giving right to purchase bonds out of your ECU50 million holding. In six months the bond will have a remaining life of six years. Your research department has produced the following theoretical calculations, and you are asked to form a view.

	Warrant premium (%)	
Exercise price	6-month exercise period	12-month exercise period
96.25	1.22	1.76%
96.50	1.11	1.61%

Expectations for the decline in yields do not go beyond six months and the 12-month option may be abandoned. Using the second example, if the warrant premium is added to the exercise price, we derive a global cost to the investor of 96.50 + 1.11% = 97.61%. A calculation on the HP-12C produces a redemption yield at this price of 8.14 percent (that is, assuming a six-year life, a coupon of 7⅝ percent, and repayment at par). For comparison purposes, if the price of the existing bond remained unchanged (96¼ percent) in six months, the redemption yield on a six-year remaining life would be 8.475 percent, or a yield differential of 33.5 basis points.

Clearly, the higher the buy-in yield, the sooner the warrant acquires intrinsic value (assuming expectations of falling yields are verified) and the more the investor is prepared to pay for it. Although the exercise period of the warrant is short, the yield differential of 33.5 basis points is nevertheless low, and other hypothetical scenarios may be drawn up as follows:

	1	2	3
Exercise price	97.00	97.00	97.00
Price of warrant	2.00	1.50	1.00
Total	99.00	98.50	98.00
Break even (6 year) redemption yield	7.84	7.95	8.06

The first and second solution produce differentials of 63.5 and 52.5 basis points, respectively (against the notional yield of 8.475% on the existing bond with a price of 96⅛ percent unchanged in six months). The second solution shows a lower warrant cost and increases the investor's leverage. A head of bond sales or head trader might well sanction either solution depending on how "bullish" were his or her expectations of falling ECU interest rates.

The economics of the second solution for the bank can be itemized as follows:

Purchase of bonds at NMI's price: (96.43)

Revenue from the sale of each warrant (ignoring fees): 1.50

Funding of holding of bonds for six months:

1. Yield (assume the bonds are bought and sold to investors at the same price of 96.43); the yield is therefore the current yield of:

$$\frac{7.625}{96.43} = 7.907$$

This figure is a per annum bond yield.

2. Funding (assume 6-month LIBOR is 7.3125% p.a.) This is a money market yield and expressed in annual bond terms of 7.55% p.a.

3. The yield exceeds the funding; therefore, there is a profit of positive carry of 35.7 basis points per annum, or 17.85 basis points for six months.

Sale price of bonds on exercise of warrants (if exercised): 97.00

Summary Cash Flow. This is a cash flow with four payments: the first two are made on day one and include the purchase price of the bonds and the proceeds from the warrant sales. The second two payments take place six months later and include the sale of bonds and the positive carry.

Purchase	(96.43)
Warrant proceeds	1.50
	(94.93)
Positive carry	0.1785
Sale of bonds	97.00
	97.1785

The IRR of the cash flow is 2.36859 percent. On a principal amount of ECU50 million, this produces a profit of:

$$50,000,000 \times \frac{2.36859}{100} = ECU1,184,295$$

Forward Swaps
and Swap-Options

Where an issue has a call feature, the issuer has an option to redeem the issue before the scheduled maturity. The issuer confident of a fall in interest rates may choose to sell an option in the form of naked debt warrants in anticipation of exercising the call option. The warrants may be structured so that their exercise would be coterminous with the call date. The warrants would be exercisable into bonds of the same maturity or longer, which would in effect serve to refinance the old bond issue but at a lower cost.

An alternative refinancing strategy would be to enter into a forward swap whereby the issuer commits to an exchange of debt service payments at a future date, that is, the call date. Under this scheme, the issuer redeems the issue on the call date and refinances by arranging a bank loan at a floating rate of interest. The issuer simultaneously enters into a swap whereby he receives floating-rate payments (with the same floating-rate interest base as the bank loan) and, in exchange, makes fixed-rate payments on the same amount as the bond issue, but at a lower rate, until the final maturity of the issue. The effect of the swap is to produce a new fixed-rate financing at a lower cost. The floating-rate payments offset each other but for the margin on the loan.

The issuer might choose a third strategy, which is to sell its call option and forgo the opportunity of early redemption. Selling the option to the existing investors is not practical. Instead the issuer sells on a swap, or *swaption,* to a third party, such as a financial institution seeking a guaranteed level of income over the period from the call date to final maturity of the issue. The third party then exercises the option if yields fall below the coupon of the bond by the date of exercise.* In practice, the sale of the call is structured as the sale of an option on a swap, or a swaption. If the swaption is exercised, the issuer prepays the issue and simultaneously refinances with a bank loan and implements the swap contract with the buyer of the swap-option whereby he undertakes to make fixed-rate payments at the same rate and on the same principal amount as the bond issue and receives in return floating-rate payment at, say, interbank deposit rates.

The price of swaptions may be calculated theoretically in much the same way as debt warrants. Both constitute an option on a flow of payments. In the case of the swaption, the issuer also puts a value on the renunciation of the call, which may be crudely expressed as the difference in the bond price structured with and without the call feature. However, this value would have to be adjusted for changing interest rate expectations at the time the swaption was sold. A further consideration is the scarcity of swaptions, which places a premium on their market price.

---

* If the rates are the same as the coupon on the bond, the option may nevertheless be exercised if there is an expectation of falling rates.

Exercise: Benelux Associated Satellite Television (BLAST) has an outstanding DM80 million issue, paying 8¼ percent per annum and maturing in November 1994. There is a call option providing for early redemption in November 1990 at 101.50 percent. The issue was launched in November 1987 at par. The fees were 2¼ percent plus a listing fee of ½ percent. The issue is currently yielding 6.25 percent. With DM yields currently at their lowest level for some years, BLAST would like to refinance the issue on the basis of today's rates. You are an issuing house without a strong relationship with BLAST, but with a strong technical support in-house to assist in making proposals. The date is November 1989. What are your choices?

A financing in DM with Reinvestment of the Proceeds Until the Call Date. A five-year public bond issue launched today would duplicate BLAST's funding until the call date, but the excess funding could be reinvested until the old issue is redeemed in November 1990.

To offer a current market yield of 6.25 percent at the full selling concession of 1½ percent: (1) what would the coupon on the bond have to be (to the nearest ⅛ percent)? Work out (2) the issue price (rounded to the next lowest ⅛ percent) and (3) the all-in cost, assuming issuance fees of 2 percent plus ½ percent listing; (4) could you save on a public DM bond issue?

Solutions

1. Given a yield of 6.25 percent at 98.50 percent (100 percent minus ½ percent), a life of five years and repayment at 100 percent, a calculation on the HP-12C produces a coupon of 5.89 percent—say, 5⅞ percent.

2. Inputting the coupon of 5⅞ percent (instead of 5.89 percent) and solving for *PV,* we derive a price of 98.43 percent. In other words, at a price of 98.43 percent, the redemption yield of a five-year bond with a 5⅞ percent coupon is 6.25 percent. Adding back the selling concession of 1½ percent, we obtain an issue price of 99.93 percent or, rounded down to the nearest ⅛ percent, 99⅞ percent.

3. A bond with an issue price of 99⅞ percent, a coupon of 5⅞ percent, a five-year maturity and 2½ percent fees (including listing) has an IRR of 6.5068 percent.

4. A private placement would have a higher coupon but lower fees. On a five-year maturity, the coupon would increase by an ⅛ percent to 6 percent, fees would be ⅜ percent less and fall to 1⅝ percent. Given an issue price of 99⅞ percent, and ignoring expenses, the financing has an IRR of 6.4202 percent.

You opt, therefore, for a private placement and reinvest the proceeds for one year on the money market. One-year DM LIBOR is 4.25 percent bid. (1) What is the return on the deposit? (2) Write down the cash flow of the old bond with and without early redemption; and the cash flow of the new five-year private placement, including its reinvestment for one year. (3) Combine the old bond with early redemption with the private placement and derive the IRR of the combined financings. What is the saving per annum on the cost of the old bond?

Solutions

1. The net proceeds of the private placement are 98.25 percent (99⅞ percent minus 1⅝ percent) of DM80 million or DM78 million, ignoring expenses.
   Interest for one year at 4¼ percent per annum on a money market basis:

$$78,600,000 \times \frac{4.25}{100} \times \frac{365}{360} = 3,386,896$$

2. Cash flows are as follows:

End of year	Old bond without redemption	Old bond with redemption
0	+77,800,000	+77,800,000
1	−6,600,000	−6,600,000
2	−6,600,000	−6,600,000
3	−6,600,000	−87,800,000*
4	−6,600,000	
5	−6,600,000	
6	−6,600,000	
7	−86,600,000	
IRR: 8.7926%		

* This amount comprises: −6,600,000 − 80,000,000 − 1,200,000 = −87,800,000

	New private placement	Reinvestment
2	+78,600,000	−78,600,000
3	−4,800,000	+81,986,896
4	−4,800,000	
5	−4,800,000	
6	−4,800,000	
7	−84,800,000	
IRR: 6.42%		

3. Combined cash flow of private placement and reinvestment is as follows:

2	NIL
3	+77,186,896
4	−4,800,000
5	−4,800,000
6	−4,800,000
7	−84,800,000

Combined cash flow of old bond with early redemption, private placement, and reinvestment is as follows:

0	+77,800,000
1	−6,600,000
2	−6,600,000
3	−10,613,104
4	−4,800,000
5	−4,800,000
6	−4,800,000
7	−84,800,000
IRR: 8.4241%	

This represents a saving of 36.85 basis points (annual) on the IRR of the old bond, or DM294,800 per annum.

An Issue of Debt Warrants. You have the option to issue debt warrants exercisable until September 1990 into a fixed-rate bond with a current market coupon and a maturity of four years.

Advantages:

- Warrant proceeds reduce the cost of the original financing regardless of the degree of exercise.
- Bonds arising out of the exercise of the warrants are issued without payment of commission.
- Exercise date coincides with limit date for the notice of call (say, 60 days). If a sufficient proportion of warrants are exercised, BLAST redeems the old issue to avoid duplication of funding. The proportion of the issue not replaced can be financed by a bank loan and swapped, if necessary, into fixed-rate debt.

Drawbacks:

- Rates are at a historic low point, so there is perhaps little scope for further decline.
- DM rates have low volatility.
- Degree of exercise is not guaranteed.
- There may be duplication of funding for a short period.

Conclusion: Abandon scheme.

Refinancing through a Forward Swap. Your swap department advises you that a DM interest rate swap may be arranged with a start date to coincide with the call date one year hence, at a rate of 6½ percent against one-year DM LIBOR.

Your banking department tells you that a bank loan can be arranged for BLAST with effect from the call date, subject to no change in the credit or market conditions, at a spread of ⅛ percent over one-year DM LIBOR. Is this a cheaper solution? (1) Write down the cash flow of the bank loan and swap. (2) Write down the combined cash flow of the old bond with redemption, the bank loan, and the swap and derive the IRR.

Solution: The principal amount of the swap and the loan is DM80 million. The spread element of interest on the bank loan, at the rate of DM LIBOR plus ⅛ percent, is calculated as follows:

$$80,000,000 \times \frac{1}{100} \times \frac{12.5}{100} \times \frac{365}{360} = 101,389$$

1. Cash flows (from BLAST's standpoint):

End of year	Bank loan (ignoring fees and expenses)		Swap
3	+80,000,000	—	—
4	−DM LIBOR − 101,389	+DM LIBOR	− 5,200,000
5	−DM LIBOR − 101,389	+DM LIBOR	− 5,200,000
6	−DM LIBOR − 101,389	+DM LIBOR	− 5,200,000
7	−80,101,389 − DM LIBOR	+DM LIBOR	− 5,200,000

2. Combined cash flow of old bond, bank loan and swap:

0	+77,800,000
1	−6,600,000

2	−6,600,000
3	−7,800,000
4	−5,301,389
5	−5,301,389
6	−5,301,389
7	−85,301,389
IRR: 8.1934%	

The forward swap produces a saving of 59.92 basis points over the original bond issue, or DM479,360 per annum.

Refinancing through a Swap-Option.   Your swap department proposes to purchase from BLAST an option to receive BLAST's interest payment flows from the call date in exchange for one-year DM LIBOR. This entails the renunciation of BLAST's call option on the bond issue, whose exercise would then be subordinated to the exercise of the swap-option by your swap department.

By entering into the swap-option, BLAST pays 8¼ percent per annum until the maturity date of the old bond issue, come what may. If your swap department decides to exercise its option (assuming interest rates are lower in a year), then BLAST must:

- prepay the issue
- contract a bank loan for DM80 million at say DM LIBOR plus ⅛ percent.
- implement the swap-option whereby it (1) receives one-year DM LIBOR and (2) pays 8¼ percent per annum.

If the swap department does not exercise its swap-option, it is because rates have gone higher and the swap department will have no interest in a flow of receipts at 8¼ percent. BLAST continues to pay the bondholders as before. Since yields will have risen higher, no borrowing opportunity will have been lost, but the overall cost of the original bond issue will have been reduced in any event by the income of the option premium.

What level of swaption premium must BLAST receive to make this solution more attractive than a forward swap?

Solution: The cash flows comprise:

- the old bond with early redemption at the end of year 3
- the payments under the swaption of 8¼ percent per annum against DM LIBOR flat from the end of year 3
- the bank loan interest from the end of year 3 at a rate of DM LIBOR plus ⅛ percent

These cash flows are identical to the cash flows in the example of the forward swap except for the fixed-rate payments from year 4 to year 7, which continue to be at the rate of 8¼ percent per annum. Again, as in the previous scheme, the DM LIBOR flows cancel out.

The combined cash flow may then be set out as follows:

0	+77,800,000
1	−6,600,000
2	−6,600,000
3	−7,800,000 + ?

4	−6,701,389
5	−6,701,389
6	−6,701,389
7	−86,701,389
IRR: 9.0912%	

The premium on the swaption is payable at the end of year 3 and the level of premium is ascertained by trial and error to achieve an overall IRR on the cash flow of below 8.19 percent. If BLAST can secure from your swap department a premium of DM4.7 million, the net outgoing at the end of year 3 falls to DM3.1 million and the IRR falls to 8.1774 percent. At this point, this is the most attractive solution.

10

The Anatomy of a Eurobond Issue*

This chapter discusses, first, the legal nature of a Eurobond and, in particular, the means by which it is transferable and the legal and commercial consequences that flow therefrom. Second, it will describe the documentation and procedures by which Eurobonds are typically issued into the market. This will involve consideration of the terms and conditions to which Eurobonds are subject (which will include the tax treatment of payments under Eurobonds and typical "negative pledge" convenants and events of default).

The Legal Nature of a Eurobond

It is a fundamental, and for all practical purposes essential, requirement of a Eurobond that it be transferable; and its transfer should be straightforward and simple. Transferability can be achieved by a number of techniques, but two particular methods are generally employed. These two methods are represented by the bearer bond, where the issuer promises to pay the bearer of the physical instrument, and the registered bond, where the promise is that payment will be made to the person whose name appears on the register as the holder of the bond.

Since payment on a bearer bond is due to the physical holder of the bond, the right to receive that payment can be transferred by physical delivery of the bond itself by one person to another. No formalities or writing are

* By Stephen Hood and Andrew Taylor of Clifford Chance, Capital Market Department.

required and, when stamp duty was levied in the United Kingdom on written instruments by which transfers of loan capital were effected, no stamp duty was due.

Bearer bonds are not only transferable, but usually also negotiable. Negotiability is distinct from transferability: by no means all transferable instruments are negotiable. Bearer bonds usually are, but registered bonds are not. Negotiability can be acquired under English law in two ways.

The Bills of Exchange Act of 1882 confers negotiability on bills of exchange, checks, and promissory notes. Although bonds are often likened to promissory notes, the detailed terms and conditions to which bonds are subject are generally held not to satisfy the act's requirements regarding certainty of amount and unconditionality. Bonds are therefore not negotiable by virtue of the 1882 act.

Negotiability can also be acquired by custom or mercantile usage: an instrument can acquire negotiability simply by being so treated by the financial community. The custom need not be very long-standing, as long as the frequency of relevant transactions is sufficiently high. This particular point may not be relevant in relation to bonds, which appear to have been acknowledged as being negotiable for many years, but is relevant in relation to more recently emergent instruments. In consequence, there seems to be little doubt that London certificates of deposit and Euro-commercial paper are (since about 1966 in the former case and 1984 in the latter) to be treated as negotiable under English law.

The Consequence of Negotiability. The concept of negotiability operates in favor of a "holder in due course." The holder of a negotiable instrument will be a holder in due course if he or she has physical possession of the bond and received it in good faith and for value and without actual notice of any defect in the title of the person who transferred it. A negotiable instrument may be transferred by mere delivery so as to pass complete title, free of any equitable interests, to a transferee who is a holder in due course. Such a transferee will have the right to sue in his or her own name the issuer of the bond, although the particular terms of a trust deed may limit this right.

A holder in due course acquires property in the bond and the benefit of the issuer's obligations under it, all free of any defect in the title, and free of any setoffs or defenses that the issuer might have had against any previous holder. It therefore follows that:

- A holder in due course can get better title than the person he took it from.

- A holder in due course can (subject to any limitations in a related trust deed requiring claims to be made by the trustee on behalf of the holders) sue the issuer in his own name without needing to join any previous holder in the action.

- A holder in due course will be entitled to payment in full, notwithstanding any setoff or defense that the issuer might have had against any previous holder.

- If a Eurobond is lost or stolen, the issuer will not normally issue the unfortunate holder with a replacement unless he receives an appropriate indemnity against the risk of the original bond being presented for payment (when the issuer will prima facie be obliged to pay the original bond as well as the replacement bond).

Other consequences of bonds being in bearer form include the following.

1. *Anonymity.* Payments are made through paying agents, and usually an issuer would not know the identity of the holders.
2. *Risk of theft, loss, etc.* Most bearer bonds are held by Euroclear or Cedel, which effect transfers by entries in their books.
3. *Risk of forgery.* Security printing makes forgery both difficult and expensive.

Documentation

The documentation involved in and required for an issue of bonds is imposing in its bulk and apparent complexity. The "bible" of documentation prepared for record purposes after the completion of an issue will contain many documents, including the usual principal ones listed below.

1. The form of bonds in definitive form
2. Bonds in temporary global form
3. Mandate telex
4. Invitation telex
5. Allotment telex
6. Listing particulars (the offering circular, placing memorandum, or prospectus)
7. Subscription agreement (or purchase agreement)
8. Agreement among managers
9. Auditors' report (set out in the listing particulars) and consent letter
10. Auditors' comfort letters
11. Agent bank agreement (FRN issues only)
12. Legal opinions
13. Various payment instructions and receipts
14. Fiscal agency agreement (or simply a paying agency agreement if there is a trust deed)
15. Trust deed (where a trustee is appointed for bond holders)

These documents are described in more detail following.

The Definitive Bonds. There are two formats: the AIBD format and the Euroyen format. The AIBD format is specified by the Association of International Bond Dealers (AIBD) in conjunction with the International Organisation for Standardisation (IOS) and is the most common. The Euroyen format is used only for Euroyen issues where the fiscal or principal paying agent's specified office is in Tokyo.

Basic Features. These are the same for both formats, and are as follows:

- *On the face of the bond:* a simple promise to pay principal and interest (subject to certain terms and conditions), executed by the issuer in facsimile and, in most cases, authenticated manually by the fiscal or paying agent. However, if there is a trustee, the trust deed will contain the primary promise to pay, so the face of the bond may merely record the entitlement of the bearer to the benefit of the trusts constituted by the trust deed.

- *On the reverse of the bond:* the terms and conditions (fine print—see following) and the names and addresses of the paying agents.

- *Attached to the right-hand side of the bond:* coupons that have to be surrendered in order to claim interest payments.

- *On the reverse of each coupon:* the names and addresses of the paying agents.

- *On the face of the bond and each coupon:* a machine-readable OCR code.

Terms and Conditions of Eurobonds. The conditions normally found in the fine print can be summarized thus:

1. *Preamble.* A recital of the authorization of the issue, any trust deed constituting the issue, and the fiscal or paying agency agreement and any agent bank agreement.

2. *Form, denomination and title.* A reference to the bonds being in bearer or in registered form, the denomination of each bond, and a statement about the title to the bond and who is recognized as enjoying it.

3. *Status.* Normally unsecured, ranking pari passu with all other unsecured indebtedness, but may be secured or subordinated.

4. *Negative pledge.* Usually much less onerous than for a commercial banking transaction. Generally it does no more than prohibit the encumbrance of assets (and, sometimes, the giving of guarantees by any third party) to secure any comparable debt (such as publicly issued or listed debt instruments) of the issuer, unless the identical security is also granted equally and rateably to the bondholders. All it does is ensure that the issuer of unsecured bonds does not subsequently issue secured (or guaranteed) bonds; but it does nothing to prevent any other secured borrowings. Bondholders, in practice, accept such a limited clause because the free transferability of bonds and the extreme dif-

ficulty of arranging for any subsequent waiver of breach or modification of terms means that the issuer does not have the ability to ask existing bondholders for their consent to the creation of any subsequent encumbrance. While this argument may not hold good for an issue where there is a trustee (who can, if the trust deed is appropriately worded, grant waivers or agree to modifications), in practice the negative pledge clauses for such issues are not usually much stronger.

5. *Interest.* Terms governing the accrual and calculation of interest, which may be at a fixed or floating rate. Methods of determining floating rates can vary a great deal. LIBOR (both by reference to the Reuter Monitor Money Rate Service and by reference to reference banks) is common but by no means invariable. Other common benchmarks are Libid, Limean, the T-bill rate, LTPR (for yen), the Bank Bill Rate (for Australian dollars) and formulas that vary an otherwise fixed interest rate by reference to the performance of various stock indices (such as the FT-SE 100 or the Nikkei 225). Three different bases are commonly used in calculating interest payments:

365/365: applies the annual rate to the principal sum and divides the result by the number of days in the relevant period. This is the basis employed by the clearing banks for domestic loans.

365/360: the annual rate is applied to the principal sum as if X percent per annum meant X percent per 360 days, so that, for a calendar year, slightly more than X percent will accrue. This is the basis employed by issuers of Eurocurrency loans and floating-rate notes.

360/360: each calendar month is treated as having 30 days, so that one-twelfth of the annual rate will accrue for each month. Thus, the same amount of interest will accrue in February (28 days) as in December (31 days). This is the basis of calculation used for fixed-rate notes and bonds.

6. *Payments.* The mechanics of payment require the surrender of the bond for payment of principal and the surrender of the relevant coupon for payment of interest. Surrender and payment are made through paying agents that act for the issuer.

7. *Problem.* What if a bond is for any reason redeemed early and, when surrendered, any future coupons are missing? The issuer does not want to have to pay interest on principal that it has already repaid. There are two different solutions. For floating-rate notes, all future coupons are rendered void and no payments will be made in respect of them. For fixed-rate notes and bonds, missing coupons, if eventually presented before they become prescribed, will be paid at their face value. However, the amount of principal paid to the holder of the note or bond from which the coupon was missing will be reduced by the face amount of the missing coupon.

8. *Taxation.* Investors in Eurobonds do not want to receive interest less any withholding tax levied by the taxing authorities of the issuer.

Accordingly, there is invariably a withholding tax grossing-up clause to ensure that the investor receives the full amount that it expects. The grossing-up obligation is usually restricted to taxes withheld by the issuer's own country or that of any guarantor. It is also usually qualified to exclude from grossing up any holder that suffers withholding by reason of any of the following:

- any connection between the holder and the issuer's country
- its own failure to make any necessary declaration of nonresidence or claim for exemption
- a significant delay by the holder in claiming payment

9. *Redemption and purchase.* The conditions dealing with these matters are normally subdivided as follows:

   Redemption at maturity. Bonds are normally redeemable on or after their scheduled maturity date at par, but index-linked issues may provide for redemption at a premium or a discount by reference to a stock index or some other external factor.

   Redemption for taxation reasons. The entire issue is usually callable for redemption if a change in law or practice gives rise to a need to gross up payments of principal and interest under the bonds. However, if the effect of the change is merely to impose withholding tax on interest payments on any on-lending of the proceeds of the issue, the International Primary Markets Association (IPMA) says that early redemption should not be permitted. The IPMA recommendation was inspired by the revocation in 1987 of the USA/Netherlands Antilles tax treaty, when various Netherlands Antilles issuers threatened to redeem early because of the imposition of withholding tax on interest payments from their U.S. parent companies, to which they had on-lent the proceeds of issues.

   Redemption at the issuer's (a call option) or the holder's (a put option) option. These options are by no means invariably present. The issuer's call option, if present at all, would generally be exercisable in relation to floating-rate issues only on specified interest payment dates.

10. *Purchases.* As a matter of general law, there is no reason why the issuer should not purchase its own bonds, and the terms and conditions will often make specific provision for this. However, if the bonds are listed on the International Stock Exchange in London, there will be limits on the price at which any such purchase can be made. The terms and conditions of such purchases will normally provide for the cancellation of the bonds, but issuers that are banks may wish to retain the ability to resell them.

11. *Events of default.* As is the case with negative pledge clauses, these conditions will be less onerous than those applying to commercial banking transactions. Nonpayments will have grace periods, as a matter

of course; and cross-defaults (if any) will usually be confined to external and/or public indebtedness, and/or subject to a high threshold.

12. *Replacement of bonds and coupons.* Replacements are available for lost, stolen, mutilated, defaced, or destroyed bonds and coupons. The need for an indemnity in the case of loss or theft is discussed above.

13. *Notices.* Notice is given to bondholders and coupon holders by means of newspaper advertisements. The *Financial Times* is normally used, but notices should also appear in the *Luxembourg Wort* when the issue in question is listed on the Luxembourg Stock Exchange.

14. *Meetings of bondholders and modifications.* These are complicated and standardized. Bearer form gives rise to the need for formal notices to be given of any meetings and for rigorous quorum requirements to be met before any modification of the terms and conditions may be approved.

15. *Governing law and jurisdiction.* The law governing the bond is usually English and the jurisdiction is nonexclusive.

Bonds in Temporary Global Form. Bonds are issued initially in the form of a single temporary global bond for two reasons. The first is that lack of time precludes the printing and authentication of bonds in definitive form by the closing date of the issue. The second is that U.S. securities law often (but not always) requires a "lock-up" procedure, under which the following occur:

- The bonds are represented initially by a temporary global bond (which is a bearer instrument) held by a common depositary for Euroclear and Cedel.

- Bonds in definitive form are not available in exchange for the temporary global bond until 90 days after the completion of the distribution of the issue.

- Completion of the distribution is determined by the lead manager to have occurred once each of the co-managers has sent it an all-sold telex; this states that the co-manager has sold all the bonds it purchased under the allotment telex and the subscription agreement.

- Even after the exchange date, bonds in definitive form will be issued in exchange for the temporary global bond only against a certification given through Euroclear and Cedel that the beneficial owner of the relevant bonds is not a U.S. citizen;

- Any payments of interest made in respect of bonds while represented by the temporary global bond will be made only against a similar certification as to non-U.S. beneficial ownership.

It should be noted that this 'lock-up' procedure will be subject to modification under the U.S. Securities and Exchange Commission's Regulation S, which is, at the time of writing, scheduled for imminent release. The temporary global bond is a typewritten document, executed manually by the issuer and often authenticated by the fiscal or principal paying agent. It has a schedule on which exchanges for definitive bonds and payments of interest are noted.

Mandate Telex. This usually consists of an exchange of telexes between the issuer and the lead manager setting out the principal terms of the issue and authorizing the lead manager, on the issuer's behalf, to announce the issue and invite co-managers into the management group. In other words, the lead manager is awarded a mandate to arrange the issue on the terms summarized in the mandate telex.

Invitation Telex. This is required by the International Primary Market Association (IPMA) and usually preceded by a screen (Reuters and/or IPMA) and/or telephone invitation. IPMA Recommendation 1.1 states: "The invitation telex should be considered as the basis of the syndicate participant's commitment, subject to the signed syndicate agreements."

IPMA stipulates that the invitation should, as a minimum, set out the commercial terms of the issue and cover matters specified in a checklist. "An early positive response to a screen or telephone invitation may be reversed upon receipt of the invitation telex only if there are changes in or additions to the basic commercial or non-commercial terms of the issue. If there are subsequent material changes in or additions to the invitation telex (whether in the agreements or otherwise), commitments may be withdrawn but for these reasons only." (IPMA, Recommendation 1.3.)

Stabilization. The rules made by the Securities and Investment Board (SIB) on stabilization changed on March 1, 1989. To avoid contravention of S.47(2) of the Financial Services Act, 1986 (FSA), the invitation telex must (if there is any prospect of the lead manager stabilizing the issue) contain the disclosure "Stabilisation/SIB," indicating that stabilization transactions may be effected and, if so, will be effected in conformity with the SIB Conduct of Business Rules. It is no longer necessary to put any fuller legend into the invitation telex for fear of the telex, say, being used as a press release, because under the revised SIB rules the same disclosure will suffice for a press release.

But what is stabilization? The pricing of an issue involves a combination of issue price, coupon (the interest rate), management and underwriting commissions, and a selling concession (the discount from the issue price allowed to the managers). IPMA places responsibility for correct pricing on the lead manager, and an issue price would be deemed to be incorrect (that is, too high) if its market price during primary distribution were to fall below the selling price (the issue price less the selling concession). For reasons of prestige, lead managers will therefore buy bonds in the market if the market price is otherwise likely to fall below the selling price. This is called *stabilization.* Such stabilizing purchases are made for the account of the managers as a syndicate, but the lead manager can require co-managers to contribute to stabilization losses only to the extent of their underwriting commissions—their management commissions are sacred. (See IPMA, Recommendation 1.7.)

Allotment Telex.   This is also required by IPMA. The invitation telex, as well as inviting co-managers to assume an underwriting commitment, will also ask them to specify their selling interest—the number of bonds they actually want for sale to customers. The allotment telex allots (in the lead manager's discretion) bonds to each manager and gives directions as to the payment and transfer instructions that need to be given to Euroclear and Cedel in connection with closing.

IPMA Recommendation 1.2 requires final allotments in prepriced offerings syndicated among managers to be made only within the next business day following the launch. However, in cases where, for any reason, a pro-spectus has been or is being prepared for the purposes of Part III and Schedule 3 of the Companies Act 1985, S.82 of that act prohibits allotments "in pursuance of a prospectus issued generally" until the beginning of the third business day after the issue of the prospectus. Whether allotments made in the normal way before the issue of the prospectus would actually contravene this is not clear, but the safe approach is to give indications only of proposed allotments in advance, formal allotment being delayed until the third business day.

Listing Particulars.   If the bonds are to be listed on a stock exchange, the relevant authorities have to approve the listing particulars or prospectus. In the case of Luxembourg, these are the Luxembourg Monetary Institute and the Luxembourg Stock Exchange; in the case of London, the Quotations Department and the Listing Committee of the International Stock Exchange of the United Kingdom and the Republic of Ireland Limited.

In each case, contact with the relevant exchange is through an intermediary. In Luxembourg this is a listing agent, which must be a Luxembourg bank that is a member of the Luxembourg Stock Exchange; in London this is a sponsor, which must be a member firm of the Stock Exchange or a firm authorized by The Securities Association.

In each case, the requirements of the exchange derive from three EC directives: (1) the Admissions directive, (2) the Listing Particulars directive, and (3) the Interim Reports directive.

In practice, there is a difference in the level of rigor between the two exchanges, whose detailed requirements are to be found in Luxembourg in the *Requirements Concerning the Listing of Debt Securities on the Luxembourg Stock Exchange* (available in translation from various listing agents), and in London in the *Admission of Securities to Listing* (known as the *Yellow Book*). The contents of London listing particulars are specified in Section 3 of the *Yellow Book,* but Section 7 specifies which parts of Section 3 apply to Eurocurrency securities (which would normally include Eurobond issues). Section 7 also requires compliance with parts of Section 9. More immediately useful is

Euro-currency Debt Securities: a Guide to Listing (known as the *Blue Book*), which summarizes and extracts the relevant parts of the *Yellow Book*. (This is not entirely reliable, so is not a complete substitute for the *Yellow Book*.)

A detailed discussion of the requirements of listing particulars would take a chapter on its own, but the following are the broad components of typical listing particulars for an issue by a new corporate applicant.

Front cover, giving the title of the bonds and their outline terms.

Inside-front cover, containing a responsibility statement, health warnings regarding securities laws, and a contents list. If there is any prospect of the lead manager stabilizing the issue, the statement specified in Note 3 to Table S1 of the SIB stabilization rules must appear "reasonably prominently" (that is, in bold type). The specified wording is: "In connection with this issue (name of stabilizing manager) may over-allot or effect transactions on (name of specified exchange) which stabilise or maintain the market price of the Bonds at a level which might not otherwise prevail on that exchange. Such stabilising, if commenced, may be discontinued at any time."

This wording should not be altered except as permitted by Note 4 (which deals with the situation where there are a number of stabilizing managers that stabilize in different countries on different exchanges).

Terms and conditions of the bonds.

Use of proceeds, which is usually most uninformative (saying something like "for general corporate purposes").

History and business of the issuer, including a fairly up-to-date statement of the issuer's equity and long-term indebtedness (known as a capitalization table).

Issuer's audited financial statements, for at least two years.

An auditors' report on the financial statements.

A description of the withholding tax treatment of the bonds in the issuer's country and, in the case of a London listing, in the United Kingdom.

Subscription and sale, containing a recital of the subscription agreement and details of the selling restrictions applicable to the bonds (which will have to deal with the United Kingdom, the United States, the issuer's country and, sometimes, the country of the relevant currency).

General information, including statements as to the absence of any material adverse change or material litigation; notice of the availability for inspection of constitutional documents, agency agreements, the trust deed, etc.; details of the Euroclear and Cedel numbers; and anything else that does not fit anywhere else.

Graveyard or *football team,* giving the names and addresses of the issuer, trustee, agents, lawyers, auditors, listing agents, etc.

Listing particulars are normally printed in booklet form, but this is not essential. Until very recently, London listing particulars had to be printed in the form of an Extel Card for distribution through the Extel service, but that requirement has now been relaxed, so that conventionally printed or even typewritten listing particulars are permitted.

In each case, admission to listing is a two-stage process. The first stage is approval of the listing particulars, carried out through the Luxembourg Monetary Institute or the Quotations Department of the International Stock Exchange in London. Once approved, the listing particulars can be published on the date of signing the subscription agreement. Shortly before the scheduled issue date, the listing application is considered by the Luxembourg Stock Exchange or the Listing Committee of the International Stock Exchange, which will approve the listing subject to the actual issue of the bonds.

Subscription Agreement. This is the agreement under which the issuer agrees to issue and sell to the managers (and the managers agree to purchase from the issuer, and pay for) the bonds. Also covered are the following:

1. Representations by the issuer, both as to law and as to fact (including the truth and accuracy of the listing particulars).

2. Indemnities by the issuer to the managers in respect of any misrepresentation.

3. Selling restrictions on the managers (and, sometimes, indemnities by the managers to the issuer in respect of any breach of selling restrictions). Most countries have a statutory framework regulating the offer and sale of securities. Criminal sanctions are imposed for breach. It is customary, therefore, for the managers to agree to certain selling restrictions which, if complied with, will avoid the distribution of the bonds involving anything in breach of the relevant regulatory frameworks. (The statutes applicable in the United Kingdom are the Companies Act, 1985 and the Financial Services Act, 1986. In the United States the principal statute is the Securities Act, 1933 and regulations made thereunder.)

U.S selling restrictions have, over a period of several years, settled down into something approaching a standard form. United Kingdom selling restrictions have been confused because of the gradual introduction of relevant provisions of the FSA. However, they have been rescued by an informal working party of city firms of solicitors, which has agreed on a pair of flowcharts and a series of annexes, covering just about every situation likely to be encountered in practice. So far as selling restrictions are concerned, however, specific legal advice will generally be required for each transaction.

- Commissions, costs, and expenses.

- Conditions precedent to the closing of the issue, which would normally include:

  delivery of legal opinions

  delivery of auditors' comfort letters

  delivery of a closing certificate, by which the issuer confirms the continued truth and accuracy of the representations and the absence of any material adverse change

  approval of the listing application by the relevant stock exchange

  no material adverse change

- Force majeure. According to IPMA (Appendix CIX), managers are normally to be discharged from their underwriting obligations if certain events occur between the date of the subscription agreement and the closing date. "Underwriters should be able to assume that the lead manager will negotiate a clause which is sufficiently broad to afford reasonable protection against unforeseen developments."

Note: The liability of the managers under the subscription agreement is joint and several (as opposed to a syndicated loan facility, which gives rise only to several liability according to the commitments of the banks). The subscription agreement does not specify the commitments of the managers, and each manager is jointly and severally liable for the full amount of the issue. (This is known as the "European-style" underwriting; the "American-style" operates by way of several commitments.)

Agreement among Managers. The prime purpose of this is to regulate the liability of the managers among themselves so that, as between themselves, the bonds are underwritten pro rata to their underwriting commitments, which are stated. Also covered are the following:

1. Payment of management and underwriting commissions and, in particular, the extent (if any) to which these are subject to reduction on account of stabilization losses or unreimbursed costs and expenses of the issue

2. Prohibition of any stabilizing activity by any manager other than the stabilizing manager

3. Delegation to the lead manager of discretions and powers that are in the subscription agreement given to "the managers"

Auditors' Report. This appears in the listing particulars and is normally a restatement of the auditors' report in the issuer's most recent financial statements. Indeed, it may simply be a reprint of it, so that its date is that of the actual audit report. A formal consent letter (a letter by which the auditors consent to the publication of their report in the form and context in which it appears in the listing particulars) is a formal requirement of a London listing (see paragraph 1.8 of Chapter 2 of Section 3 of the *Yellow Book*) and of a Luxembourg listing where the listing particulars are also a prospectus for the purposes of Part IV and Schedule 3 of the Companies Act, 1985 (see Companies Act 1985 S.61 and S.74). However, for a "normal" Luxembourg listing, a consent letter would often not be obtained, the auditors merely being asked to sign a copy of their report in the listing particulars in final form.

Auditors' Comfort Letters. The conjunction of the audited financial statements in the listing particulars, the auditors' report, and the auditors' consent letter will do no more than verify the issuer's financial position up to the date of its last audited accounts. That may well be as much as 18 months out of date. The purpose of comfort letters is to obtain the following:

- external verification that there has been no material adverse change in the issuer's financial position since the relevant audit date, usually taking the backhanded form of a statement that nothing the auditors have seen causes them to believe that there has been any such change except as may be disclosed in the listing particulars

- external verification of the unaudited financial information in the listing particulars (such as any interim financial statements, summary financial information in the section on history and business, and the capitalization table)

Usually a full comfort letter is written on the date of the subscription agreement and listing particulars; on the closing date a short letter updating the original comfort letter is provided.

Agent Bank Agreement. In the case of an FRN issue it is normal for the bank that has responsibility for calculating the rate of interest applicable to each interest period to enter into an agreement with the issuer. The operative clause is usually restricted to an undertaking by the agent bank to do everything that the terms and conditions of the notes say it will do.

Legal Opinons. Legal opinions will be required as conditions precedent to closing. One or possibly two opinions will be obtained from lawyers practicing in the jurisdiction of the issuer. These will cover matters such as the due incorporation of the issuer; governmental consents (if any); due authorization by the board of directors or other governing body of the issuer; the local tax and stamp duty position; and the enforceability of a judgment obtained, say, in England in the relevant jurisdiction. In addition, the lead manager's lawyers in London, in the case of issues documented under English law, will be required to give an opinion concerning the legal, valid, and binding nature of the documents under English law. In giving such an opinion the lead manager's lawyers will assume the correctness of the opinions relating to the law of the jurisdiction of the issuer.

The opinions will customarily be addressed to the managers and, if there is one, to the trustee.

Various Payment Instructions and Receipts. These items are self-explanatory.

Fiscal Agency Agreement. The convention is that this should be called a paying agency agreement if, and only if, the issue is constituted by a trust deed. The difference in terminology notwithstanding, the fiscal agent and the principal paying agent are otherwise indistinguishable from each other. The fiscal agency agreement makes provision for the following matters:

- authentication of the temporary global bond (if required)
- exchange of the temporary global bond for definitive bonds and authentication of the definitive bonds (if required)
- issue of replacement bonds in the case of theft, loss, destruction, mutilation, or defacement
- payments of principal and interest through the relevant agents to the holders of bonds and coupons
- keeping of records of issue, payment, redemption, and destruction of bonds and coupons
- meetings of bondholders (unless there is a trust deed, in which case this will mostly be dealt with in the trust deed)
- fees and expenses for the agents

Trust Deed. Probably only a minority of issues involve a trust deed. There are advantages in having a trustee for both the issuer and investor.

For the issuer, the advantage is that it vests in a sensible and rational trust corporation the right to accelerate the bonds upon an event of default, which gives a degree of protection against "barmy bondholders" seeking to accelerate for merely technical events of default. Also, because a trustee can be given and can exercise discretions, its presence opens opportunities for future amendments to negative pledges or events of default, for the giving of waivers, and for the substitution of primary debtors without the need for bondholders' meetings.

For the bondholders, the advantage of a trustee is that, in the case of a substantive (rather than a merely technical) event of default, there is someone to pursue the interests of the bondholders, as a class, with a degree of vigor and skill, sharing the costs among the bondholders as a group.

Where there is a trustee, it is usually advised, and the trust deed drafted, by a partner in the same firm of lawyers as those acting for the lead manager, but in a different group.

Trading Bonds in the Primary and Secondary Markets*

Introduction

Trading is the purpose and function of the market and the mechanism whereby demand and supply of a commodity can be equated. Through this single activity trading houses implement a variety of business strategies which, in the Eurobond market, may include:

- making markets
- investing (or disinvesting) for its own account
- underwriting new issues
- acting as brokers to third parties

The most important role is that of the market maker which, by virtue of the capital commitment, often undertakes all four activities to underpin the business. At the other end of the spectrum are brokers, who have traditionally confined themselves to brokering between clients but who recently have been obliged to undertake limited market making to compensate for a lesser demand for brokering services.

The essence of being a market maker is to quote two-way prices to all comers. This activity generates positions, i.e., an investment or disinvestment in bonds as a result of being "hit" or "lifted" on prices quoted. Added to these positions may be those which the market maker creates intention-

---

* Contributed by Robert Chillcott.

ally for its own account. The sum of a trader's positions are the "book" and, at any one moment, the trader seeks to achieve a composition of holdings which reflects his or her—or the employer's—views of the market. Composition here refers not merely to a range of credit risk, maturities, or currency of exposure but also to the balance between long and short positions. Long positions are bonds owned by the trader and short positions are the trader's commitments to deliver bonds which he or she has sold but does not own.

Being short of stock can be expensive. If, because of an uncovered or short sale, delivery cannot be made on settlement day, then the purchaser does not pay on that day and settlement does not take place until bonds are in the purchaser's account. However, the purchaser retains all rights to the bonds as if settlement had taken place on the original date.*

The Markets

Traders in existing Eurobonds deal in what is called the *secondary market*. Liquidity is provided mainly by the market makers, but also by brokers acting between market makers and/or end investors. In adverse bond conditions, market makers are prone to go on the defensive by "dropping" issues or going "basis only." A *basis only* price is no more than an approximate indication and a client cannot deal on the price. The trader's intention is that by furnishing such information the customer will reveal his or her intentions and give a tame, risk-free order with scope for a large profit margin. To all intents, the trader acts here as a broker but without providing the broker's professional service.

When an issue is launched, investors and traders may start dealing even though the bonds themselves are not issued until the payment date, which is between two and five weeks after the launch date. This is the duration of the primary or gray market, and trades concluded in this period are settled on the same day as the payment date of the issue, instead of the usual seven-day interval which applies in the secondary market. The prolonged payment date appeals to speculators who have a long delay before settling their trades.† Deals on the gray market are said to be on an "if, as, and when issued" basis, i.e., the deals will stand if there are only minor changes (if any) to the terms of the issue or its launch (e.g., the settlement date) but

---

* The potential cost is illustrated by an example: not delivering bonds worth $5,100,000 for 10 days with interest of 9.5 percent would cost $5,100,000 × (10/360) × (9.5/100) = US$13,458.33. The cost of being short can be reduced by borrowing bonds, which is normally done through Euroclear or Cedel.

† The enthusiasm to deal can sometimes be costly. Dealing often starts before a prospectus has been issued and those dealing will have only sketchy details of the terms of the issue. In 1986 an FRN issue with a 99-year maturity was launched by a Canadian bank. The conditions of the issue were not favorable to investors, but this was not realized until the next day when a newspaper prefaced its report of the issue with the headline "Flawed Floater."

will be voided if the issue is withdrawn or pulled by the issuer or canceled by the issuing house after invoking the force majeure clause.

Cancellation can be a blessing in relation to other risks of dealing in the gray market. At the time of launch, managers are under pressure to sell the issue quickly in case adverse yield movements render the terms unattractive. Here the lead manager enjoys significant advantages over other members of the group by:

- placing bonds before inviting co-managers to join the management group
- denying the co-managers their requested allocations or allotments of bonds if the issue is selling well*
- taking a (legitimate) praecipuum on the entire issue which enables the lead manager to sell bonds at a lower price than the co-managers and still make a profit

Straight bonds denominated in currencies such as U.S. dollars or sterling and which are priced in terms of a margin over the yield of the corresponding government debt are vulnerable to yield movements in the underlying government security. Thus, in the case of a Eurodollar bond issue launched at a 50-basis-point spread over U.S. Treasury stock, the price of the bond will fall if the price of the underlying Treasury security falls and the 50-basis-point spread is maintained. By contrast, FRN issues present a lesser risk because the first coupon is fixed only after several days or weeks and there is no direct interest rate exposure for the managers.

Techniques

A number of techniques are associated with the dealing activities of traders, reflecting their policy towards the market.

- *Staying flat.* The trader neutralizes the effect of his or her trades on the book by promptly entering into equal and opposite transactions, mainly with other market makers. The trader holds neither long nor short positions and, as a technique, this is unlikely to lead to good profits unless the trader has a good flow of customer orders. In practice, much turnover in bonds arises from traders' efforts to stay flat, particularly in times of volatile interest rates and currencies.

---

* The lead manager might also deny co-managers their allotments if the issue were selling very badly, in which case the lead manager would seek to control as large a percentage of the issue as possible to avoid exaggerated adverse price movement triggered by short selling and/or co-managers selling their bonds into the professional market rather than to end investors. If the lead manager controls a sufficient amount of paper, short sellers may not cover their exposure and are "squeezed" by the lead manager who may then dictate—and raise—the price of the issue.

- *Balancing shorts and longs.* The trader seeks to manage his or her book to the extent of balancing the total short and total long positions. For example, if a trader were taken short of US$5 million of an issue and it were not possible to cover easily, then a purchase of US$5 million of a similar issue would be made, which would reduce the exposure to interest rate fluctuation. The purchase, however, has to be funded, and the new holding in itself does not help the cost of running a short position.

- *Ramping.* Ramping is the practice of aggressive buying of an issue with the intention of manipulating the market price upwards by taking dealers short. This activity is clearly frowned upon by its victims, but can be effective. In the period 1984–1986, many houses became traders in FRNs and it became common to quote a small dealing spread of 10 cents (e.g., 98.65–98.75) with a deal size of up to US$5 million in issues whose size was less than US$100 million. These issues were prone to be ramped, particularly on a late Friday afternoon. Dealers unable to cover faced the high cost of being short over the weekend and the prospect of loss on eventual covering. The technique, however, could rebound against rampers themselves when ramped issues were subsequently dropped by all other market makers and the ramper was left holding a substantial unsalable position.

- *Wipe-out.* The greatest danger confronting a trader is to become a victim of a swiftly moving market. The trader sells bonds only to find when negotiating later to replenish the book that a much higher price is being quoted. When the losses sustained in a short time are significant in relation to the trader's capital resources or a normal year's profits, then a wipe-out has occurred. Avoiding a wipe-out can be achieved by employing professional staff and by not quoting in excessive size.

- *Hedging.* Traders acquire positions which are not always possible to unwind, and hedging instruments such as futures, options, or alternative debt securities (e.g., U.S. Treasury stock) can occasionally mitigate the exposure. Take a trader, for example, with a square book just before close of business when a customer sells US$10 million of a 10-year straight Eurodollar bond. It is too late to call other traders to unwind the position and, rather than carry the risk of interest rates rising overnight, a *short* or uncovered sale of US$10 million, 10-year U.S. Treasury stock could be made as a hedge through the New York market. However, hedges involve expense and often the hedging instrument has a correlation of significantly less than 1 with the hedged position.

- *Funding.* Long positions, even if held only overnight, require to be funded. Often these are financed day-to-day at "overnight" money rates, but in times of rising interest rates, it is clearly worthwhile to fund longer term. Holdings of fixed-rate and especially floating-rate notes have been funded through a managed pool of below-LIBOR finance arranged

246

through a series of bond issues with currency and interest swaps attached. An extreme example of long-term funding of financial investments is the practice of zaitech by Japanese corporate institutions who arrange low cost yen finance through Eurodollar bond issues with equity warrants and cross-currency swaps attached and reinvest the proceeds in higher-yielding yen securities.

Charts

The widespread use of information technology is often blamed for the low profitability of making markets in Eurobonds and, indeed, one of its applications, the screen-based dissemination of price information throughout a market, reduces if not eliminates the opportunity for arbitraging price differentials in a given security at any one moment.

Yet the technology only conveys the information and is not to be confused with the causes behind it. As markets move up or down, financial commentators produce a posteriori explanations resting largely on fundamental economic data and which serve only as an analysis of history. A trader needs to form a view ahead of developments both in the market as a whole and in the particular securities in which he or she makes markets or holds positions. Here it is the potential buyers and potential sellers who hold center stage, and prices of bonds are determined in the short term by supply and demand. An excess of demand causes prices to rise and a surplus of sellers causes prices to fall. The trader has no way of knowing whether buyers or sellers will prevail except by observing the market and acquiring a "feel" for its behavior. However, information technology in the form of charts can assist the assessment by often indicating clear trends in the price of a security.

This is not to belittle the relevance of fundamental economic data which are important in so far as they change potential buyers into potential sellers and vice versa. Such changes, however, tend to be gradual and little affected by individual economic indicators which are published on a periodical basis. If a market is "expensive," it will not necessarily be right to stay out. If potential investors have cash to spare and no appropriate investment alternative, the market could become even more expensive. The Tokyo stock market has been a good example of this for many years.

Charts have attracted their adherents and their opponents with strong and opposite views on the use of charts and technical analysis. It is argued here that a middle view is the most sensible. Charts can be obtained from written publications or from screen services, but the most useful are those prepared by oneself on graph paper since this guarantees the application of some thought to the task at hand. A point and figure chart is helpful to eliminate periods of little price fluctuation. An X is drawn to indicate a move up and an O is drawn for a move down.

To analyze a chart, the first step is to draw trend lines. These are often self-evident, but there are variations such as flags, double tops, double bottoms, and parallel trend lines. Resistance levels appear when trading carries on for a prolonged period at a similar price level. This may indicate buying support, for example, from central banks or the reverse (i.e., major sellers who have a price target for liquidating their holdings). Related markets should also be considered—and the similarities between them. For example, the trend in the Eurodollar straight bond under consideration may be upwards but should be corroborated or not by the chart of U.S. Treasury stock in the same maturity. As a general guide, the key in analyzing a chart is to consider the current position in relation to the current trend line. A position above the line is generally bullish (i.e., indicating further movement upwards) while a position below the line suggests a movement downwards.*

Charts are accessible to traders, and it is not necessary to be a technical analyst to interpret them. They serve as a vital tool in decision making by enabling the trader to relate the chart of the price of a security to fundamental economic data and the current "feel" of the market. Thus, charts should be reviewed each day with fresh eyes in order to determine whether a trader's positions are appropriate in relation to the outlook of the market.

The charts that follow illustrate some of the points just outlined.

1. The chart of the FT-SE 100 Index (Figure A-1) shows a distinct uptrend for nearly a year, which is then decisively broken. Consolidation then took place in 1988.

2. The chart of U.S. Treasury bond yields (Figure A-2) shows a decisive double bottom occurred in 1988.

3. The chart of the Deutsche mark/sterling exchange rate (Figure A-3) shows a prolonged resistance level at 3.00, which was due to Bank of England intervention. On breaking this level, the move was decisive.

4. The chart of the Swedish kroner/sterling exchange rate (Figure A-4) shows a distinct uptrend throughout. However, the double top indicates the possibility of a downturn.

Exercises

1. Consider the chart of six-month LIBOR (Figure A-5a). What would your stance on Eurodollar interest rates be?

2. Consider the chart of the Dow Jones index (Figure A-6a). Does it make one bullish or bearish?

---

* It can be shown mathematically that for most markets, the following equation applies at most times:

$$x(2) = x(1) + a. \, [x(1) - x(0)]$$

where $x(0)$, $x(1)$ and $x(2)$ are levels of a market at uniform time intervals and a is a positive constant with a value of less than 1. From this it may be shown that the trend of a market will indicate whether the next move is more likely to be up or down.

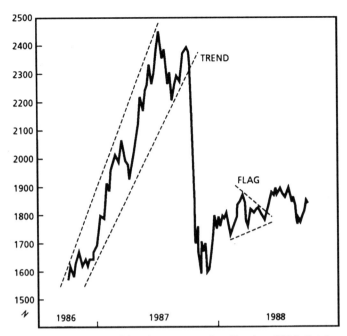

Figure A-1. FT-SE 100 index: price index (October 1986–October 1988). *(Source: Datastream.)*

Figure A-2. U.S. Treasury bonds 30-year redemption yield (October 1986–October 1988). *(Source: Datastream.)*

Figure A-3. Deutsche mark against sterling: exchange rate. (October 1986–October 1988). *(Source: Datastream.)*

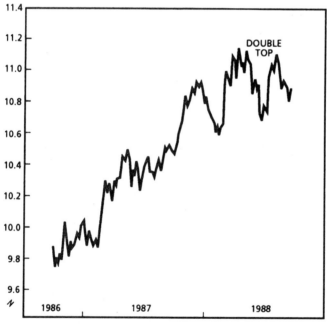

Figure A-4. Swedish krona against sterling exchange rate. (October 1986–October 1988). *(Source: Datastream.)*

250

Solutions

1. Six-month LIBOR chart from 2 October 1987 to 29 April 1988:
   The downtrend from the December peak to the low point in February (Figure A-5a) was decisively broken in the middle of February. Since then, a clear uptrend is evident which has been operating for more than two months and remains intact. Historical trading evidenced by the chart shows no indication of a significant resistance level which might hurt the uptrend. Verdict: Interest rates are likely to continue rising.
   The next chart (Figure A-5b) shows just how long and long-lasting the uptrend turned out to be.

2. Dow Jones Index from 20 October 1987:
   The first chart (Figure A-6a) shows the index has been meandering throughout the period of the chart. It would be unwise to reach any dramatic conclusion from the chart, but perhaps a policy of "buy on weakness" would be in order. However, there is a gentle uptrend in evidence which is confirmed by the second chart (Figure A-6b), which shows the index continuing to rise in the same manner (i.e., meandering but with a gentle uptrend).

Information Systems

The introduction of advanced information systems is the most important development in post war securities markets. Often hailed as a threat to the survival of market participants, these systems have on the contrary served to open up new markets, acted as a catalyst to greater transparency of dealing and protection of investor interests, and enabled the design of trading and hedging techniques to facilitate the management of debt. They are an essential tool for traders, salespeople, syndicate managers, product and derivative specialists, as well as for the customers, issuers, and investors whom they serve.

1. *Reuters.* The Reuters service, incorporated in the United Kingdom is used universally and provides a very extensive range of information on markets in debt and equity securities, foreign exchange and money markets, Euro-commercial paper and company news. Eurobonds are assigned individual codes and details of an issue can be accessed by entering the dedicated code. Bond prices are published on Reuter screens by market makers and serve as a guide to dealing prices at any one moment. The Reuters Rich system enables dealers to reduce the number of screens on their desks by channeling different systems through the same screen. Further developments are designed to add value through facilities for calculating yields or end costs of funds by linking the information provided on several screens and thus taking over to some extent the work of the issuing house.

2. *Telerate.* Telerate is the major competitor of Reuters and is developing from a home base in North America. It is best known for its U.S. Treasury bond prices, yield curves and charts but also provides a wide range of information, news, and comment on all aspects of financial markets. It operates a Eurobond price service called VIGIL, run jointly with the

(a)

(b)

Figure A-5. London Eurocurrency US$ 6-months: middle rate (October 1987–April 1988); (b) London Eurocurrency US$ 6-months: middle rate (October 1987–October 1988). *(Source: Datastream.)*

252

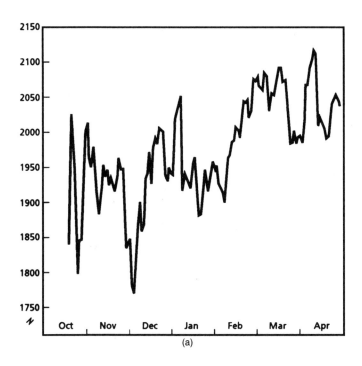

(a)

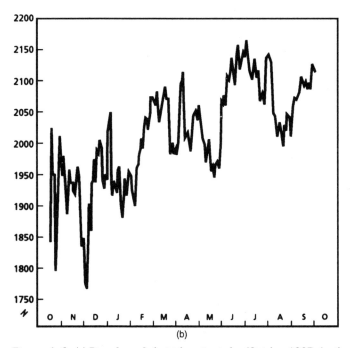

(b)

Figure A-6. (a) Dow Jones Industrials: price index (October 1987–April 1988); (b) Dow Jones Industrials: price index (October 1987–October 1988). *(Source: Datastream.)*

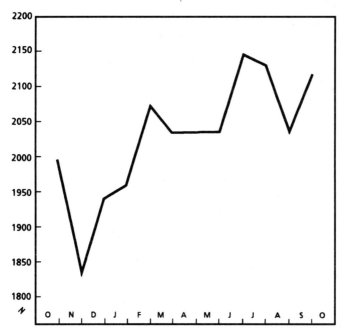

Figure A-7. Dow Jones Industrials: share price index (end period). (*Sources: Datastream,* Wall Street Journal.)

International Financial Review magazine, which compares well with Reuters. The system was acquired by Dow Jones & Co. at the beginning of 1990.

3. *Datastream.* Datastream is based in the United Kingdom and is mainly used by the U.K. domestic fund managers and dealers. It contains a multitude of charts and a wide range of data on bonds, companies, and currencies.

4. *Bloomberg.* Bloomberg is of U.S. origin and, though a relative newcomer, has met with considerable success with the introduction of databases comprising live dealer-entered prices. With the help of this information, it provides charts comparing similar bonds and related information on yields, yield curves, etc.

Other information sources serving the Eurobond market offer publications including:

1. The Association of International Bond Dealers (AIBD) publishes the following:

The *Bond Manual* (also known as the "Bible") is a large tome containing comprehensive details of the terms and conditions of public Eurobond issues.

The *Weekly Bond* guide is a smaller, user friendly handbook containing a list of outstanding issues, current prices, and abridged terms.

The *Members' Register* is a list of Eurobond dealers which is published on a periodic basis.

2. The Extel bond service is a system of cards setting out the terms and conditions of issues.

3. Other significant publications serving the Eurobond market include a number of widely read periodicals such as:

- *Euromoney* magazine (monthly)
- *Institutional Investor* (monthly)
- *International Insider* (weekly)
- *International Financial Review* (weekly)

4. Major Eurobond houses such as Merril Lynch, CS First Boston, Morgan Stanley, and Deutsche Bank publish economic research and market commentaries.

Subjective Probability

Subjective probability is not a well-known topic and yet millions of people enjoy betting, particularly on horse races, while traders often talk imprecisely of the risk/reward ratio. The essence of the subject that concerns both is set out in the pages that follow together with the implications for dealing room trading policy.

Probability

Define the probability of an event, A, as having a value of a, where a has a range of values from 0 to 1.

If A has no chance at all of occurring, then $a = 0$. If A is certain to happen, then a has a probability of 1.

Consider the toss of a coin. Define A as the event of a "Heads" result. The probability of this occurring is 0.5.

Now, in tossing a coin the result may be "Tails." Call this event B. Event B also has a probability of 0.5.

Since there are two possible events, A or B, their probabilities must sum to 1. Thus $a + b = 1$, or $0.5 + 0.5 = 1$.

Note that events A and B are mutually exclusive and b is both the probability of event B occurring and the probability of event A *not* occurring.

The tossing of a coin is a simple example of a "trial." In general, the outcome of a trial is essentially of interest and (usually) uncertain.

If there are more than two possible outcomes of a trial, say, A,B,C,D,E . . . (each event being mutually exclusive), then the sum of the probabilities of each outcome is still 1. For example, if there are the three possibilities of A, B, or C, then $a + b + c = 1$.

Why are probabilities interesting? The main use of probabilities is in forecasting. Financial repercussions of different outcomes can be great. How can one assign probabilities?

1. *Theoretically.* This may be by mathematical theorem or otherwise. For example, a coin should obviously yield "Heads" 50 percent of the time.

2. *By extensive observations of trials.* This can provide excellent results but it is not always possible to reproduce exactly the same trial many times. With a small number of trials, accuracy in assigned probability is not likely to be possible.

3. *Subjectively.* Probabilities can be assigned by subjective assessment. Factors which can be used include: concrete data and experience in similar situations, pure "guesswork" and "feel." In this chapter, from now on, only subjective probability will be considered.

Utility Functions and Utility Values

1. *Utility functions* are used to describe how much outcomes of trials are liked. Values or utility functions are assigned subjectively and can be on any scale.

   For example, consider the toss of a coin, where US$1 is gained for a Heads result and US$1 is *lost* for a Tails result. Fred might have a utility function (UF) as follows:

   $$+1 \text{ for Heads } (= \text{gaining US\$1})$$

   $$-1 \text{ for Tails } (= \text{losing US\$1})$$

2. *Utility values* tell us whether or not to act. The utility value (UV) is obtained by multiplying the numbers chosen by Fred, to represent how much he likes the possible outcomes of tossing a coin, by the probabilities of such outcomes.

   From section 1, the probability of a Heads or Tails event is 0.5. In this example, therefore:

   $$UV = [1 \times 0.5] + [-1 \times 0.5]$$

   $$= 0$$

The utility value is neither negative nor positive: therefore Fred should be indifferent as to whether he bets on the toss of a coin in such circumstances.

In general, if there are, say, three possible outcomes with a utility function represented by the corresponding values A,B,C each with subjective probability a,b,c of occurring, then:

$$UV = [A \times a] + [B \times b] + [C \times c]$$

Keeping the same UF as before, Fred might actually think that by tossing the coin himself he can increase the probability of a Heads result to 0.6 His UV then becomes:

$$UV = [1 \times 0.6] + [-1 \times 0.4]$$

$$= 0.2$$

Since this is positive, Fred should engage in this activity.

Now consider Bill, who does not like losing money. His UF is as follows:

+1 for gaining US$1

−3 for losing US$1

Like Fred, he thinks he can achieve Heads with a probability of 0.6. Should he bet and spin?

In his case the UV becomes:

$$UV = [1 \times 0.6] + [-3 \times 0.4]$$

$$= -0.6$$

Since the result is negative, Bill should not spin.

From these simple examples the same method can be used to broaden to cases of several possible outcomes and to cater for different utility functions.

Subjective Probability and Financial Markets

In dealing rooms all over the world traders are taking views on markets, positioning, losing and gaining money. All too rarely does management really consider whether the overheads and risk of loss are controlled enough to justify the trading activities.

The most common view that traders have of their jobs is that they are paid "to get it right" more often than they "get it wrong." Thus, trading is often viewed as a form of gambling and traders feel they must be dealing virtually all the time. A stream of profits and losses ensues. This notion of trading is very dangerous and can be viewed as "negative sum" game: one trader's profits are often another's losses and, in addition, there are technology and settlement costs to meet. There is the further temptation of reducing or even canceling trading losses by effecting further purchases of the stock as the price falls, which lowers the *average* bought-in price. However, each purchase increases exposure in the stock, as some trading rooms have found to their cost.

Consider this type of trading in terms of subjective probability. The "trial" may be considered to have two possible outcomes: money is gained or money is lost. This will usually equate to the market going up or going down. The *UF* can be simply expressed as:

+1 for gaining one unit of money, e.g., US$1000

−1 for losing one unit of money, e.g., US$1000

Since a trader will want to trade almost all of the time, the subjective probability for the first event of making a profit is about 0.6. Therefore the subjective probability of making a loss is 0.4.

In this case the *UV* becomes:

$$UV = [1 \times 0.6] + [-1 \times 0.4]$$
$$= 0.2$$

The UV is positive, if small. It might be suggested, therefore, that all is well. However, great caution is in order. The risk of losses is significant, which may not be acceptable to management or shareholders. Also, the trader's assigned probability of 0.6 is perilously close to 0.5—the position where tossing a coin would be as good. Years of experience in trading rooms shows that most dealers, most of the time, cannot do better than 0.5—which is not enough to meet dealing room overheads. The current trend to indexed funds and the low profitability of dealing room operations support this view. Thus, pure continuous trading is an activity of dubious propitiousness and it is prudent to avoid it.

Better than continuous trading is occasional trading. The essence of this method is that the trader watches the market continuously but deals only occasionally when he or she has a very confident feeling of the immediate trend. Unfortunately, many dealers are not able or willing to subject themselves to this discipline. Many feel the need to be seen to be dealing in the market at all times, a need compounded by managements, who tend to be uneasy about paying a dealer who is not busy dealing most of the time. Nevertheless, occasional positioning is best, and it is now examined in terms of subjective probability.

In practice, most managements want to make money but are not keen to concede the possibility of a loss. A typical *UF* would be like Bill's, that is:

+1 for gaining US$1

−3 for losing US$1

Now consider a trading strategy where positions are only taken if the trader's subjective probability is equal to or greater than 0.8.

In this case, the utility value becomes:

$$UV = [1 \times 0.8] + [-3 \times 0.2]$$
$$= 0.2$$

Since the result is positive, the action should be taken.

Obviously, it is possible to extend the number of outcomes and to complicate the *UF*, but the simple example given illustrates the heart of the principle. Rather than a policy of systematic continuous dealing, the trader's approach should be to ascertain the utility value of each trade before taking action. In practice, this implies a more selective and analytical attitude to trading.

Appendix B
Syndicate Invitation Telex

Attn.: New Issues Department

(Name of Borrower)
(Currency/Amount)
(Coupon/Maturity)
[- (Unconditionally and irrevocably) guaranteed by (Name of Guarantor) the 'Guarantor' -]
(Securities Index Number)

On behalf of (Name of Borrower), we are pleased to confirm our telephone conversation in which you agreed to participate as Co-Manager in the above issue, details of which are set out below:

1. Management group

	Underwriting Commitment in (Currency)
LEAD-MANAGER	00,000,000. -
	00,000,000.-

The issue is to be fully underwritten by the Management Group. There will be no sub-underwriting group or selling group.

The total commissions of xxx pct. will be divided as follows:

zzz pct. selling concession (re-allowance discretionary)

www pct. combined management and underwriting commission, subject to deduction, if any, for stabilization costs and un-reimbursed expenses, which will be distributed among the managers in proportion of their underwriting commitment after deduction of a praecipuum of vvv per cent for (Lead-manager name) [and Co-Lead manager name].

261

Appearance in publicity

First line: (Lead-manager name)

Second line: [Co-Lead manager(s) if any]

Third line: to be followed by Co-Managers in alphabetical
                                     order

2. *Proposed time schedule*

.... 1989   Despatch of Invitation telexes to management
                                     group.

.... 1989   Deadline for Co-managers' acceptance

.... 1989   Deadline for selling indications to be received
                                     by (Lead-manager).

.... 1989   Expected allotment. Allotments are expressed
                                     to be subject to signature of the Subscription/
                                     Purchase Agreement and related documents.

Still open   Signing of Subscription/Purchase Agreement
                                     and related documents will be communicated
                                     later.

.... 1989   Expected payment and delivery

3. *Description of Borrower and Guarantor*

4. Summary of the principal terms and conditions of the Issue

   Borrower: **(Name)**
                                     (Location)
                                     (Country)

   [Guarantor:.   Name, Location, Country]

Amount:	(Currency/Amount)
Interest:	. . . per cent p.a., payable annually in arrears on . . . , commencing on . . . . 1990.
Issue Price:	. . . per cent.
Maturity:	. . . ,199. at par
Status:	Direct (unsecured) obligation of the Borrower.
[Rating:	The Borrower's outstanding issues (in the U.S. market are rated by Moody's and . . . . . . by Standard and Poor's)]-
Form and denomination:	Bearer bonds in denomination of (Currency) (1),000 [and other denomination(s) respectively].
Optional Redemption:	[None, except for tax reasons]; [otherwise, insert redemption dates].
Tax redemption:	In the event of imposition of [home country of Borrower] or [home country of Guarantor] withholding taxes affecting the Notes/Bonds, the Borrower will be entitled to redeem all, but not part only, of the outstanding Notes/Bonds at par on any interest payment date, but not earlier than the interest payment date immediately preceding the date of such imposition.
Taxation:	Payments to be made without deduction for or on account of (home country of Borrower) or (home country of Guarantor) withholding taxes (subject to customary exceptions, as set forth in the Information Memorandum).

[Guarantee:	The Notes/Bonds will be unconditionally and irrevocably guaranteed by (Guarantor name) for the due payment of principal, [premium, if any] and interest].
Negative Pledge:	With respect to any other indebtedness in form of any bonds, notes, debentures or other debt instruments, (including any guarantee or indemnity assumed therefor) of the Borrower [and with respect to International Bond Issues as defined in an undertaking (including any guarantee or indemnity assumed therefor) of the Guarantor].
Cross default:	In respect of any bond or note issue of the Borrower [and of the Guarantor].
Listing:	Application will be made to list the Notes/Bonds on the Luxembourg Stock Exchange.
Force Majeure:	Standard Euromarket provision.
Payment:	Expected to be on . . . . 1989 with settlement on a delivery against payment basis. Procedures will be fully described in the Allotment telex. The Notes/Bonds will be represented initially by a temporary Global Bearer Note/Bond without interest coupons which is expected to be deposited with a depositary common to Euroclear and Cedel S.A. in Paris/Luxembourg/etc. on or about
. . . .	(the 'Settlement Date' and will be exchangeable for definitive Notes/Bonds not later than 120 days after the payment date [upon certification of non-US beneficial ownership].
Governing Law:	English law
Sales Restrictions:	Sales restrictions as contained in the Subscription/Purchase Agreement, a draft copy of which will be mailed to you, **will be imposed** on offers and

sales in the United States of America. The Notes/Bonds have not been and will not be registered under the United States Securities Act of 1933 and may not be offered or sold, directly or indirectly in the United States of America, its territories or possessions, or to nationals or residents thereof, as part of the distribution of the Notes/Bonds. Customary restrictions on distribution of documents in or from Great Britain will also apply (add sales restrictions for other countries, if applicable).

Expenses: IPMA recommendation. There will be no reimbursement for Managers' expenses by the Borrower/ there will be a reimbursement by the Borrower/Issuer in respect of Managers' legal, travelling, telephone and telex expenses up to an amount of [currency, amount] payable to (Lead-manager name).

This is not an offer of Notes/Bonds. It is expected that subject to signature of the Subscription/Purchase agreement, offers will be made at the discretion of the undersigned on . . . . (allotment date).

A draft Information Memorandum will be mailed to you.

Please indicate the extent of your selling interest to (Lead-manager name) (Attn: Ms. Isadora Duncan, Syndicate dept. **Telex** No. 000 000) as soon as possible, but in any event not later than ..00 HRS London time on

. . . . 1989

5. Acceptance **of invitation**

Please confirm your acceptance of this invitation to co-manage the above issue by return telex to (Lead-manager name) Attn: Ms. Isadora Duncan, Syndicate department, Telex No. 000 000 as soon as possible but in any event not later than . . . . 00 HRS> **London time on**

. . . . 1989 in the following form:

Quote

(Name of Borrower)
(Currency/Amount)
(Coupon/Maturity)
[- (Unconditionally and irrevocably) guaranteed by (Name of Guarantor) the 'Guarantor']
(Securities Index number)

We confirm our acceptance of your invitation to co-manage the above issue with an underwriting commitment of (Currency) (please complete) principal amount of Notes/Bonds on the terms and conditions of your telex dated . . . . 1989.

The name of our institution should appear in all legal documentation as (. . . . .)

By:

Date:

Unquote

On behalf of the Co-managers

(Lead-manager name)

By: (Lead-manager)
      Syndicate Department

Draft Allotment Telex

Date, 1989

(Name of borrower)
(Currency/Amount)
(Coupon/Maturity)
- [Guaranteed by (Name of Guarantor)]
- (Security Index Number)

Subject to signing of documents we hereby allot you

    (Currency/Amount) . . . .

Principal amount of Notes/Bonds

Payment for your Notes/Bonds must be made at the rate of . . . . . . (Currency/Amount) per (Currency) (1,000/5,000/10,000) principal amount of Notes/Bonds representing the issue price of . . . . pct. less . . . . pct. selling concession.

Receipt of and payment for your allotment will be executed by way of a book entry clearance against payment in either Cedel or Euroclear.

You must immediately decide in which clearing system you wish to receive your allotment and

(1) inform (the Lead-manager, att. Ms. Isadora Duncan, Telex No. 999 999) about the chosen clearing system not later than . . . . 1989 and

(2) instruct the chosen clearing system not later than . . . . 1989 according to the instructions set out below

Instructions can not be changed after 10.00 hrs. (Central European Time) on . . . . , 1989.

IF YOU SELECT CEDEL

You must submit to Cedel S.A., New Issues Section, not later than . . . . 1989 by 10.00 hrs, Luxembourg time if by tested telex or mail, or validated by 10.00 hrs, Luxembourg time, if by Cedcom, A 41 clearance receipt against payment instruction, reference (Lead-Manager name)'s New Issues Securities Clearance Account A/C No. 000 000 'Ref (Quote Issue)' as the counterpart. The Notes/Bonds have been accepted for clearance through Cedel (Reference No . . . .).

IF YOU SELECT EUROCLEAR

You must submit to the Euroclear, New Issues section, not later than . . . . 1989, by 10.00 hrs, Brussels time, if by tested telex or mail, or validated by 10.00 hrs Brussels time if by Euclid, A 01 clearance receipt against payment instruction, reference (Lead-manager's name) New Issues Securities Clearance Account A/C No. 000 000 'Ref (Quote Issue)' as the counterpart. The Notes/Bonds have been accepted for clearance through Euroclear (Reference No . . . .).

Cedel and Euroclear are able to open temporary accounts for non-members, but arrangements must be made prior to . . . . 1989.

If you maintain an account in Cedel and in Euroclear you may split your allotment between the clearing systems provided your instructions are given for the specific amounts as set out above.

On . . . . 1989 a temporary Global Bearer Note/Bond representing the Notes/Bonds will be delivered to a depositary in Luxembourg/Brussels/Frankfurt/Paris/London for the account of participants in Cedel and Euroclear. Upon receipt of the Global Bearer Note/Bond, your account with Cedel or Euroclear will be credited with your allotment against receipt of your payment to the credit of (Lead-manager)'s account No. 333 333 in Cedel or account No. 444 444 in Euroclear. The temporary Global Bearer Note/Bond will be exchangeable for definitive Note/Bonds in bearer form not later than 120 days after the payment date [upon certification of non-US beneficial ownership].

You are particularly reminded that the Notes/Bonds have not been registered under the United States Securities Act of 1933 and may not be offered or sold or delivered directly or indirectly in the United States of America, its territories or possessions, or to any nationals or residents thereof, as part of the distribution of the Notes/Bonds. Customary restrictions on offers and sales in Great Britain (and the Netherland Antilles) also apply. [To be checked against selling restrictions in invitation telex].

On behalf of the Co-managers

(Lead-manager name)

Syndicate department

Index

About the Author

Business International Corporation, a member of the
Economist Group, is the world's leading provider of business,
economic, financial, and political information related to global
business.

Noël Clarke is managing director of Capital Markets Partners
Limited, a capital market consulting firm based in London,
England, which is the principal center worldwide for the
issuance and trading of Eurobonds. Mr. Clarke is involved in
international debt financing for borrowers in Latin America,
Europe, and Africa.